For Elina

HISTORY'S MYSTERIES

People,
Places,
and
Oddities
Lost in
the Sands
of Time

By

Brian
Haughton

NEW PAGE BOOKS
A division of The Career Press, Inc.
Franklin Lakes, NJ

Copyright © 2010 by Brian Haughton

HISTORY'S MYSTERIES
EDITED BY JODI BRANDON
TYPESET BY EILEEN MUNSON
Cover design by Jeff Piasky
Printed in the U.S.A. by Courier

To order this title, please call toll-free 1-800-CAREER-1 (NJ and Canada: 201-848-0310) to order using VISA or MasterCard, or for further information on books from Career Press.

The Career Press, Inc., 3 Tice Road, PO Box 687,
Franklin Lakes, NJ 07417
www.careerpress.com
www.newpagebooks.com

Library of Congress Cataloging-in-Publication Data

Haughton, Brian, 1964-
   History's mysteries : people, places, and oddities lost in the sands of time / by Brian Haughton.
      p. cm.
   Includes bibliographical references and index.
   ISBN 978-1-60163-107-7 – ISBN 978-1-60163-732-1 (ebook) 1. Civilization, Ancient--Miscellanea. 2. Curiosities and wonders. 3. Geography, Ancient. 4. Historic sites. 5. Historic buildings. 6. Antiquities. 7. Prehistoric peoples. 8. Biography—To 500. I. Title.

CB311.H345 2010
930.1--dc22

                                                                    2010003633

Acknowledgments

Thanks to Elina Siokou for reading the manuscript,
Michael Pye at New Page,
and my agent, Lisa Hagan, of Paraview.

Contents

Unexplained Artifacts

Enigmatic People

Introduction

What is an ancient mystery? The distant past will more often than not be mysterious by its very nature. We can uncover buildings, artifacts, and sometimes even texts, but we do not know how the people of these ancient societies felt, what they believed, or what motivated them to behave in the way they did. Nevertheless, modern science is allowing us the kind of access to secrets of the past that was only dreamed of a few decades ago. DNA studies, for example, of modern inhabitants of parts of Syria, Palestine, Tunisia, Morocco, Cyprus, and Malta have shown extraordinary connections with the ancient Phoenicians, who once had colonies in those areas. Ongoing study, conservation, and sampling of the Uluburun Shipwreck, the remains of a 3,300-year-old ship and its extraordinary cargo from the coast of southern Turkey, are discovering fascinating connections between ancient Canaan, Egypt, Mycenaean Greece, Italy, and even the Baltic Sea area of Northern Europe.

Science alone, however, will not give us a complete picture of the ancient world. But when combined with the study of mythology, folklore, and sometimes simply a sharp change of viewpoint when looking back at the ancient world, science can be extremely enlightening. Indeed, it is surprising what can be accomplished by turning oneself off from a technology-obsessed 21st-century mindset—for example, in terms of understanding what the priorities may have been for the inhabitants of Nabta Play in the Egyptian desert 11,000 years ago, or the builders of Tenochtitlan in Mexico around 700 years ago. Nevertheless, even if we could somehow project ourselves back into antiquity, one suspects that the magic and mystery that were undoubtedly a part of the lives of many of these ancient civilizations would remain elusive.

It is often said by "alternative" historians that a certain controversial ancient site or artifact will turn conventional wisdom on its head. "Conventional" archaeologists (*conventional* presumably meaning those who have studied and are qualified as archaeologists) are criticized for not being open-minded enough to accept new theories and ideas. Generally this is not the case. Witness the (often-heated) discussions surrounding genuinely challenging archaeological puzzles such as the extraordinary Turkish site of Göbekli Tepe, the enigmatic "Venus" figurines of the last Ice Age, the abandonment of Mesa Verde, or the volcanic eruption that destroyed the Mediterranean island of Thera. Spurious "ancient" artifacts or sites (such as the Oak Island Treasure or the Dendera Lamps) are anything but a challenge to "conventional" archaeology. The furor surrounding these subjects on the Web and in various print publications is the result of speculation based on the preconceived agenda of the writer, and as such has no place in history or archaeology. It is this distinction between genuine and bogus ancient mysteries that *History's Mysteries* attempts to clarify. Sometimes a few hours of research and a modicum of critical thinking can dispense with anything in the second category.

History's Mysteries is an investigation into 35 archaeological mysteries from across the globe, organized by geographical region. As with my previous book, *Hidden History*, this work separates its collection of enthralling ancient riddles into three sections: Mysterious Places, Unexplained Artifacts, and Enigmatic People. The choice of subjects was made to include a wide range of cultures, and a mixture of both the well-known and the relatively obscure. Consequently you will read about India's celebrated Taj Mahal and the biblical Temple of Solomon, as well as the little-known Royston Cave in the UK, the infamous Rennes-le-Château in France, and the forgotten site of Great Zimbabwe in South Africa.

In writing *History's Mysteries*, I have not attempted to justify any personal prejudices regarding the enigmas of the ancient world. Rather, I have been guided by the facts, even if, in the end, they can sometimes be unsatisfactory. This has to be the case, especially when we are dealing with prehistoric cultures that left no writing. We do not know—perhaps will *never* know—all the answers. In this brief work I have tried to present a summary of the current level of knowledge for a small selection of archaeological mysteries. I leave it to my readers to pursue in more detail these riddles left to us by our ancient ancestors.

MYSTERIOUS PLACES

Lyonesse
(England)

St. Michael's Mount.

The story of the drowned land of Lyonesse, often referred to as the "English Atlantis," is told in medieval Arthurian tales and may also be connected to older Celtic legends of cataclysmic floods. The country of Lyonesse is said to have had many towns, woods, and fields, and 140 churches, but all this was all lost underneath the waves in one catastrophic inundation. According to local tradition, only one person escaped the flood: the hero Trevilian, who rode a white horse to the safety of high ground. Lyonesse is most commonly located between the English county of Cornwall and the Isles of Scilly, 28 miles to the southwest of the United Kingdom, but does this legendary land have real geographical coordinates?

The earliest extant sources for the story of Lyonesse, which are in Old French literature, do not go back any further than the 12th century. However, the legend seems to have been brought to Northern France from older Celtic sources that have not survived. Lyonesse appears as *Loenois* in the early French versions of the legend of *Tristan and Iseult* by Béroul, and that of the Anglo-Norman poet Thomas of Britain (c. 1155–1185). The tragic romance *Tristan and Iseult* tells the story of the adulterous love between the Cornish knight Tristan (whose native land is called Loenois), nephew of King Mark of Cornwall, and the king's bride, the Irish princess Iseult.

Although the story *Tristan and Iseult* originated outside of the contemporary cycle of stories of King Arthur and his knights, the two became intertwined at an early date. In Arthurian literature Lyonesse is sometimes described as the birthplace of King Arthur's wife, Guinevere, and even of King Arthur himself. Lyonesse (written *Liones*) is mentioned a number of times in Thomas Malory's 15th-century *Le Morte d'Arthur*, though there is no reference to it being destroyed by a great flood. Alfred, Lord Tennyson's Arthurian epic *Idylls of the King*, published between 1856 and 1885, describes Lyonesse as the site of the final battle between Arthur and his nemesis, Mordred.

Is there any reality behind these tales of the lost land of Lyonesse? The collection of annals known as the *Anglo-Saxon Chronicle* (compiled over a period spanning the ninth to 12th centuries) mentions disastrous sea floods on November 3, 1099, and St. Martin's Day, November 11, 1099. Some researchers have connected these floods with the inundation of Lyonesse, but the *Chronicle* does not give a specific location for the events. The fact that these sea floods were important enough to be recorded at all probably indicates that they affected the city of London—that is, the areas near the River Thames, a very long way from Cornwall. It was to protect against such tidal surges that the large flood control structure known as the Thames Barrier was built between 1974 and 1982.

It was not until the 15th century that the possibility of Lyonesse being a real place seems to have been first realized. William of Worcester (c. 1415–c. 1482), writing in his *Itinerary*, describes woods, meadows, fields, and 140 parish churches, submerged beneath the ocean between St. Michael's Mount (Cornwall) and the Isles of Scilly. He does not give this lost land a name. In the *Description of Cornwall* by topographer John Norden (1548–1625), however, this sunken land is given the name Lioness. An account of Lyonesse in William Camden's *Britannia*, written in Latin and first published in 1586, was taken from Cornish antiquary Richard Carew. It appeared in Carew's own *Survey of Cornwall* in 1602. In this work, Carew talks of the reality of the existence of Lyonesse:

> …that such a Lioness there was, these proofs are yet remaining. The space between the Land's End and the Isles of Scilly, being about thirty miles, to this day retaineth that name, in Cornish Lethowsow, and carrieth continually an equal depth of forty or sixty fathom (a thing not unusual in the sea's proper dominion), save that about the midway there lieth a rock, which at low water discloseth his head.

This rock, Carew says, is "called…by the English, Seven-stones," and was thought to be the last remnants of the land of Lyonesse. In Cornish, the area around Seven Stones was known as *Tregva*, "dwelling." Seven Stones reef lies about 18 miles west of Land's End and 8 miles northeast of the Isles of Scilly. The rocky reef is a navigational hazard for shipping and has caused many shipwrecks, including that of the supertanker the *Torrey Canyon*, which struck Pollard's Rock in the Seven Stones reef in March 1967, causing an environmental disaster.

The Cornish legend of the lost land of Lethersow seems to originate at least in part from the Breton tradition of Ker-Is, a great city thought to lie under the Bay of Douarnenez in Brittany, northwestern France. The monastery on Mont-St.-Michel, a tidal island in Normandy, northern France, was the mother house to the Norman priory on its English counterpart, Mount St. Michael in Cornwall. The story of Lyonesse may have come from records kept by Benedictine monks on Mont-St.-Michel mentioning the drowned Ker-Is. In Breton legend Ker-Is (or Caer Ys) was a great city built below sea level by Gradlon, King of Cornouaille (Kerne in Breton). The name Cornouaille is the French for Cornwall, as emigrants from Cornwall settled this area of Brittany. Apparently Ker-Is developed a reputation as rather a wicked place and was condemned by the Breton Saint Winwaloe, who warned of God's wrath and punishment, but was ignored. One night King Gradlon's daughter, Dahut, left the sea gate open during a terrible storm and the city was engulfed by a huge wave. Only King Gradlon managed to escape by galloping away on his magic horse. The parallels between the tales of Lethersow/Lyonesse and Ker-Is are obvious, and point to them being the same story.

There are, however, some indications that the identification of Lethowsow as Lyonesse is a mistake. Loenois, the name of Tristan's native land in the early French versions of *Tristan and Iseult,* is the Old French name for Lothian, in Scotland. Further support for a possible Scottish origin comes from the fact that the name Tristan is a Pictish royal name (written "Drust," or Latinized "Drustanus"). The Picts ("painted people") were a confederation of tribes living in what was later to become eastern and northern Scotland, from at least the third century AD until around the 10th century. Apart from the Pictish connection with Tristan, however, there seems to be no other evidence linking Lyonesse/Lethersow with Lothian. In fact further evidence for linking Tristan with Cornwall comes in the form of a weathered 9-foot-high monolith, near the town of Fowey in Cornwall. The stone, known as the Tristan (or Drustan) Stone, bears a Latin inscription that reads "Drustanus Hic Lacit Cunomori Filius" ("Drustanus lies here, son of Cunomorus"). The inscription dates to the sixth century AD, and Drustan is a known variant of the name Tristan. The stone appears to have been moved at some time in the past, and the location of the original burial is unknown. Though the Tristan Stone represents a tantalizing piece of historical evidence for the existence of an important royal person named Tristan, we don't know if it was the legendary prince of the story *Tristan and Iseult* who was once buried beneath it.

The tradition of a drowned land off Cornwall must have been based partly on the fact that local people could easily observe that the land around the coast at Land's End was once more extensive, before it had been flooded by the sea. Indeed, during the past 5,000 years or so, many coastal parts of western Cornwall and the Isles of Scilly have sunk below sea level. The tidal island of St. Michael's Mount, located around 0.2 miles off Cornwall's Mount's Bay, is known in Cornish as *Carrack Looz en Cooz* ("The Grey Rock in the Wood"), perhaps a folk memory of the time before the area was flooded. On occasion the remains of trees have been reported in the water at low tide, probably the remnants of a submarine forest, and in the past fishermen are said to have drawn up pieces of doors and windows in the area.

In 1752 Cornish antiquary William Borlase recorded lines of stones running out from the shore in the tidal flats near Samson, one of the Isles of Scilly. Though some researchers believe these are medieval or later fish traps, the fact that they do not follow marine contours makes this explanation questionable. If these walls are man-made, perhaps they are the remains of prehistoric stone field boundaries, possibly Bronze Age (c. 2000–650 BC). Querns for grinding grain were discovered incorporated into the structure of some of these walls. Oceanographers, however, doubt that there would have been a sufficient rise in sea level during the past 3,000 years (more than 12 feet would be required) to submerge such fields. Furthermore, land submergence around the coast would have been a gradual process, not a single cataclysmic event, which would be etched on the memories of the local population for centuries to come.

Though no evidence of a lost land lying between Cornwall and the Isles of Scilly has ever been discovered there is some evidence that Scilly itself was once a single island. If this was the case, could the Isles of Scilly themselves be the location of Lyonesse? Current research suggests that the Scillies may once have consisted of a single land mass, but the melting of the ice sheets and rise in sea level meant that by 3000 BC, low-lying areas had been submerged, leading to the formation of a number of separate islands. Toward the end of the Roman period (late fourth–early fifth centuries AD) today's islands began to appear, though the Roman names for the Islands, Sylina Insula and Siluram Insulam ("The Scilly Island") are interestingly singular, not plural. Even into medieval times the majority of the Scilly Isles would have been connected at low water, and today it is possible to walk between some of the Scilly Islands at certain low tides. Again, however, the essence of the story of Lyonesse is a cataclysmic sudden event, not the submergence of land by a gradual rise in sea level through hundreds, if not thousands, of years.

Should we be looking for an historical Lyonesse at all? Perhaps the legend is merely a British version of the biblical moralizing tale of Sodom and Gomorrah. Since at least the time of Plato's Atlantis, around 2,500 years ago, tales of drowned cities have fascinated Western Europe. The British Isles and northern France have several tales of sunken lands broadly similar to Lyonesse and Ker-Is, including that of Cantref Gwaelod, Cardigan Bay, Wales; Kenfig, near Swansea, southeast Wales; Lough Neagh, Northern Ireland; and Lomea (Goodwin Sands), Kent, southeast England. Generally, these stories concern towns destroyed by floods as an example of divine wrath provoked by wicked living. Perhaps the common elements in the flood tales of Wales, Cornwall, and Brittany originate, at least in part, from their common (Celtic) linguistic inheritance or in the moralizing character of Welsh and Cornish Methodism, and Breton Catholicism.

There certainly seem to be elements of Celtic mythology present in the tale of Lyonesse and Ker-Is. Stories from Irish, Scottish, and Welsh folklore of an overflowing well or fountain that forms a lake are particularly relevant here. According to one such legend, the Cailleach Bheur, a blue hag said to frequent parts of the Scottish Highlands, was in charge of a well on the summit of Ben Crauchan in Argyll. Every sunset it was her task to cap the flowing water with a large flat stone and then release it again at sunrise. One evening, tired from a long day herding goats, the Ben Cruachan fell asleep on her watch, and the water overflowed down the mountain, creating a loch and drowning the local people and cattle. Another similar tale comes from the 11th-/12th-century *Book of the Dun Cow*, one of the oldest-known manuscripts in Ireland. In this story, known as *The Death of Eochaid Mac Mairid*, Eochaid's daughter, Lí Ban, is put in charge of a magic well but one day forgets to replace the covering stone and the water overflows, drowning Eochaid and all but two of his children, and forming Lough Neagh.

These Celtic legends of overflowing wells seem to be the source of much of the material contained in British, Irish, and French stories of drowned lands. It is such ancient tales, combined with glimpses of submerged parts of the former coast at low tides off Land's End, the Isles of Scilly, and the Bay of Douarnenez, that constitute the origins of the tales of Lyonesse and Ker-Is.

But the mystery of Lyonesse still lingers on. A fascinating new project that may throw further light on the fabled drowned land was begun in 2009: The Lyonesse Project, co-ordinated by Cornwall Council's Historic Environment Projects Team, will attempt to reconstruct how the physical environment of the Isles of Scilly evolved during the Holocene (beginning about 12,000 years ago) and will also examine "the progressive occupation of this changing coastal landscape by early peoples and their response to marine inundation." We await their results with interest.

⧗

Chapter 2

The Mysteries of Royston Cave (England)

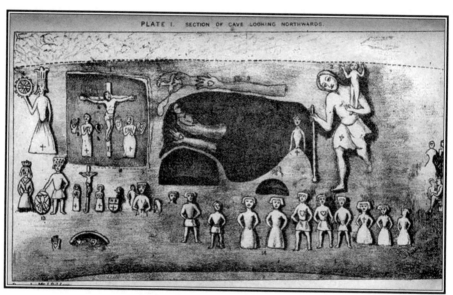

Plate from Joseph Beldam's 1884 book showing some of the carvings at Royston Cave.

Located in the small market town of Royston, Hertfordshire, about 40 miles north of London, Royston Cave is a curious site, relatively unknown outside the UK. Since its discovery in the mid-18th century, this enigmatic artificial cavern has attracted the interest of antiquarians, archaeologists, and New Age followers, and continues to fascinate visitors today. In recent years, the cave and its strange carvings have been linked with pre-Christian pagan worship, the Knights Templar, and the Holy Grail, but what was its real function and why was it built?

In August 1742, workmen in Royston were busy digging out footings for a new bench in the Butter Market when they came upon a buried millstone. The men dug around the stone and lifted it up only to discover, to their amazement, that it had been covering up an entrance shaft leading down into the chalk. After having established by plumb-line that the shaft was 16 feet deep, and curious to know what they had discovered, they sent a small boy down the narrow passageway on a rope. When he came back up the boy reported that he had seen a cavern with an earthen floor. Soon rumors of buried treasure began to circulate through the town, and hordes of curious onlookers gathered at the site to see what would be brought up from the strange underground cave. When digging began the crowds were so troublesome that it was impossible to carry on, and the work had to be undertaken at night. The workers soon discovered that the cavern was more than half filled with soil; consequently they had to widen the entrance and perform the arduous task of emptying out cartloads of soil in order to reach bedrock.

Unfortunately, in keeping with the attitude of the time, the discovery of treasure was the main object of most of those involved in the excavation, so the fragments of bone and pottery discovered in the soil were regarded as worthless and left unexamined. As a result, vital evidence was lost that today's archaeologists could have used to try to construct a history of the site. One of the few finds noted from the clearance of the cave was recorded by Reverend George North (1706–1772), vicar of the village of Codicote and a man with a keen interest in antiquities. Reverend North described a brown earthenware cup with yellow spots, a type of vessel common in the early post-medieval period, making it late 16th century at the earliest. Other finds noted by North, none of which were kept, were a human skull, various animal or human bones, and a piece of copper alloy plate.

Later the same year antiquary William Stukeley (1687–1765), pioneer of archaeological investigations at the Neolithic sites of Stonehenge and Avebury, visited Royston Cave but discovered nothing more than what seems to have been a piece of a common clay tobacco pipe decorated with a fleur-de-lys. The commercial exploitation of Royston Cave began in 1790, when the owner of the cave, a wealthy builder named Thomas Watson, cut a new entrance into the structure, consisting of a sloping passageway down to its floor. Watson then opened the cave to the public, and since that time it has remained open. Excavations were undertaken in Royston Cave in 1853 by local antiquary Joseph Beldam (1795–1866) and Edmund Brook Nunn (1833–1904). Beldam claimed to have found material of pre-medieval date and subsequently identified the structure as a Romano-British tomb, but, as he did not keep a record of the artifacts he discovered, this theory remains unproven. Further excavations of the cave floor in 1976 discovered what could be a post-hole and beam slots, all of undetermined date.

Beldam's investigations revealed that the cave at Royston is a bell- or bottle-shaped manmade structure cut into the chalk bedrock, measuring 26 feet in height and 17 feet in diameter. The entrance to the cave is located on Melbourn Street (formerly Icknield Way), close to where the road crosses Ermine Street. Ermine Street was a major Roman road that ran from London northward to Lincoln and York, and Icknield Way is one of the oldest roads in the UK, already ancient when the Romans arrived in Britain in AD 43. Icknield Way runs from Ivinghoe Beacon in Buckinghamshire, in the southeast, in a northeast direction to Knettishall Heath in Norfolk, in the east of England.

It has been speculated that the position of the cave close to the ancient crossroads in the town has some kind of sacred significance dating back into pre-Christian pagan times. The base of a stone cross known as Royston Cross (*Crux Roasie*) marks the site of this crossroads, and the settlement takes its name from this object. Royston was first known under the name *Crux Roasie* ("the cross of a woman named Rohesia") in 1184, but by the 14th century this had become *Roisia's Town, Roiston*, or Royston. The Rohesia in question was probably Rohese Fitzrichard De Clare, who was the wife of Eudo Dapifer (c. 1047–1120), a Norman aristocrat. This would place the naming and therefore the possible origins of the town of Royston somewhere in the late 11th/early 12th century, certainly not back into the pagan Iron Age more than a thousand years earlier. No traces of a Roman settlement have ever been discovered at Royston, nor is there mention of the town in the Domesday Book (a record of a great survey of England completed in 1086), facts that would support an origin for Royston and its cross late in the 11th or early in the 12th century.

Royston Cave is justly celebrated for the curious low relief carvings that cover its walls. Despite the fact that these carvings are generally crude and simplistic, and obviously not the work of professionals, they have a certain antique charm and an undoubted air of mystery. The scenes on the cavern walls are predominantly religious in nature, and many are fairly easily identifiable, such as depictions of the Passion of Christ, and legends of various martyrs and saints such as St. Christopher, St. Catherine, and St. Laurence. However, the identities of some of the other figures shown are more controversial. For example, supposed representations of Plantagenet royalty (monarchs who ruled England from 1154 until 1485), such as King Henry II of England, King Richard I (Richard the Lionheart), and Queen Berengaria, are far from certain.

Another unexplained carving is a depiction of a naked woman, which in some respects resembles a Sheela na Gig, a figurative stone carving of a naked womon displaying an exaggerated vulva. Such figures are found mainly on churches and castles dating from the 11th to the 13th centuries, particularly in Britain and Ireland, but also in France, Spain, Norway, and a few other countries. The Sheela na Gig has been interpreted variously as a warning against lust, a protection against evil, a survival from pagan Celtic times, a representation of the Earth Mother, and a fertility goddess. Given the motif's appearance on medieval churches, the appearance of a Sheela na Gig among the religious carvings at Royston would not be unusual, whatever the origin and date of this particular example.

During the two and a half centuries or so since the carvings were discovered, there has been much debate about their dates. After his work at the cave in the 1850s, Joseph Beldam concluded that some of the carved figures on the walls were of a much later date than others. Indeed a number of figures show traces of alteration, which indicates that the carvings were made by a number of people over many years. Beldam also discovered vestiges of red, blue, and yellow on the carvings, which suggests that at least some of them were originally colored.

The problem in authenticating the artwork at Royston is that no detailed record of it was made before Beldam's account. William Stukeley's drawings from 1742 are not particularly thorough, and the figures have been modified by him to fit his idea of what he thought their original appearance was. Beldam believed the carvings dated from the 12th or 13th century, based on the facts that the men were depicted without beards and the knights did not wear full plate armor. It was previously thought that two dates in Arabic numerals carved into the chalk in the cave—"1347" and "Martin 1350 February 18"—supported an early date for the carvings. However, the use of Arabic numerals in the 14th century would be highly unusual (Roman numerals were the norm), and it is much more likely that the carved dates read "1547" and "1550." These dates fit within the Tudor period (1485 to 1603), when relief carvings such as those at Royston became popular in England. Some carvings at Royston are even later than that. For example, the initials "WR" on the chest of a crowned figure have been identified as definitely 17th century in style.

The question of the function and origin of Royston Cave is an even more controversial subject than the dates of its artwork. One of the earliest and most eminent visitors to the cave who propounded a theory as to its use was William Stukeley. Shortly after his visit to the cave in 1742, Stukeley published *Palaeographia Britannica; or, discourses on Antiquities in Britain no. 1: Origines Roystonianae; or an account of the oratory of lady Roisia, foundress of Royston, discovered in Royston in August 1742*. In this work, the distinguished antiquarian claimed that the cave was constructed around AD 1170, as an oratory, by Lady Roisia ("Rose") the widow of Geoffrey de Mandeville II, First Earl of Essex (died 1144), the supposed founder of Royston. Stukeley attempted to back up his idea by claiming that the human skull discovered by workmen in the cave belonged to Lady Roisia, but his book failed to convince most people that the cavern was her final resting place. Reverend Charles Parkin (1689–1765), rector of Oxborough in Norfolk, disagreed strongly enough to pen a response entitled *Answer to Dr. Stukeley's Origines Roystonianae*, in which he pointed out that Lady Roisia was actually buried in the Chapter House at Chicksands Priory, in the neighboring county of Bedfordshire.

Another hypothesis was put forward in 1834 by antiquary John Yonge Ackerman, who was of the opinion that the cavern functioned as a Roman tomb. Joseph Beldam later expanded on this idea by suggesting that the cave was originally constructed as a shaft and was later enlarged to become a Romano-British mausoleum, or *columbarium* as he called it. Beldam also conjectured that hundreds of years later, during the

Crusades (11th–13th centuries AD), the cave was used as an oratory (a room for prayer) attached to a hermitage, and remained in use until the middle of the 16th century, with the coming of the Reformation, when the Church of England first broke away from what was seen as the corrupt authority of the Pope and the Roman Catholic Church. Beldam compared Royston with what he interpreted as similar caves in the Holy Land, and thought the carvings within were probably the work of Crusaders. From this seed seems to have grown the connection between the site and the Knights Templar, now the most popular and romantic theory regarding the origins and use of Royston Cave.

Sylvia P. Beamon, an archaeologist local to the Hertfordshire area, began researching Royston Cave in the 1970s and in 1992 published a book illustrating her theories: *The Royston Cave: Used by Saints or Sinners?—Local Historical Influences of the Templar and Hospitaller Movements* (Cortney Publications). Beamon believes that the Knights Templar held a weekly market at Royston, traveling the 9 miles to the town from Baldock, their English headquarters between 1199 and 1254. Her theory is that the Cave was divided into two levels by a wooden floor, one to act as a cool store for their produce and the other as a chapel. Beamon regards the post-hole and possible beam slots discovered in the 1970s excavation at Royston as the remains of this hypothetical structure.

One of the parallels Sylvia Beamon found for the Royston carvings was at the Château de Chinon, in the Indre-et-Loire department, central France. In the keep (*donjon*), known as the Tour de Coudray, Templar Knights, imprisoned there in 1308 after the brutal suppression of their Order the previous year, carved strange symbols into the limestone walls of their cells. However, although Beamon has claimed that these symbols bear a close resemblance to the carvings at Royston, the similarities between the two sets of carvings are not particularly striking, and may be the result of the fact that they were possibly carved at the same period rather than anything else. Closer parallels to the artwork in Royston can be found in the prisoner carvings in a small cell within the Keep of Carlisle Castle (Cumbria, UK), where they have been dated to the 1480s.

Beamon's work on the Templar connection with Royston has been extremely influential on other researchers through the years, so much so that even the official Website of the Cave (*www.roystoncave.co.uk*) has the legend "A Knights Templar Legacy" plastered across its homepage. This echoes modern popular opinion that the cave was used by the Knights Templar as a secret meeting place after the persecution of their Order began, and that some of the figures depicted on the walls represent Saints revered by the Templars. It has even been postulated that one of the carvings is an illustration of the burning at the stake of Grand Master of the Knights Templar Jacques de Molay. The present custodian of Royston cave, Peter Houldcroft, author of *A Pictorial Guide to the Royston Cave* (Royston and District History Society, 1998), takes the connections beyond the Knights Templar to include the Holy Grail and the Illuminati, though based on what evidence is not clear.

Although the possibility of the Knights Templar using Royston Cave as a place of refuge is not unfeasible, it has to be born in mind that the bloodthirsty persecution of the Order in France did not extend to England. This is one reason why between October 1307 and January 1308, Templars fled to the country for safety. Though a few Templars were arrested in England, and there was a trial that took place from October 22, 1309, until March 18, 1310, most remained free to find another place in society after the dissolution of their Order. Subsequently, many Templars joined the Knights Hospitaller, and others joined the Cistercian order. Despite the romantic appeal of the idea of Templars at Royston, in light of the situation in England at the time it seems unlikely that the Order would have found it necessary for clandestine subterranean meetings in places such as Royston Cave.

The most probable explanations for the construction and use of Royston Cave are decidedly more prosaic than those discussed here, but interesting nonetheless. The late-13th-century castle of Sloup, situated on a remote sandstone cliff 2 1/2 miles east of Nový Bor, in the Liberec Region of the Czech Republic, has interesting parallels with Royston Cave. There is a chamber in the castle of a similar bottle-shape to Royston, and that seems to have been used as a prison, and later, in the 17th century, after the castle had been mostly destroyed by the Swedish, as a hermitage. Carvings illustrating religious themes have been discovered on the walls here. Taking the discoveries at Sloup together with the prisoner carvings at Carlisle castle previously mentioned, it is a distinct possibility that Royston Cave was used as a prison at some stage in its history. Documentary evidence in the form of a rental (an agreement between a landlord and a tenant) from 1610 states that there was a prison in the middle of "Icknell Street" in Royston. Could this be referring to Royston Cave? And were the carvings on the walls meant to give spiritual solace to prisoners?

Royston Cave was almost certainly being used as a hermitage in the late 15th/early 16th century. Under the date 1506, the Churchwarden's book of the parish of Bassingbourn, just over the Hertfordshire border into Cambridgeshire, mentions a hermit living in Royston who bequeathed a sum of money to the parish of Bassingbourn. In this light it seems probable that the cave originated as a hermitage, probably for use by anchorites from the nearby 12th-century Augustinian Priory, and was later converted into a prison.

Certain aspects of Royston remain enigmatic, however. There is no agreement as to its exact date, with some researchers suggesting that the structure could even have originated as a Neolithic flint mine around 5,000 years ago, though there is no direct evidence of this, and the quality of flint in the area is not particularly high. If the Sheela na Gig carving is genuine, and not a 17th-/18th-century addition, could there have been a pagan aspect to the use of the cave? A number of other carvings on the cave walls have also not given up their secrets. Bearing in mind the uniqueness and importance of Royston Cave, one wonders what a full investigation into the carvings and a survey/re-excavation of the cave floor would bring. If the funding were available the development of such a project would undoubtedly prove extremely rewarding.

Rennes-le-Château (France)

The Tour Magdala.

During the last few decades, the small village of Rennes-le-Château in southern France has become the center of a number of sensational conspiracy theories. The story began in the 1950s with rumors of hidden treasure discovered by a priest in the 19th century and through time has expanded to include a secret society known as the

Priory of Sion, Mary Magdalene and the Holy Grail, and the Knights Templar. The mystery of Rennes-le-Château came to international attention after its inclusion in *The Holy Blood and the Holy Grail* by Michael Baigent, Richard Leigh, and Henry Lincoln in 1982, and the village attained instant mythical status after the publication of Dan Brown's hugely popular fiction thriller *The Da Vinci Code* (2003). Does anything real lie behind the mass of conflicting information and the endless conspiracy theories regarding Rennes-le-Château?

Rennes-le-Château is a small medieval castle village in the Aude department of the Languedoc-Roussillon region of south-central France. The village is magnificently situated on a hill overlooking the valley of the Aude and the village of Couiz. The area of Languedoc is particularly rich in history, home to Phoenicians and Greek colonies, Celts, Romans, Visigoths, Saracens, and the Cathar religious movement mercilessly put down by the Roman Catholic Church in the 13th century. Little of this history is in evidence in the village of Rennes-le-Château, however. One of the few historic buildings in the village is the small Romanesque Church of Mary Magdalene, which dates to the 10th or 11th century, though it may have been built on the site of an older structure.

When a locally born priest named Bérenger Saunière arrived in the village in 1885, this church was in a ruined state. During his time as village priest, Saunière refurbished the Church of Mary Magdalene, which included adding some new features, such as various statues, stained glass windows, and a mysterious inscription above the front door: *Terribilis est locus iste* ("This is a place of awe"). He also renovated several other buildings in the village and embarked on ambitious building projects, which included a personal library modeled after the Tower of David in Jerusalem (*the Tour Magdala*) and a large mansion (*the Villa Bethania*), which he built for himself between 1901 and 1902. According to the popular account, it was during the renovation work on the Church of Mary Magdalene in 1887 that Saunière made an incredible discovery.

During the removal of a large stone that constituted part of the altar of the church, Saunière found that a pillar supporting the slab was hollow and contained four parchments. Two of these manuscripts contained genealogies; the other two were written in a code that

Saunière had to have decrypted in Paris. Apparently one of the coded messages read *A Dagobert II Roi et a Sion est ce tresor et il est la mort* ("To King Dagobert II and to Sion belong this treasure, and he is dead there"). These messages were apparently written by Abbe Antoine Bigou, who was the priest in the village a century before Saunière arrived. Saunière continued his extensive investigations in and around the church, finding another mysterious stone slab under the church floor, the details of which he kept a secret.

Suspicions began to arise as to how a poor village priest could afford to finance so many elaborate renovation and construction projects. Unfortunately Saunière died of a heart attack in 1917, only revealing the secret of his incredible wealth to his housekeeper, Marie Dénarnaud, who in turn promised to reveal it on her deathbed to Noel Corbu, to whom she sold the Saunière estate in 1946. However, Dénarnaud suffered a stroke that left her unable to speak or write, and, when she passed away in 1953, the secret died with her. Speculation was rife as to just what the source of Saunière's incredible wealth could have been, but no one was able to come up with a satisfactory explanation.

In 1982 a controversial book by Michael Baigent, Richard Leigh, and Henry Lincoln, called *The Holy Blood and the Holy Grail*, was published. The sensational central hypothesis of the book was that Saunière had unearthed documents at Rennes-le-Château that proved that Jesus Christ had survived the crucifixion and had come to live in southern France with Mary Magdalene. The couple had a child named Sarah who founded a bloodline that eventually became the Merovingian dynasty of southern France. This bloodline was protected by the Knights Templar, and later by the Freemasons and a secret society known as the Priory of Sion, allegedly founded in Jerusalem during the First Crusade and boasting luminaries such as Leonardo da Vinci, Isaac Newton, Victor Hugo, and Claude Debussy among its members. *The Holy Blood and the Holy Grail* claimed that Saunière had in fact discovered nothing less than the Holy Grail at Rennes-le-Château, but it was not the legendary cup that held the blood of Christ, but was itself a bloodline—*sang real* in Old French ("royal blood"). According to the book, this incredible secret—the revelation of which could turn Christianity on its head—has been kept secret for two thousand years by the mysterious Priory of Sion.

One of the authors of *The Holy Blood and the Holy Grail*, English writer and actor Henry Lincoln, stated that he had been influenced by a 1967 book titled *Le Trésor maudit de Rennes-le-Château* ("The Accursed Treasure of Rennes-le-Château") by French author Gérard de Sède. This book tells the popular story of Saunière and his mysterious discovery more or less as we know it today and obviously had a huge influence on *The Holy Blood and the Holy Grail*.

More notoriety was to come for Rennes-le-Château in 2003. Although Dan Brown's best-selling novel *The Da Vinci Code* never specifically mentions Rennes-le-Château, it utilizes many of the elements from the Saunière mystery established by *Le Trésor maudit de Rennes-le-Château* and *The Holy Blood and the Holy Grail*. In *The Da Vinci Code* we read about the marriage of Jesus and Mary Magdalene, the Jesus bloodline theory, and the Priory of Sion; one of the characters is even named Saunière. The extraordinary popularity of Dan Brown's book still draws thousands of visitors to Rennes-le-Château today.

If it was *Le Trésor maudit de Rennes-le-Château* that first popularized the mystery of Rennes-le-Château, though, where had Gérard de Sède obtained his information about Saunière and his incredible discovery? Were there documents proving the truth of the discovery of a great secret in Rennes-le-Château? Unfortunately for conspiracy theorists, the real story of the Rennes-le-Château mystery only goes back to 1956, with Noël Corbu. In 1946, Corbu had purchased Saunière's former estate, which comprised the Villa Béthanie and the Tour Magdala, and, in 1955, opened a restaurant in the Villa Béthanie called the *Hotel de la Tour*. In order to attract customers to his restaurant, Corbu began spreading rumors current in the area at the time that in 1892 Father Saunière had discovered parchments while renovating his church. These manuscripts had led the priest to the treasure of Blanche of Castile (1188–1252), wife of Louis VIII of France. The stories were serialized in the local newspaper, *La Dépêche du Midi*, between January 12 and January 14, 1956, in the form of interviews with Corbu and his brother Charles. These sensational articles brought the little village of Rennes-le-Château to national attention, and visitors armed with treasure-hunting equipment flocked to the area. One of those attracted by the legends surrounding Rennes-le-Château was a French draftsman named Pierre Athanase Marie Plantard.

In May 1956 Plantard and a group of three friends had founded the *Prieuré de Sion* (Priory of Sion) in the town of Annemasse in eastern France. The group, which was named after a local feature called *Montagne de Sion* (Mount Sion), a mountain south of Annemasse, was ostensibly organized to promote spiritual retreats on this mountain. However, the group's real aim seems to have been to endorse affordable housing in the area. Plantard was a rather unsavory character, a right-wing fantasist who had previously founded a French nationalist organization known as *Alpha Galates*, and had spent time in prison for fraud and embezzlement. The Priory of Sion produced a dozen or so newsletters and little else, and soon ceased activity—but this is not the last we hear of Pierre Athanase Marie Plantard.

Plantard's dream had always been to play an important role in the history of France. To help realize this ambition, he concocted a bizarre and elaborate scheme suggesting that he was a descendant of a royal dynasty—the last of the Merovingians—and thus the current vessel of Christ's holy blood and the legitimate heir to the throne of France. During the 1960s, Plantard reanimated the Priory of Sion and, adapting the claims of Noël Corbu about Bérenger Saunière's discoveries at Rennes-le-Château, he and some friends fabricated a series of documents—the so-called *Dossiers Secrets d'Henri Lobineau* ("Secret Files of Henri Lobineau")—which they deposited at the Bibliothèque nationale de France in Paris. Among the documents deposited, which included forged genealogies and encrypted messages referring to the Priory of Sion, were fake medieval parchments that Plantard's artist friend Philippe de Cherisey had put together.

Remember that the case for the existence of the mysterious Priory of Sion, as described in *The Holy Blood and the Holy Grail* and *The Da Vinci Code*, is based entirely on these forged manuscripts. During the 1960s Plantard passed on these documents regarding the Priory of Sion to his friend Gérard de Sède, telling him they were real. They then became the inspiration for de Sède's *Le Trésor maudit de Rennes-le-Château*.

In 2005, Channel Four Television in the UK filmed a documentary entitled *The Real Da Vinci Code*. This insightful documentary included interviews with some of major players in the Rennes-le-Château mystery, including Henry Lincoln, Michael Baigent, and Arnaud de Sède, son of Gérard de Sède, as well as archive footage of Pierre Plantard. During his interview Arnaud de Sède stated unequivocally that his father and Plantard had invented the existence of the Priory of Sion. The forger of the medieval documents, Philippe de Chérisey, made several confessions through the years regarding his part in the affair.

So if the whole Rennes-le-Château was a hoax engineered mainly by Noël Corbu and Pierre Plantard, what about Father Saunière's unexplained sudden wealth? As early as 1896 Saunière had been under the suspicion of his superiors at the Bishopric of Carcassonne for selling masses. Investigations found that Saunière had advertised in religious magazines, journals, and papers worldwide, resulting in so many requests for masses that the priest was unable to honor all of them. During 1910–1911, Saunière was brought to trial for "trafficking in masses," selling masses he never performed, on a huge scale and was consequently suspended from priestly duties.

Receipts still in existence show that the sum of money Saunière gained from selling masses was respectable but not huge. In 1913, for example, his estate was only valued at 18,000 Francs by the Crédit Foncier de France (a French national mortgage bank) when Saunière was desperately trying to negotiate a loan from that bank by mortgaging his property. What is known is that, when he died in January 1917, Saunière was relatively poor; in fact, Marie Dénarnaud could not even afford to pay for his coffin until June of that year. Contrary to what is written in *The Holy Blood and the Holy Grail* regarding Saunière imparting a terrible secret to a horrified priest just before he died, the Abbé Rivière, who was at Saunière's bedside in his last moments, heard his confession, lifted his suspension from the priesthood, and administered the last sacraments.

The strange inscription put above the entrance to the Church of Mary Magdalene by Saunière—"This is a place of awe"—is often quoted in isolation in books about the Rennes-le-Château mystery as if to suggest that something of earth-shattering consequences is contained inside the church. In reality the phrase is taken from the Common Dedication of a Church, from Genesis 28:17, which in full reads "How awe-inspiring is this place! This is no other but the house of God, and this is the gate of heaven." When Italian researcher Massimo Polidoro visited the village museum at Rennes-le-Château in July 2004 he located the hollow pillar discovered by Saunière that allegedly contained the parchments. When he examined the pillar he found that it was not hollow at all, but only contained a CD-sized slit, far too small to have contained any hidden manuscripts.

When looked at more critically, the so-called "facts" of the mystery begin to crumble to dust before our eyes, and the unavoidable conclusion is that Bérenger Saunière did not in fact discover a mysterious treasure in the Church of Mary Magdalene and become a wealthy man because of it. The popular story of the Rennes-le-Château mystery, and its connection with Jesus Christ, Mary Magdalene, the Templars, the Priory of Sion, and the Merovingians, is based on superficial research, a lack of critical judgement, and good old-fashioned wishful thinking—not that it all doesn't add up to an exciting and highly enjoyable read, which *The Da Vinci Code* certainly is, but it has nothing to do with history.

Chapter 4

Cape Sounion
(Greece)

Temple of Poseidon at Cape Sounion.

Place me on Sunium's marbled steep,
Where nothing save the waves and I,
May hear our mutual murmers sweep;
There swan-like, let me sing and die.
Lord Byron—*Don Juan*
(Canto III, Stanza L16) (1819–24)

Occupying the border between the relative tranquility of the Saronic Gulf and the dangers of the open Aegean Sea, the dramatic coastal site of Cape Sounion (Soúnio), at the southeastern tip of Attica, has been sacred at least as far back as Homeric times. In the Greek myth of Theseus and the Minotaur, it is the site from which the hero's father, Aegeus, King of Athens, leaps to his death into the sea. Cape Sounion is home to a number of important ancient monuments, the most impressive of which is the Temple of Poseidon, the powerful Greek god of the sea and of earthquakes.

The sheer cliffs of the windswept Cape Sounion promontory rise 170 feet above the Aegean Sea around 43 miles south-southeast of Athens. The site has a long history. According to Homer's *Odyssey* (eighth century BC) during the arduous journey of the Greeks back from Troy (probably modern Hisarlik, northwestern Turkey) the helmsman of King Menelaus of Sparta died while steering the ship round "the sacred cape" of Sounion:

> We were sailing together over the sea from Troy, Menelaus and I, the best of friends. But when we were abreast of the sacred cape of Sunium, where Attica juts out into the sea, Phoebus Apollo shot one of his painless arrows at Menelaus's helmsman and killed him, with the tiller of the running ship still in his hands. This man, Phrontis son of Onetor, had been the world's best steersman in a gale, and Menelaus, though anxious to journey on was kept at Sunium til he could bury his comrade with the proper rites.

> (*Odyssey*, 3.276–285)

After giving his companion the proper funerary honours of cremation on a funeral pyre on the beach, the Greek ships sailed on, only to be caught in a violent storm off Cape Malea (southeast Peloponnese), where the fleet was split into two separate groups.

Further indication of the importance of the Cape Sounion promontory in ancient Greek history is its inclusion in the tale of Theseus and the Minotaur. This well-known myth tells the story of Theseus, the legendary founder-king of Athens, who volunteered to go to the island of Crete as one of the seven Athenian boys and seven Athenian girls to be devoured by the Minotaur. The Minotaur was a creature with the head of a bull on the body of a man that was kept locked up in a labyrinth by King Minos of Crete. As Crete was the main political and military force in the Aegean at the time, Athens was forced to send King Minos a yearly tribute of 14 young people to avoid being attacked by the mighty Cretan navy. On leaving for Crete, the ship carrying the hostages hoisted a black sail. Theseus vowed to his father, King Aegeus, that he would kill the Minotaur to put an end to the bloody tribute; on his return he promised he would hoist a white sail in place of the black as a sign of his success.

When Theseus arrived in Crete he was helped in his task by Ariadne, the daughter of the king, who fell in love with him. She gave him a magic sword and a spool of thread he could use to find his way back out of the narrow winding passageways of the labyrinth. After he killed the monster, Theseus escaped by ship with Ariadne and the other hostages. On their way back to Athens they stopped at the island of Naxos, where, according to some accounts, Theseus abandoned Ariadne. (She was later taken by the god Dionysus to be his wife.)

Meanwhile, King Aegeus had been watching daily from the Cape Sounion promontory for the safe return of his son. The king saw the approaching ship in the distance, but Theseus had forgotten his promise to change the sails, and the vessel's sails were still black. On seeing this, Aegeus, overcome with grief at his son's apparent death, hurled himself into the sea from the rocky heights of Sounion. From then onward, the sea was named the Aegean in the king's honor. After his father's tragic death, Theseus became the king of Athens.

Some material evidence for the Cape's connection with the Homeric Phrontis was recovered during 19th-century excavations on the lower hill at the site. During this work, excavators discovered a rectangular pit almost 50 feet deep that contained a huge amount of votive offerings dating to the Archaic period (750–500 BC). These offerings, which include small oil jars, bronze and terracotta figurines, scarabs and carved seals, and black-figured plaques, have been associated with a cult of Phrontis. One of the plaques (now in the National Archaeological Museum, Athens), which dates to the eighth century BC, bears an illustration of a warship ploughing through the waves with the helmsman (Phrontis?) clearly depicted as larger than the other rowers in the boat.

By the seventh century BC there were two sanctuaries on the Sounion promontory, a sanctuary of Poseidon on the higher ground at the southern edge of the headland, and a sanctuary of Athena about 0.3 miles to the northeast. The open-air sanctuary of Poseidon contained some of the earliest examples of monumental marble sculpture in Greek art, in the form of *kouroi*, large marble statues of young nude males. The earliest of these extraordinary statues, which dates to around 600 BC, is also one of the largest *kouroi* so far recovered, standing around 10 feet in height. The first evidence for a temple dedicated to Poseidon on this site dates to considerably later than the sanctuary, around 490–480 BC. Fragments of limestone Doric capitals, wall blocks, unfinished column drums, and architraves have been discovered built into the later temple of Poseidon and also into the structure of the sanctuary of Athena on the lower hill. The original Temple of Poseidon was never completed, and was destroyed by the invading Persians in 480 BC. According to Greek historian Herodotus (c. 484–c. 425 BC) after the Battle of Salamis (on the eastern coast of Cyprus) in 450 BC, the Greeks sacrificed a captured Phoenician warship at Sounion as retribution for the Persian violation of their temple.

The Temple of Poseidon, which now stands on the Cape Sounion promontory, was built between 444 BC and 440 BC on the debris of the earlier structure. The newer temple was constructed using white marble from local mines rather than poros limestone, as in the original building. The Temple is built on the standard Doric plan; it is rectangular in shape with a colonnade on all four sides. There were once 42 huge columns, each 20 feet high, with a diameter more than 3 feet at the base, though only 18 of these remain today. The Temple of Poseidon stood within its own walled precinct, which was approached through a monumental gateway (*propylon*) of marble and limestone. The windowless inner sanctum (*naos*) at the center of the temple would have contained the colossal cult image (probably about 20 feet in height) of Poseidon, crafted in bronze and covered in gold leaf. The Temple of Poseidon is so close in plan to that of the contemporary Temple of Hephaestus, on the northwest side of the Agora of Athens, that they may well have been designed by the same architect.

At about the same time as the Temple of Poseidon was rebuilt, a Temple of Athena Sounias was constructed on the lower hill of the promontory over the site of her former sanctuary and a previous Doric temple destroyed by the Persians. This new Ionic temple was larger than its predecessor and opened to the east, with columns on only two of its sides: 10 columns along the east and 12 on the south. This arrangement is unique in Greek architecture.

Around 412 BC, during the last decades of the Peloponnesian War (fought between Athens and its empire, and the *Peloponnesian* League, led by the city of Sparta), the entire hill was heavily fortified. The 10-feet-thick fortification wall stretched down to the sea on the north side and was strengthened by 13 defensive towers around its perimeter. The fort was built by the Athenians primarily to protect the sea-route around the cape and consequently their vital corn supply. Thus the promontory became a strategically important military station for the Athenians, and a settlement grew up around it, testified by the remains of the large central street that have been recovered in excavations. Some time later, probably during the third century BC, two gable-roofed ship sheds, referred to as "The Trireme Launch" (a trireme was an ancient warship with three rows of oars on each side) were carved into the coastal bedrock on the northwest of the cape. This facility would have enabled the inhabitants of Sounion to launch triremes to defend grain ships passing by on their way to Athens.

During the sixth century BC, there was a sharp increase in the activity at the Laurion silver mines, located just to the north of Sounion. These mines provided Athens with much of its prosperity, and, as a result, the history of the temple and fortress site of Sounion was closely tied to that of Athens. However, from the end of the fourth century BC, Laurion fell into decline and Sounion began to lose its importance. Its fort was abandoned and its temples gradually deserted. In the first century AD the Temple of Athena at Cape Sounion was dismantled and re-erected in the Athenian Agora. Writing in the second century AD, Greek traveler and geographer Pausanias notes (*Description of Greece*, 1 1.1.): "When you have rounded the promontory you see a harbor and a temple to Athena of Sunium on the peak of the promontory." Pausanias obviously mistook the Temple of Poseidon for the Temple of Athena, which had long since been moved to Athens. His statement is a clear indication that, by his time, Cape Sounion and its great Temple of Poseidon had lost its importance as a religious site.

By the 14th century, the significance of its sacred buildings long since forgotten, Cape Sounion was used as a pirate stronghold and continued to be so for centuries afterward. Indeed, when English romantic poet and philhellene Lord Byron (1788–1824) visited Sounion as part of his Grand Tour of Europe in 1810–11, he and his party narrowly escaped being attacked by pirates at the Cape. The base of one of the columns of the Temple of Poseidon bears the inscribed signature supposedly of Byron himself, though there is no direct evidence that he was responsible for the carving. Byron also celebrated Cape Sounion in his masterpiece *Don Juan*, and was to die of pneumonia while fighting for the Greek struggle for independence from the Turks, at Messolonghi (western Greece) in April 1824. Since the 19th century, Cape Sounion, with its Temple of Poseidon representing the archetypal Greek romantic ruin, has continued to attract travelers, many of whom visit the site these days as much for the spectacular sunsets visible from the summit of the promontory as for the archaeological remains.

🏛

Chapter 5

Akrotiri and the Destruction of Thera (Greece)

Ruins of Akrotiri.

The southernmost of the Cyclades group of islands, Santorini is a small, circular archipelago of rocky volcanic islands in the southern Aegean Sea. The largest of the Santorini group is the modern island of Santorini (ancient Thera), where at the height of the Greek Bronze Age (c. 2000–1650 BC) a thriving Minoan community inhabited the town of Akrotiri. The Minoans were an advanced Bronze Age civilization that arose on the island of Crete and flourished from approximately 2700 BC to 1450 BC. The volcanic eruption on Thera, variously dated from the mid-1700s BC to the mid-1600s BC, split the island in two, and buried and preserved Akrotiri much in the same way as centuries later Vesuvius buried Pompeii. The eruption was one of the biggest in the past 10,000 years and has a rating of 7 on the Volcanic Explosivity Index. The catastrophe would have affected civilization in the Eastern Mediterranean for hundreds of years after it occurred, and it has even been suggested that the devastating eruption caused the collapse of the Minoan Civilization and was the inspiration for Plato's myth of Atlantis.

The first signs of settlement at Akrotiri date back to the Late Neolithic period (fourth millennium BC at the latest). During the third millennium BC (Early Bronze Age) the site grew into a large settlement, but it was not until the Middle and Late Bronze Age (c. 20th–17th centuries BC) that Akrotiri developed into an important urban center and, because of its strategic geographical position, one of the major ports of the Aegean. Due to close similarities in fresco styles and artifacts, Akrotiri has been associated with the Minoan civilization, though it was really a well-to-do town rather than an elaborate palace-complex like those found on Crete.

Excavations at Akrotiri began in 1967 under the late Professor Spyridon Marinatos and, although only the southern edge of the substantial town has been uncovered, the finds have been nothing less than startling.

Preserved in the solidified ash of the eruption, which is a staggering 150 feet deep on some parts of the island, Marinatos discovered complexes of multi-storied buildings with remains of walls standing as high as 26 feet, streets, an elaborate drainage system (utilizing the dual-pipe system, suggesting hot and cold running water), frescoes, furniture, and pottery. Objects from Crete, mainland Greece, Anatolia, Cyprus, Syria, and Egypt show the wide-ranging trade contacts of the settlement, while a loom-workshop indicates organized textile weaving for export.

One of the major buildings excavated at Akrotiri, named Xeste 3, was a large edifice, its western half standing at least three stories high.

Each floor probably contained 14 rooms, and the building had two staircases—a main one in the entrance and a service staircase inside. Other than a few storage jars (known as *pithoi*), there were no finds of domestic material such as cooking pots or millstones from this building, indicating that it was probably set aside for public use.

One of the most interesting features of Xeste 3 was the "Lustral Basin," discovered in the northeast corner of the house. Lustral Basins are known from Minoan palace architecture, and consist of a sunken rectangular room reached by an L-shaped or dog-legged flight of steps. Once believed to have been used for bathing, it is now thought that they had a function connected with ritual purification. Some of the rooms in Xeste 3 were decorated with magnificent wall paintings, the well-preserved remains of which can still be seen. One of these frescoes is known as the "Saffron Gatherers," and shows young women wearing typical Minoan costumes gathering crocuses from which the spice and dye saffron is made. The girls bring the crocuses to a "goddess," seated on a platform supported by altars. The goddess is flanked by a monkey and a griffin in attitudes of worship. In a fresco on the north wall of the ground floor, three girls are shown, one of whom is depicted in profile seated and clutching her forehead in pain because she has injured her foot, which is bleeding. This girl wears a myrtle branch in her hair. The entire head of one of the other girls in this fresco is painted blue, probably indicating that it is shaven, which would seem to indicate the ritualistic nature of this painting.

Another edifice at Akrotiri, known as Sector B, probably comprised two separate buildings, and it was from here that two well-known wall paintings, those of the of the Antelopes and the Boxing Children, came. In the latter painting, the head of each of the boys is partially shaven (and painted blue) but for two long tresses dangling at the back and two small locks of hair just above the forehead. Each of the children is wearing a belt/girdle and a boxing glove on the right hand.

The West House at Akrotiri was a medium sized building that, when excavated, contained storerooms, workshops, a kitchen, and a considerable number of loom weights, indicative of weaving activity in the house. The most spectacular discovery from the West House was a miniature "Ship Fresco," which has been rightly described by many archaeologists as one of the most important pieces of Aegean art ever found. The fresco, also known as the "Flotilla Fresco," is an extraordinarily complex series of scenes covering all four walls of Room 5 of the house. The painting depicts a fleet of ships, escorted by dolphins, on a major naval expedition, in the course of which they visit a number of ports and towns. Scholars have been unable to agree whether this fresco represents a military invasion, a trading voyage, or some kind of ritual journey.

Sometime in the middle of the 17th century BC, the prosperous and seemingly peaceful life of the inhabitants of Akrotiri came to an abrupt end. The Minoan eruption of Thera, as it is known, was perhaps the most violent volcanic eruption ever to hit the ancient world, erupting a staggering 14 cubic miles of magma and rock into Earth's atmosphere. This is six times more than the infamous 1883 eruption of Krakatoa, which killed more than 36,000 people. However, scientists believe that just before the volcano erupted on Thera there would have been seismic tremors, warning the inhabitants of what was to come. Excavations at Akrotiri have so far discovered no bodies in the ruins of the town. The absence of portable items such as jewelry and other valuable metal artifacts indicates that the inhabitants had time to collect their most precious small items and flee.

But where did they go? Did they make it to the harbor and board ships? Because only a small portion of the site has been excavated, it may be that future excavations close to Thera's ancient seashore will uncover hoards of skeletons clutching their valuables. Excavations of the ruins of the prosperous ancient Roman town Herculaneum, destroyed by Vesuvius in AD 79 along with Pompeii, revealed few human remains, showing that the town had been largely evacuated. However, in 1982, more than 250 skeletons were found huddled together in boat houses along the shore close to the town, buried under 66 feet of volcanic material. The populace had evidently attempted to escape by sea but had been killed instantly by the poisonous sulphuric gas cloud from the eruption. Excavations in this area also discovered lamps, house keys, wax tablets, jewelry, and coins—evidently the personal possessions that the inhabitants of Herculaneum had taken with them in their attempted flight. The question of whether the populace of Akrotiri suffered the same fate or whether they managed to escape in boats—perhaps to the island of Crete around 70 miles away—can only be solved by further excavations in and around Akrotiri.

The massive eruption on Thera would have generated catastrophic tsunamis and dense clouds of volcanic ash, blocking out the sun for many days, which would have had devastating effects on coastal sites across the Eastern Mediterranean. In an article entitled "Worldwide Environmental Impacts from the Eruption of Thera" in the journal *Environmental Geology* (1995, 26:172–81), P.E. LaMoreaux states that the environmental effects of the huge blast may have been felt across the globe, from north Africa and Asia Minor, to places as far away as Norway, Ireland, China, and possibly even North America and Antarctica.

There has been speculation that that the eruption of Thera had an effect of rather a different kind: the inspiration for Plato's tale of the legendary lost city of Atlantis first recorded his dialogues *Timaeus* and *Critias*. The excavator of Akrotiri, Spyridon Marinatos, believed that Plato's story of an intellectually and technologically advanced civilization suddenly destroyed by a catastrophic event was based on the collapse of the Minoans. Aside from the fact that Plato was not writing history but a moralizing tale, there are a number of objections to Marinatos's theory. Plato was writing in the fifth century BC; the eruption took place at least 1,000 years earlier, which would be an inordinately long time for the story to survive. Plato also states clearly that Atlantis lay beyond the Pillars of Hercules (the Strait of Gibraltar), which stood at the entrance to the Atlantic Ocean—nowhere near Crete or Thera. Perhaps most importantly, in contrast to the civilization in Plato's tale, the Minoan civilization did not collapse dramatically over night. The administrative and political center of Minoan Crete—the palace complex of Knossos—did not experience a destructive episode until around 1400 BC, much later than the eruption of Thera, and anyway was soon rebuilt and functioned as before until it was finally destroyed around 1360 BC.

The dating of the eruption on Thera is a controversial topic. As mentioned, the event has often been cited as the cause of the decline of the Minoan civilization around the mid-15th century BC. However, a 2006 study led by Professor Sturt Manning of Cornell University in New York, obtained radiocarbon dates from 127 wood, bone, and harvested seeds recovered from Akrotiri, Crete, Rhodes, and Turkey, which gave a date for the eruption of Thera of between 1660 BC and 1613 BC.

A further study led by geologist Walter Friedrich of the University of Aarhus in Denmark, of a buried olive branch from Akrotiri, used dendrochronology (tree-ring dating) and radiocarbon dating to show that the tree must have died between 1627 BC and 1600 BC.

Despite these results, many archaeologists object to these early dates for the eruption, arguing that the pottery finds from Akrotiri and other sites in the Aegean, as well as Egypt, indicate a date for the event between 1500 BC and 1450 BC. They also point out that if the Thera eruption is to be dated so early as the 17th century BC then the whole of Aegean Late Bronze Age chronology must be pushed back, which would also affect the dating of several Eastern Mediterranean cultures. Exactly when Thera erupted remains controversial topic, but if the radiocarbon dating is accurate, then major chronological realignments in prehistoric Mediterranean archaeology will be necessary.

Solomon's Temple and the Jehoash Inscription (Israel)

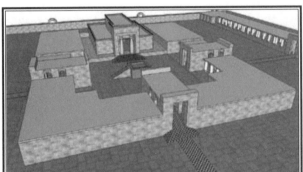

3-D computer reconstruction of Inner Court and House of the Temple.

Temple Mount, Jerusalem.

A ccording to the the Bible and the Torah, Solomon's Temple—
also known as the First Temple—was the first Jewish Temple
in Jerusalem. The huge exquisitely built structure was located on the
Temple Mount (or Haram al-Sharif; "Noble Sanctuary"), which is
associated with the biblical Mount Moriah, the place where Abraham
offered up his son in sacrifice to God. According to the Book of Kings,
Solomon is said to have secreted the Ark of the Covenant containing
the Ten Commandments in a Holy of Holies in the Temple. The Ark
subsequently disappeared when the First Temple was plundered and
burned to the ground in the sixth century BC by the Babylonians. The
structure was later rebuilt as the Second Temple, which stood from
516 BC until AD 70, when it was destroyed by the Romans during the
First Jewish-Roman War. All this is according to the Bible, but what
archaeological evidence is there for the Temple of Solomon? Could
the "Jehoash Inscription" finally constitute proof that the First Temple
as described in the Bible actually existed, or is it an elaborate fake?

The only surviving source for the First Temple of Jerusalem is a
description in the Biblical books of Joshua, Judges, Samuel, Kings, and
Ezekiel. The Book of Kings describes the Temple as follows:

> The house that King Solomon built for the LORD was sixty cubits
> long, twenty cubits wide, and thirty cubits high. The vestibule in
> front of the nave of the house was twenty cubits long, equal to the
> width of the house, and ten cubits deep in front of the house. And
> he made for the house windows with recessed frames. He also built
> a structure against the wall of the house, running around the walls
> of the house, both the nave and the inner sanctuary. And he made
> side chambers all around. The lowest story was five cubits broad,
> the middle one was six cubits broad, and the third was seven cubits
> broad. For around the outside of the house he made offsets on the
> wall in order that the supporting beams should not be inserted into
> the walls of the house. (1 Kings 6:2–6)

The Temple thus measured about 90 feet long, 30 feet wide, and
45 feet high. The Book of Kings goes on to describe that the ceiling of
the house was made of beams and planks of cedar and the floor with
boards of cypress. The huge quantities of cedar were sent by King
Hiram of Tyre, an ancient Phoenician city in modern-day Lebanon.

Solomon built within the structure an inner sanctuary of wood overlaid with gold; no stone was used for this room, which was known as the "Most Holy Place." The inner sanctuary was constructed to receive the "ark of the covenant of the Lord," which was accompanied by two huge cherubim carved of olive wood and covered in gold.

There is also a description of the Temple in the *Tanakh* (the sacred book of Judaism, consisting of the Torah, the Prophets, and the Writings), in the second Book of Chronicles (Chapters 3–7). Written several centuries later than the Book of Kings (and using it and the Book of Samuel as sources), Chronicles tells essentially the same story of the construction of the Temple, though it adds a few details. According to Chronicles, the whole building was roofed with tiles of gold, and adorned with bronze columns and precious stones. Gold nails were also used. In fact, Chronicles states that, in all, around 20 tons of gold were used in the Temple's construction. Chronicles describes the elaborate gold furnishings of the Temple thus:

> Solomon also made all the equipment in God's temple: the gold altar; the tables on which [to put] the bread of the Presence; the lampstands and their lamps of pure gold to burn in front of the inner sanctuary according to specifications; the flowers, lamps, and gold tongs—of purest gold; the wick trimmers, sprinkling basins, ladles, and firepans—of purest gold; and the entryway to the temple, its inner doors to the most holy place, and the doors of the temple sanctuary—of gold. (2 Chronicles 4: 19–22)

According to biblical accounts, in the 10th century BC, after capturing the city of Jerusalem, King David chose an area of land in a high place outside the city walls to build a sanctuary to God, an area that the Bible calls Mount Moriah. But it was to be David's son Solomon who would complete the construction of the First Temple, in 960 BC. As well as serving as the home for the Ark of the Covenant, the Temple became an important religious center, especially after Josiah, king of Judah from 641 BC to 609 BC, outlawed worship at all other sanctuaries and established Solomon's Temple as the only acceptable place for sacrifice in the Kingdom of Judah. But in 597 BC, King Nebuchadnezzar II of Babylon attacked Jerusalem and pillaged the Temple, returning again in 586 BC when he leveled the city and again plundered the Temple.

The Bible also states that after the attack Nebuchadnezzar II sent the Jews into exile in Babylon, where they would remain until Persian King Cyrus II (Cyrus the Great) conquered Babylonia and allowed them to return in 538 BC.

Soon after the return from exile, the Temple was rebuilt as the Second Temple, which was eventually completed around 515 BC. In 19 BC, in order to win favor with the Jews, King Herod the Great ordered that the Temple be heavily renovated and expanded, though work was not entirely finished until AD 63. Only seven years later, the Second Temple was completely destroyed by the Romans during their destruction of Jerusalem on August 4, AD 70, which put an end to the Great Jewish Revolt. In AD 130, during his rebuilding of Jerusalem, the Emperor Hadrian had a Roman temple to Jupiter Capitolinus constructed on the ruins of the Temple of Herod.

With all this building activity and destruction on Temple Mount through the centuries, could any archaeological evidence of Solomon's First Temple have survived? The Temple Mount in Jerusalem is believed to have been continuously inhabited for 5,000 years. We know that during the Middle Bronze Age (c. 2000–c. 1550 BC), when the city seems to have been known as Jebus, it was a small, fortified site controlled by the Canaanites. Recently the remains of a huge, 26-foot-high defensive wall that was used to protect a path leading to a spring, the area's only water source, were discovered. The wall dates from around 1700 BC and represents the oldest fortifications ever found on the Temple Mount.

The First Temple, according to the Bible, was a large complex structure and dates to around seven centuries later than the Canaanite citadel, so despite the repeated destructions on the site we should expect to find some trace of its existence, or at least some contemporary related artifacts or structures. The reality is, however, that not a single structure or artifact has been positively identified that unequivocally relates to Solomon's Temple. Indeed, because of the lack of archaeological evidence for King Solomon's time in Jerusalem, some scholars now doubt the truth of the biblical account of Solomon as the ruler of a great empire.

However, the problem with locating the supposed site of the First Temple in Jerusalem is more complex than it may first appear.

Solomon's Temple is thought by many researchers to be on the present site of a complex of holy buildings on the Temple Mount, including an Islamic shrine known as the Dome of the Rock and the Al-Aqsa Mosque. Due to the sacred nature of the site, religious leaders do not allow archaeological excavations on Temple Mount. Nevertheless, there have been a few interesting archaeological discoveries during the past couple of decades that, for some scholars, including Israeli archaeologist Eilat Mazar, suggest that the great Temple of Solomon does indeed lie hidden beneath the buildings on the Temple Mount.

In October 2007, the Israeli Antiquities Authority (IAA) reported that Muslim workers had unearthed artifacts on the Temple Mount that dated to within the First Temple period (eighth–sixth centuries BC). The objects were found by the Waqf Muslim religious trust during maintenance work on the Temple Mount and included animal bones, fragments of ceramic bowls and juglets, and the rim of a ceramic storage jar. If the dating is correct, the finds certainly indicate the presence of people on the Temple Mount during the late eighth century BC and seventh century BC, though the artifacts do not of course provide any direct evidence for the existence of the First Temple on the site.

One sensational artifact that certainly seemed at the time of its discovery to provide evidence for the existence of the First Temple was the so-called "Jehoash Inscription." This controversial artifact appeared in Israel in 2001, when it was anonymously offered to Israel's National Museum at a price reportedly more than $4 million. The stone tablet measures 10.6 inches long, 8.7 inches wide, and 2.7 inches thick, and bears an inscription in Hebrew Phoenician from the First Temple. The inscription contains details of repairs made to the Temple in Jerusalem by King Jehoash (reigned c. 837–c. 800 BC), son of King Ahaziah of Judah. The details of the inscription corresponded closely to the description of repairs made to the Temple in 2 Kings 12:5–13.

As the first royal inscription of an Israelite king ever found, the historical and archaeological potential of the Jehoash inscription was huge. From the beginning, however, the provenance of the tablet was unclear. It was said to have been unearthed either during construction work on the Temple Mount or in the Muslim cemetery outside the eastern wall of the Temple Mount. Initial examinations in 2002 by geologists from the Geological Survey of Israel (GSI) suggested that the

Tablet was indeed genuine, though there were a number of researchers who voiced doubts about the authenticity of the object. Indeed, it soon turned out that the GSI had misidentified the Tablet's rock type: it was not arkosic sandstone from southern Israel or Jordan, as they had stated, but a type of metamorphic greywacke, the nearest source of which was the island of Cyprus.

An investigation of the Tablet in 2003 by the Israel Antiquities Authority (IAA) commission concluded that, due to various mistakes in the spelling and the mixture of different alphabets in the inscription, the object was a modern forgery. Yuval Goren, professor of Archaeology at Tel Aviv University, and also a geologist, examined the patina (the layer that forms over an ancient object after many centuries) on the front of the inscription and found microfossils of marine organisms called foraminifera. Such fossils could only be found if the patina formed beneath the sea—obviously impossible if it had been formed in Jerusalem, miles from the sea. Thus Professor Goren concluded that patina on the front of the Tablet was artificial—a manmade chemical mixture to which gold and ancient charcoal had been added by hand. The charcoal had been introduced to obtain an ancient date in carbon-dating tests (one sample taken from the object gave a radiocarbon date in the region of 2,300 years old). Goren also believes that the gray/black stone used for the inscription had probably been taken from a nearby medieval Crusader castle, possibly the Fortress of Apollonia around 10 miles away. At this site there are a number of appropriate rectangular flat stones of metamorphic graywacke. Originally having served as ballast on board ships coming from Cyprus, these stones had eventually been used in the construction of the castle.

Apart from the scientific evidence, something else that initially raised suspicion as to the authenticity of the Tablet was its connection with another controversial artefact: the James Ossuary. This limestone box, which came to light in Israel in 2002, was alleged to have been the ossuary (bone box) of James the Just, the brother of Jesus. The box bears the Aramaic inscription "Yaakov bar Yosef akhui di Yeshua" ("James, son of Joseph, brother of Jesus"). Though some researchers still believe the box to be authentic, the Israel Antiquities Authority concluded after intensive investigations that it was a modern forgery. Coincidentally, the owner of both the James Ossuary and the Jehoash

Inscription was a Tel Aviv antiquities dealer called Oded Golan. Golan was also connected with a thumb-sized ivory pomegranate believed by some scholars to be a relic from Solomon's Temple. The pomegranate carries the inscription in ancient Hebrew "Belonging to the Temple of the Lord (Yahweh), holy to the priests." This relic was bought from an anonymous collector by the Israel Museum for $550,000 in the 1980s, but in 2004 was declared to be a fake.

In March 2003, police and officers of IAA's Theft Unit raided Golan's apartment and two other premises under his ownership. After a thorough search they found the Jehoash Inscription, numerous unregistered archaeological artifacts, various tools and materials used to fake antiquities, and many half-finished "ancient" artifacts. Golan and three of his associates were accused of operating an international fake antiquities ring, which had been in existence for around 20 years. In December 2004, police indicted Golan, and, as of February 2010, he was still on trial, though charges against his colleagues have been dropped. This is a sad tale of a cynical and selfish group of people whose activities have seriously corrupted the archaeological record. It is a sobering thought to think that the work of Golan and his colleagues, and others like them, could well litter the shelves and display cases of museums all over the world. The faking of biblical antiquities is now a huge and immensely profitable industry—an industry that, like it or not, is closely linked to the question of evidence for the existence of the Temple of Solomon.

⧖

Chapter 7

Göbekli Tepe
(Turkey)

Sculpture of an animal on one of the pillars at Göbekli Tepe.

Located in modern Turkey, Göbekli Tepe is fast becoming one of the most important archaeological sites in the world. The discovery of this stunning 10,000-year-old site in the 1990s sent shock waves through the archaeological world and beyond, with some researchers even claiming it was the site of the biblical Garden of Eden. The many examples of sculptures and megalithic architecture that make up what may well be the world's first temple at Göbekli Tepe predate pottery, metallurgy, the invention of writing, the wheel, and the beginning of agriculture. That hunter-gatherer peoples could organize the construction of such a complex site as far back as the 11th or 10th millennium BC not only revolutionizes our understanding of hunter-gatherer culture but poses a serious challenge to the conventional view of the rise of civilization.

Göbekli Tepe (Turkish for *"the hill of the navel"*) is a 1,000-foot-diameter mound located at the highest point of a mountain ridge, around 9 miles northeast of the town of Şanlıurfa (Urfa) in southeastern Turkey. Since 1994, excavations conducted by Klaus Schmidt of the Istanbul branch of the German Archaeological Institute, with the cooperation of the Şanlıurfa Museum, have been taking place at the site. Results to date have been astounding, especially bearing in mind the excavators estimate that their work has uncovered a mere 5 percent of the site.

Göbekli Tepe consists of four arrangements of monolithic pillars linked together by segments of coarsely built dry stone walls to form a series of circular or oval structures. There are two large pillars in the center of each complex, which are encircled by slightly smaller stones facing inward. Archaeologists believe that these pillars could have once supported roofs. The structures vary in size, between around 33 and 98 feet in diameter, and have floors made of terrazzo (burnt lime). The megaliths themselves, 43 of which have been unearthed so far, are mainly T-shaped pillars of soft limestone up to around 16 feet in height, and were excavated and transported from a stone quarry on the lower southwestern slope of the hill. Geophysical surveys on the hill indicate that there are as many as 250 more megaliths lying buried around the site, suggesting that another 16 complexes once existed at Göbekli Tepe.

Although some of the standing stones at Göbekli Tepe are blank, others display extraordinary artwork in the form of elaborately carved foxes, lions, bulls, scorpions, snakes, wild boars, vultures, waterfowl, insects, and arachnids. There are also abstract shapes and one relief of a naked woman, posed frontally in a sitting position. A number of the T-shaped stones have depictions of what appear to be arms at their sides, which could indicate that the stones represent stylized humans or perhaps gods. Although the pictograms at Göbekli Tepe do not represent a form of writing, they may have functioned as sacred symbols whose meanings were implicitly understood by local populations at the time.

The depictions of vultures at Göbekli Tepe have parallels at other Anatolian and Near Eastern sites. The walls of many of the shrines at the large Neolithic settlement of Çatal Höyük (in existence from approximately 7500 BC to 5700 BC) in south-central Turkey were adorned with large skeletal representations of vultures. One theory put forward to explain the prominence of vultures in the early Anatolian Neolithic is in the context of possible excarnation practices suggesting a funerary cult. After death, bodies were deliberately left outside and exposed, perhaps on some kind of wooden frame, to have their skeletons stripped of flesh by vultures and other birds of prey. The skeletons were then interred somewhere else. Perhaps the ritual of excarnation was the focus of a cult of the dead practiced by the inhabitants of Göbekli Tepe, as it certainly seems to have been elsewhere in Anatolia and the Near East in the Pre-Pottery Neolithic.

Curiously, Schmidt and his team have so far found no evidence of settlement at Göbekli Tepe; houses, cooking hearths, and refuse pits are all absent. The archaeologists did, however, find over 100,000 animal bone fragments, many of which exhibited cut marks and splintered edges, which shows that animals were being butchered and cooked somewhere in the area. The bones came from wild game such as gazelle (which made up more than 60 percent of the bones), boar, sheep, red deer, and different species of birds, such as vultures, cranes, ducks, and geese. All of the bones were from wild species—evidence that that the people who inhabited Göbekli Tepe were hunter-gatherers rather than early farmers who kept domesticated animals.

Due to the presence of multiple monumental complexes at such an early date, Göbekli Tepe is a somewhat unique site. However, there are some parallels with the site at the early Neolithic settlement of Nevali

Çori, on the middle Euphrates River in eastern Turkey, which lies only 12 1/2 northwest of Göbekli Tepe. The main temple at Nevali Çori was dated to around 8000 BC, perhaps a thousand years later than Göbekli Tepe. The cult complexes at the settlement had a number of features in common with Göbekli Tepe, such as a terrazzo-style lime cement floor, monolithic T-shaped pillars built into dry stone walls, and two free-standing pillars in the center of the complex area.The T-shaped pillars show reliefs of what appear to be human hands. Unfortunately, Nevali Çori is now gone, submerged under a lake created by the Atatürk Dam in 1992.

The excavators of Göbekli Tepe believe that around 8000 BC the people there deliberately buried the monuments under mountains of soil and settlement refuse, such as flints and animal bones, brought from elsewhere.

This backfilling is the main reason why the site has been preserved after so many thousands of years. Why the inhabitants of Göbekli Tepe abandoned the site is not clearly understood, though the monuments had obviously lost their relevance, which may have had some connection with the new way of life that accompanied the development of agriculture and animal husbandry that occurred around this time.

We know from typological dating (of stone tools) and radiocarbon dates that the final building phase at Göbekli Tepe dates to c8000 BC. However, the date of its very earliest occupation is far from clear. Nevertheless, radiocarbon dates (from charcoal) for the most recent part of the earliest layer (stratum III) at the site center around 9000 BC. Klaus Schmidt and his team estimate that Göbekli Tepe's stone monuments are about this age, though the structures have not been directly dated themselves. From the available evidence the site's excavators estimate Göbekli Tepe's beginnings at 11,000 BC or earlier, which is incredibly early for such a complex set of monuments.

The planning and building of such a site as Göbekli Tepe would have required a degree of organization and resources hitherto unknown in hunter-gatherer societies. Schmidt has made the intriguing suggestion that, rather than building temples and other religious structures after they had learned to farm and live in settled communities, the hunter-gatherers of the area first constructed megalithic sites like Göbekli Tepe and thus laid the foundation for the later development of complex societies. Indeed, investigations of other sites surrounding Göbekli Tepe have revealed a prehistoric village just 20 miles away, where evidence of the world's oldest domesticated strains of wheat has been recovered. According to radiocarbon dates, agriculture developed in the area around 10,500 years ago, just a few hundred years after the construction of Göbekli Tepe. Other sites in the region show evidence for the domestication of sheep, cattle, and pigs 1,000 years after Göbekli Tepe's monuments were erected. All this evidence suggests that the area around Göbekli Tepe was at the forefront of the agricultural revolution.

Perhaps the most elusive aspect of the megalithic structures at Göbekli Tepe is their function: why did hunter-gatherers construct such elaborate monuments? In Schmidt's opinion, the site was an important location for a cult of the dead, and, although no definite burials have been discovered so far, he believes they will be found underneath the floors of the circular monuments. In the absence of houses or domestic buildings of any sort in the area, Schmidt sees Göbekli Tepe as akin to a pilgrimage destination that attracted worshipers from as far away as a hundred miles. Indeed the vast amount of animal bone discovered at the site certainly suggests that that ritual feasting (and even sacrifice) regularly took place here. There is perhaps a parallel here with the much later site at Durrington Walls, close to Stonehenge, in Wiltshire, England. Dating to around 2600 BC, Durrington Walls was a huge ritual timber circle where enormous amounts of animal bone, mainly pigs and cattle, were discovered, which suggested to its excavator, Professor Mike Parker-Pearson, that ritual feasting was an important feature of the site.

Intriguingly, in recent excavations at Göbekli Tepe, Schmidt's team has uncovered pieces of human bones in soils that came from the niches behind the stone pillars at the site. Schmidt believes the bones show that corpses were brought into the ritual areas demarcated by the engraved T-shaped stone, where they were then laid out and left to be stripped of their soft tissue by wild animals. Such activity would make Göbekli Tepe both a cemetery and a center of a regional death cult.

It is difficult to believe that the barren semi-desert where Göbekli Tepe is located was once a region of green meadows, woods, and fields of wild barley and wheat. The area would also have been thronging with vast herds of gazelle, flocks of geese, and ducks. Indeed the animal and plant remains indicate such a rich and idyllic scene that Göbekli Tepe has been linked with the biblical story of the Garden of Eden. For those who take the story as a literal truth, the biblical location of Eden—at a point where four rivers descend—has been interpreted as within the Fertile Crescent. The ancient Fertile Crescent is defined as an agriculturally rich region in western Asia, which consists of present-day Iraq, Syria, Lebanon, Israel, Kuwait, Jordan, southeastern Turkey, and west and southwestern Iran. The four rivers of the biblical Eden include the Tigris and Euphrates, and believers in the connection between the two sites, such as the author David Rohl, point out that Göbekli Tepe lies between both of these. The Book of Genesis also states that Eden is ringed by mountains, as is Göbekli Tepe.

Other researchers believe that the Eden narrative in the Bible could be better interpreted as an allegory for the transition from a hunter-gather lifestyle to agriculture, though biblical accounts were recorded millennia after this transition took place. Interestingly, it is Klaus Schmidt's opinion that the shift from hunting to farming in the area brought about the decline of Göbekli Tepe. With the intense work required for agricultural societies to succeed there was no longer the time, or perhaps the need, for the monuments of Göbekli Tepe. In the surrounding area, trees were chopped down, soils became exhausted, and the landscape was gradually transformed into the arid wilderness we see today.

As long as only a tiny fraction of the incredible site of Göbekli Tepe has been excavated, we can never know for sure why it was built, and why it was buried and abandoned. Future work at the site will undoubtedly cast further light not only on these enigmas, but on our understanding of a critical stage in the development of human societies. One thing is certain: Göbekli Tepe has many more secrets to reveal.

⌛

Chapter 8

The Tower of Babel in Ancient Babylonia? (Iraq)

The Tower of Babel by Pieter Brueghel the Elder (1563).

The biblical story of the enormous tower built in the city of Babel after the Great Flood is familiar to people the world over. But is the account in the Bible based on historical events? If so, where exactly was the Tower of Babel, and does any archaeological evidence for its existence survive today? The word *Babel* comes from the Akkadian (the main language of Babylon) word *Bab-ilu* meaning "gate of God."

Babel is the Hebrew name for Babylon, an ancient city-state of Lower Mesopotamia (modern Iraq), so if the Tower of Babel actually existed, then it is logical that it would have been located somewhere in ancient Babylonia—that is, southern Mesopotamia. The "land of Shinar" mentioned in the Bible in connection with Babel is also generally accepted as referring to as southern Mesopotamia.

The story of the construction of the Tower of Babel is told in Genesis 11:1–5 (King James Version) as follows:

> And the whole earth was of one language, and of one speech. And it came to pass, as they journeyed from the east, that they found a plain in the land of Shinar; and they dwelt there. And they said one to another, Go to, let us make brick, and burn them thoroughly. And they had brick for stone, and slime had they for mortar. And they said, Go to, let us build us a city and a tower, whose top may reach unto heaven; and let us make us a name, lest we be scattered abroad upon the face of the whole earth. And the Lord came down to see the city and the tower, which the children built.

We don't know exactly what happened to the Tower. The Bible does not mention it being destroyed, though other sources give some details as to its demise. One of these sources is the *Book of Jubilees,* also known as the *Lesser Genesis.* The *Book of Jubilees* is an ancient Jewish religious work, probably written in the second century BC, which recounts the biblical history of the world from creation to Moses; it is not part of the biblical Canon. In the *Book of Jubilees,* God sends "a mighty wind" and destroys the Tower, which had stood "between Asshur and Babylon in the land of Shinar." Greek scholar Cornelius Alexander, who flourished in the first century BC, also mentions the Tower being toppled by a great wind, as does first-century Jewish historian Josephus (*Antiquities* 1.4.3). In the *Mishnah* (or *Mishna*), an early form of the Jewish oral law or tradition compiled into written form between the second century BC and the second century AD, one-third of the tower is destroyed by fire, one-third subsides into the earth, and the last third is left standing.

If the Tower of Babel was located within the city Babylon itself, where exactly was it? We know that ancient Babylon was completely razed to the ground in 689 BC by Assyrian King Sennacherib. Its remains are located near the modern town of Hilla, on the eastern bank of the River Euphrates, about 55 miles southwest of Baghdad. Unfortunately many of these ancient ruins have been heavily damaged by the Iraq/U.S. war. In his destruction of Babylon, King Sennacherib also claimed to have destroyed the *Etemenanki* ("temple/house of the foundation of heaven and earth"), a ziggurat (stepped temple tower) dedicated to the all-powerful Babylonian god Marduk. The ziggurat seems to have been originally built around the time of Hammurabi (1792–1750 BC), the sixth king of Babylon. After the destruction of Babylon by Sennacherib, the city was rebuilt by Nabopolassar, the first ruler of the Neo-Babylonian Empire (ruled 625–605 BC) and his son Nebuchadnezzar II (c. 630–562 BC), the last great king of Babylon.

The ziggurats of the ancient Mesopotamian valley and western Iranian plateau were built of sun-baked mud brick (there was little stone available), and could be hundreds of feet high, with temples to the city god on their lofty summits. A large number of these structures were built between the early third millennium BC and the sixth century BC, and the remains of around 32 are known today, mostly from modern Iraq and a few from Iran. It is the *Etemenanki* of ancient Babylon that many researchers believe could have been the biblical Tower of Babel. Indeed some scholars, including Stephen L. Harris, professor emeritus of humanities and religious studies at California State University, Sacramento, believe the biblical story of the Tower of Babel was influenced by the Etemenanki during captivity of the Hebrews in Babylon.

The Etemenanki is described in a cuneiform (one of the earliest forms of written script) tablet from Uruk dating to 229 BC, though copied from an older text. The clay tablet states that the Tower has seven stories, a height of "seven stocks" (around 300 feet), and a square base of 300 feet on each side. Fifth-century Greek historian Herodotus also mentions the Etemenanki in his Histories, though he never seems to have visited Babylon. He calls it the temple of the Akkadian god Bêl:

> The temple of Bêl, the Babylonian Zeus [...] was still in existence in my time. It has a solid central tower, one stadium square, with a second erected on top of it and then a third, and so on up to eight. All eight towers can be climbed by a spiral way running round the outside, and about half way up there are seats for those who make

the ascent to rest on. On the summit of the topmost tower stands a great temple with a fine large couch in it, richly covered, and a golden table beside it. The shrine contains no image, and no one spends the night there except (if we may believe that Chaldaeans who are the priests of Bêl) one Babylonian woman, all alone, whoever it may be that the god has chosen. The Chaldaeans also say—though I do not believe them—that the god enters the temple in person and takes his rest upon the bed.

(Herodotus, Histories 1.181–2; tr. Aubrey
de Sélincourt)

In 1917, excavations at the site of ancient Babylon by German architect and archaeologist Robert Johann Koldewey (1855–1925) recovered the ruins of the Etemenanki, including the remains of a large stairs and a gate. Koldewey's excavations also discovered an important black stone stele (upright inscribed stone) inscribed in cuneiform script and dating to around 604–562 BC. The stele is carved with an image of the standing figure of Nebuchadnezzar II, and also illustrates the Etemenanki tower from the front, clearly showing seven steps including the temple on the top; above this is a line drawing of the ground plan of the temple showing both the outer walls and the inner arrangement of rooms. The inscription on the stele reads:

Etemenaki, I made it the wonder of the people of the world, I raised its top to heaven, made doors for the gates, and I covered it with bitumen and bricks.

(The Schøyen Collection, MS 2063,
The Tower of Babel Stele,
*www.schoyencollection.com/babylonianhist.
htm#2063*)

One alternative site for the location of the Tower of Babel has been suggested at the ancient city of Borsippa (modern Birs Nimrud), which was located about 11 miles southwest of Babylon on the east bank of the River Euphrates. The name Borsippa means "Tongue Tower," which some researchers believe connects it with the biblical story of the Tower of Babel and the confusion of tongues. The ziggurat at Borsippa, one of the best preserved of all such monuments and still an impressive 172 feet high, was dedicated to Nabu, the god of science and the son of Marduk, by Nebuchadnezzar II. Excavations at the site by archaeologists from the Leopold-Franzens-Universität Innsbruck, Austria, have revealed that the building was constructed over the ruins of a smaller tower from the second millennium BC, and consisted of seven terraces built of millions of mud bricks. The structure rose up to a height of more than 230 feet, and archaeologists have discovered that the first two levels were covered with bitumen and were black; the third, fourth, and fifth were decorated with blue-glazed bricks and perhaps also images of bulls and lions; and the sixth and seventh terraces, closest to the sanctuary, were made entirely of mud brick.

Among the number of cuneiforms inscriptions from Borsippa, an inscription of Nebuchadnezzar II, known as the "Borsippa Inscription," records how he restored the temple of Nabu using "bricks of noble lapis lazuli." The inscription refers to the Tower as "the temple of the seven spheres." However, there is another text from Borsippa that seems to discount it as the site of the biblical Tower of Babel. This inscription states that Nebuchadnezzar wanted the Borsippa Tower built on the same design as that of the Tower of Babel at Babylon and that "Nabu's tower" should reach the skies and be just as grand as that of Babel.

Parallels to the biblical story of the Tower of Babel can be found in the Sumerian legend *Enmerkar and the Lord of Aratta*. The Sumerian civilization emerged about 4000 BC on the flood plain of the lower reaches of the Tigris and Euphrates rivers in southern Mesopotamia, and lasted roughly until 2000 BC. *Enmerkar and the Lord of Aratta* was composed around the 21st century BC and describes a golden age when all peoples spoke in one language, before the god Enki changed their speech. The epic describes the Sumerian ruler Enmerkar of Uruk (an ancient Sumerian city located east of the present bed of the Euphrates River) building a huge ziggurat in the city of Eridu. To help in the construction of the vast tower, which was to be raised in honor of the goddess Inanna, the king demanded a tribute of precious metals and gemstones from the land of Aratta.

The site of Eridu (Sumerian—"mighty place") is now called Tell Abu Shahrain, and is located around 13 1/2 miles from the Iraqi city of Nasiriyah, and about 196 miles southeast of Baghdad. Eridu was the earliest city in southern Mesopotamia, occupied between about 5000 and 2000 BC. The unfinished Ziggurat of Amar-Sin (c. 2047–2039 BC) at Eridu, which was built over 18 previous temples on the site, has been suggested as the origin of the story of the Tower of Babel. British Egyptologist David Rohl believes that this structure, much larger and older than the *Etemenanki* at Babylon, is the biblical Tower of Babel. Rohl also notes that one title of Eridu was *NUN.KI* (Sumerian—"the mighty place"), which much later became a name for Babylon. If the ancient city of "Babel" was not in fact Babylon, but rather the more ancient Eridu, then Rohl's theory must at least warrant further research.

Despite these interesting hypotheses, no structure has yet been firmly identified as the Tower of Babel, and there is consequently no proof of the historicity of the biblical story. For many the Genesis story is an explanatory myth, to give a reason for the diversity of languages and the distribution of people after the legendary Great Flood. Nevertheless, the biblical account of the building of the Tower could well have been suggested by one of Mesopotamia's numerous ziggurats. The composer of the lines in Genesis was obviously familiar with the construction methods of using sun-dried brick and bitumen in the great multi-story temple towers. Although recent events in Iraq have severely hindered all archaeological work in the area, it is possible that one day future survey and/or excavations at the ancient sites of Eridu and Babylon will uncover more clues to the origin of the enduring story of great temple tower of Babel.

Chapter 9

The Taj Mahal
(India)

The mausoleum of the Taj Mahal.

An immense, white-domed mausoleum of translucent marble, the Taj Mahal has become a symbol of India, instantly recognizable the world over. The monument was built between 1631 and 1648 on the orders of the Mughal emperor Shah Jahan in memory of his favorite wife, Arjumand Banu Begum (Mumtaz Mahal), and has thus been often described as the ultimate "monument to love." Thousands of artisans and craftsmen were employed on the huge building project, and, according to some legends, many of them were viciously mutilated, tortured, and even murdered by Shah Jahan, so they would never be able to build such a unique structure again. More recently, controversy has surrounded claims that a Hindu king, rather than a Muslim sultan built the Taj Mahal.

The Taj Mahal is located in the city of Agra, on the banks of the Yamuna River in the northern state of Uttar Pradesh, India. The monument was built by Shah Jahan (from Persian meaning "King of the World"), fifth ruler of the Mughal Empire, who was in power from 1628 until 1658. The name "Mughal" is a corruption of the Persian word for Mongol. The Mughals were an Islamic imperial power who originated in Central Asia, and were descended from the Mongol rulers Genghis Khan (c. 1162–1227) and Timur (Tamburlaine; 1336–1405). Between the mid-16th century and the early 18th centuries, the Mughal Empire was the dominant power in the Indian subcontinent. Before they moved their capital to Delhi in 1637, the Mughal Empire was governed from the Great Red Fort of Agra, a walled palatial city named after its red sandstone ramparts, located 1 1/2 miles northwest of the Taj Mahal.

In the construction of the Taj Mahal, Shah Jahan is said to have used the best architects and craftsmen in the land. Legend says that after the completion of the monument Shah Jahan was so astonished at the feat that he ordered the hands of all the craftsmen involved to be chopped off, so they would never be able to duplicate their work on the Taj Mahal anywhere else. The Emperor also ordered that their eyes be gouged out to make sure that the craftsmen would never be able to witness anything more beautiful and awe-inspiring than the Taj Mahal. Another legend has it that Shah Jahan wanted to build another Taj Mahal in black marble, across the River Yamuna, to be his own final resting place (and perhaps also for symmetry). The two Taj Mahals would have then been connected by a silver bridge, where the souls of the king and the queen would meet on every full moon night. Unfortunately, before he could realize his grand project, the emperor was deposed by his son. Historians have understandably found no proof of these stories, though such romantic and gory legends do help to attract more visitors to the monument.

In 1631, Shah Jahan's third wife and queen, Mumtaz Mahal, died in the town of Burhanpur while giving birth to their 14th child. The emperor was so devastated by the loss of his wife that his hair and beard are said to have turned snow white within a few months of her death. Shah Jahan began the construction of his wife's memorial around a year after her death and work was not was completed until around 1648, with the surrounding buildings taking another five years to finish. The monument was named for Mumtaz (Mumtaj) Mahal ("the Palace favourite"). According to official court historian Abdul Hamid Lahori, and other official chroniclers of the Emperor's reign, twenty thousand people are said to have been employed to work on the Taj Mahal. These workers included masons, stonecutters, inlayers, carvers, painters, calligraphers, and various other artisans requisitioned from all corners of the empire and also from Central Asia and Iran. Accounts of the construction state that more than 1,000 elephants were used to transport building materials from all over India and Asia to the site.

The exquisite white marble for the Taj Mahal came from Rajasthan, the jasper from Punjab, the jade and crystal from China, the turquoise from Tibet, the Lapis lazuli from Afghanistan, the sapphire from Sri Lanka, and the carnelian from Arabia. The monument was designed by a group of architects under imperial supervision, who included Abd ul-Karim Ma'mur Khan, Makramat Khan, and Persian architect Ustad Ahmad Lahauri, who is said to have been the chief designer of the Taj Mahal.

In September 1657, Shah Jahan became ill, and rumors spread rapidly through the land that he was close to death. Potential successors to his throne prepared themselves, and after a rebellion led by his son Aurangzeb in 1658, Shah Jahan was deposed. He was subsequently put under house arrest in the Agra Fort, where, eight years later, in January 1666, he died, aged 74. After Shah Jahan's death, Aurangzeb buried him in the in the crypt of the main tomb of the Taj Mahal, next to his beloved wife.

The Taj Mahal is without a doubt the finest example of Mughal architecture, a style that combines elements from Persian, Indian, and Islamic architecture. Although the principal mausoleum is the most famous aspect of the Taj Mahal, it is one component in a complex of related structures that include several additional mausoleums, including those of Shah Jahan's other wives, a monumental gateway, a mosque, and a formally laid-out walled garden. The Taj Mahal is built on a raised square platform of red sandstone topped by a huge white marble terrace. In certain conditions this arrangement gives the illusion that the vast monument, set at the end of a long shimmering canal, is somehow floating above the ground. The mausoleum is 190 feet square in plan, with its central dome rising to a height of almost 200 feet. The famous dome of the structure is flanked by four detached tapering minarets, each with an octagonal base and cylindrical body, which soar up to around 137 feet in height. The minarets were deliberately built leaning outward so that if they toppled over (during an earthquake, for example) they would collapse not onto the tomb but away from it. Architecturally, these mosques serve to balance and frame the central structure of the mausoleum.

The interior of the mausoleum contains a central chamber, a crypt underneath this, and four octagonal corner rooms originally constructed as the graves of other members of the royal family. The main feature of the mausoleum and the heart of the Taj Mahal is the central octagonal chamber, with its spectacular lofty domed ceiling. The chamber contains the two cenotaphs of Shah Jahan and Mumtaz Mahal; their actual tombs are in a crypt immediately below this room and are relatively plain stone coffins, as Muslim tradition forbids elaborate decoration of tombs. This lower level is no longer open to the public.

The empress's stone cenotaph, slightly smaller than her husband's, is located directly beneath the dome of the structure; that of Shah Jahan is to the left and at a slightly higher level, thus representing the only asymmetrical feature of the Taj Mahal. Mumtaz Mahal's cenotaph stands on a marble base of around 5 feet by 8 feet. Both the cenotaph and the base are inlaid with precious and semiprecious jewels including jasper and jade. The monument is also decorated with inscriptions of verses from the Koran and an epitaph that reads *"Marqad Munavvar Arjumand Ban Begum Mukhatib bah Mumtaz Mahal Tanifiyat ferr sanh 1040 Hijri"* ("Here lies Arjumand Bano Begum called Mumtaz Mahal who died in 1040 A.H." [or AD 1630]). The cenotaph of Shah Jahan is also inlaid with precious and semiprecious gems, and is inscribed in

Persian: "*Marqad Mutahar Aali Hazrat Firdaus Ashiyani Sahib-qiran Saani Saani Shah Jahan Badshah taab surah sanh 1076 Hijri*" ("The sacred sepulchre of his most exalted Majesty, dweller of Paradise, the second lord of constellations, the king Shah Jahan, may his mausoleum ever flourish, 1076 A.H." [AD 1666]). The two monuments are surrounded by an elegant marble screen set up in 1643 to replace the original gold-enameled one that was made in 1633.

One interesting feature of the octagonal chamber is the acoustics, perhaps originally designed in this way to echo music and chants from the Koran. A whisper can be heard from the other side of the room, and it is said that if you shout your name inside the chamber, the echoes will reverberate forever.

In 1989, a controversial book entitled *Taj Mahal: The True Story*, by Indian writer Purushottam Nagesh Oak (1917–2007), was published. In this book, Oak maintained that the Taj Mahal is actually an ancient Hindu temple of Lord Shiva that was usurped by invading Mughals during the 17th century. Oak, who is sometimes referred to on the Web as "Professor" Oak, though he appeared to have no academic credentials, was well known for his historical revisionism and claims that the origins of the Taj Mahal and a number of other historical monuments in India ascribed to Muslim sultans have a Hindu origin. His also claimed that Christianity and Islam are both derived from Hinduism.

One of the pieces of evidence cited in Oak's book (and on many Websites) to support his theory that the Taj Mahal predates the Mughal Empire is a radiocarbon date taken from a sample from the riverside doorway of the monument. According to Oak, a certain Marvin Miller (or Mills) a professor (in other accounts a student) at the Pratt institute, a private college in New York City, smuggled a piece of the wooden door of the Taj Mahal out of India and gave it to Dr. Evan Williams, director of the Brooklyn College Radiocarbon Laboratory. Apparently Williams analyzed the sample and dated it to 300 years before the time of the Shah.

However, subsequent research has failed to find any Marvin Miller who has ever been a member of the faculty at the Pratt Institute. The results of the radiocarbon dating of the wood were allegedly published in the academic journal *Radiocarbon* (Volume 19; 1977). However, although an examination of back issues of *Radiocarbon* for 1977 (available at *www.radiocarbon.org*) does indeed show an article by Dr. Evan Williams ("Brooklyn College Radiocarbon Dates I," Volume 19, Number 1, 1977), nowhere in this article is there mention of the dating of a piece of wood from the Taj Mahal. With such levels of research it is not surprising that the work of P.N. Oak is not taken seriously in academic circles. In July 2000, the Supreme Court in New Delhi, India, dismissed Oak's petition to declare that a Hindu king built the Taj Mahal.

The Taj Mahal attracts from two to four million visitors annually and in 1983 was added to UNESCO's prestigious World Heritage Site list. The UNESCO Website (*whc.unesco.org/en/list/252*) fittingly describes the monument as "the jewel of Muslim art in India and one of the universally admired masterpieces of the world's heritage." However, in recent years the exquisite monument has suffered from environmental pollution, due to automobile fumes, a nearby wood-burning crematorium, emissions from factories, and acid rain from the Mathura Refinery, owned by Indian Oil Corporation. This pollution has gradually turned the marble on the Taj Mahal from glistening white to yellow. Although the Supreme Court of India announced a set of expensive measures to protect the Taj Mahal in the 1990s, it still remains at risk from air pollution today. A particularly worrying development is that the green belt, which has been created around the Taj Mahal, is being slowly converted into commercial space with land already being allotted for new hotels. One hopes that the celebrated white marble dome of India's most famous monument will not one day be hidden behind the concrete walls of "modernization."

Chapter 10

Nabta Playa
(Egypt)

Map showing the approximate position of Nabta Playa (circled).

The remote site of Nabta Playa in the Egypt's southwestern desert (now part of the Sahara) has become well known in archaeological and alternative history circles over the last couple of decades. Its excavators have courted controversy by claiming that the site contains megalithic structures that constitute the oldest-known archaeoastronomy site in the world, that it provides some of the earliest known evidence of domesticated cattle and illustrates the probable desert origins of the ancient Egyptians. What are we to make of these grand claims for such an apparently isolated and primitive site? Is there genuine evidence that Nabta Playa played such an important role in the development of North African civilization 4,000 years before it began in the Nile Valley?

The archaeological site of Nabta Playa is located about 70 miles west of the Temple site of Abu Simbel in the south of Egypt and approximately 500 miles south of Cairo. The site itself lies in a natural depression west of the River Nile and covers an area of around 20 square miles. Egypt's southwestern desert is now one of the driest areas on earth, but it was not always so. Up until around 11,000 years ago, this region was far too arid to support permanent human settlement, but a shift in weather patterns meant that the summer monsoons of Central Africa began to reach further north. These summer rainy seasons, though usually only providing about 4 to 8 inches of rain, caused enough water to accumulate to create large temporary lakes (Spanish—*playas*), which became a natural focus for seasonal occupation by both humans and animals over several millennia.

From the early Holocene epoch (a geological period that began approximately 11,700 years ago) the seasonal flooding of Nabta Playa attracted Nomadic pastoralists with their cattle to its shore. These nomads created seasonal camps, herded cattle, and made ceramic vessels. The first of the three periods of occupation at Nabta Playa is dated by radiocarbon (controversially, it must be added) to the Early Neolithic (9,800–7,500 BC). Archaeological remains recovered from the site that date to this early period include the bones of gazelle, hare, and cattle, stone tools and hearths, and the first house on the site, which was built around built 8,500 BC. During the Middle Neolithic (7,100–6,700 BC) at Nabta Playa settlements expanded and became more sophisticated, the first domesticated sheep and goats appeared, and storage pits and wells were dug. These deep wells would have provided more stability for larger settlements around the lake. The Late Neolithic period (6,500–4,800 BC) provides evidence of agriculture and the remarkable and controversial megalithic structures that Nabta Playa has become so famous for.

The site of Nabta Playa was not discovered until 1973, when a group of researchers led by Fred Wendorf, anthropology professor at Southern Methodist University in Texas, came upon it by accident when traveling from the Libyan border. Wendorf subsequently revisited Nabta Playa many times and undertook excavations at the site in the 1990s along with Romuald Schild, professor at the Institute of Archaeology and Ethnology, Warsaw Polish Academy of Sciences. In 1997, Fred Wendorf, Romuald Schild, Ali A. Mazar of the Egyptian Geological Survey, and J. McKim Malville, astronomy professor at the University of Colorado at Boulder, surveyed the site of Nabta Playa using GPS satellite technology. Later that same year Wendorf and his colleagues sent a letter to the scientific journal *Nature* (*http://www.nature.com/ nature/journal/v392/n6675/abs/392488a0.html - a4e*), the publication of which (*Nature* 392, 488–91, April 2, 1998) sparked off a controversy that still continues today. In the letter the researchers stated that they had discovered a number of megalithic alignments and stone circles next to Middle and Late Neolithic settlements at Nabta Playa, which they believed were aligned to cardinal and solstitial directions.

The remains of the stone structures at Nabta Playa, which mostly date to the seventh and sixth millennium BC, consist of numerous large unshaped megaliths, some of which are still standing, though many have toppled over or have been deliberately knocked down. The blocks of quartzite sandstone used by the builders of Nabta Playa, some of which measured about 6 feet wide by 9 feet high, had to be transported from their origin around 0.3 miles away. Around 10 tumuli (mound of earth/stones raised over a grave) have so far been discovered at the site, some of which contained the burials of sheep, goats, and, in one case, an entire sacrificed young cow, in clay-lined, roofed chambers.

Wendorf and Schild have identified five megalithic alignments radiating outward from megalithic structures, which may have had a funerary function, at Nabta Playa. The most significant of these structures is what appears to be a 12-foot-diameter stone circle that contains within it four sets of small upright sandstone slabs. Two pairs of these slabs were aligned in a north-south direction; the second set provided a line of sight in the direction of sunrise on the summer solstice about 6,000 years ago. Wendorf and his colleagues believe that this stone circle was a calendar used by Neolithic farmers to predict the winter and summer solstices. In effect, they claim that the stone circle at Nabta was Egypt's, if not the world's, earliest astronomical measuring device. Whether this is true or not, a method of anticipating the rainy seasons that followed the solstice, especially as rainfall became increasingly more erratic as the climate shifted, would certainly have been essential to the inhabitants of Nabta Playa. The megaliths at Nabta Play certainly represent public architecture and thus reflect the increasing social complexity of the local population.

In his book *The Origin Map: Discovery of a Prehistoric, Megalithic, Astrophysical Map and Sculpture of the Universe* (iUniverse, 2002), astrophysicist Thomas G. Brody put forward the theory that the three northern stones inside the circle at Nabta Playa mapped out the stars in the constellation Orion, between 6400 BC and 4900 BC . The other three stones inside the circle, Brody contended much more controversially, are a diagram of the head and shoulders of Orion as they appeared on the meridian on the summer solstices around 16,500 BC. Why the people of Nabta Playa would have bothered with such alignments, particularly that dating back 10,000 or so years before their time, when the region was an uninhabitable desert, is not made clear, however. In *The Origin Map*, Brody also maintains, much like Robert Bauval and Adrian Gilbert in their book, *The Orion Mystery* (1992), that the pyramids of Giza match the celestial alignment of Orion at the dates 11,772 BC and 9420 BC.

The erection of such complex megalithic structures at Nabta Playa indicates a society at Nabta Playa that was both sophisticated and highly organized. Parallels have been drawn between the Nabta Playa stone circle and the much larger, 200-foot-diameter wooden henge outside of Goseck henge in eastern Germany. The Goseck Circle has been dated to around 4600 BC and is often touted as the world's oldest solar observatory. The difference between the two structures, apart from their size, is that, whereas the shape and structure of the Goseck Circle can be seen clearly on aerial photographs and the results of a magnetometer survey of the site, the Nabta Playa alignments look more like random extensive rock scatters. Many of the megaliths at Nabta Playa are not in situ, others have disappeared, and, although the megaliths at the site may have served an astronomical function, much more research needs to be done before we can say for certain that this is the case.

Wendorf and Schild also caused further controversy when they announced the presence of early domestic cattle among the archaeological remains from Nabta Playa. Cattle were vital to the people of Nabta Playa for easy access to food, including milk, blood, and meat, as well as playing a role in their cultic activities, as evidenced from the burial of the young cow.

Researchers believe that cattle were first domesticated in the Middle East during the Neolithic period, about 8000 BC. Wendorf's claim of the presence of domestic cattle at Nabta Playa as early as 8100 BP, would make it the earliest evidence from the African continent. However, a study by Dr. Caroline Grigson (published in *Origins and Development of African Livestock: Archaeology, Genetics, Linguistics and Ethnography*, 2000) concluded that cattle from all periods at Nabta Playa were morphologically wild. Another study by Andrew B. Smith, emeritus professor in the department of archaeology at the University of Cape Town, found that cattle at Nabta Playa were morphologically wild prior to and including the period 7050–6150 BC, at the site, but domesticated from 5900 BC to 5500 BC onward. These later dates would integrate Nabta Playa into the wider pattern of herding economies in other parts of Egypt and Sudan.

Around 4,800 years ago, there was a climate change, and the African monsoons shifted back southward to approximately where they had been prior to 11,000 years ago. The Western Desert became super-arid, and the people of Nabta Play were forced to leave the region and migrate to a more hospitable area. Based primarily on the prominence of cattle in Pre-Dynastic and Old Kingdom Egyptian religion, and the cosmic alignments of some of the megaliths at Nabta Playa, Wendorf and Schild believe that the population may have moved to the Nile Valley and influenced the rise of pharaonic Egypt. However, this point is hotly disputed by many Egyptologists, who see the situation as much more complicated, involving multiple influences, including borrowings from Mesopotamia and Syria.

Within Egypt itself there is evidence of pastoralism and cultivation of cereals by peoples in the East Sahara as early as the seventh millennium BC. Furthermore, sites of the Fayoum Neolithic (The Fayoum Oasis is a basin in the desert immediately to the west of the Nile south of Cairo) represent the earliest-known fully agricultural economy in Egypt, beginning round 5200 BC. In 2006 archaeologists from the University of California, Los Angeles (UCLA) and the University of Groningen (RUG) in the Netherlands, excavating at the Fayoum Oasis, discovered the earliest evidence of an ancient Egyptian agricultural settlement, dating back to around 5200 BC. The archaeologists uncovered domestic wheat and barley; the remains of domesticated animals such as pigs, goats, and sheep; pits for cooking; floors for what appeared to be dwellings; and evidence of fishing and hunting. Such evidence shows that the populations living in the East Sahara in the seventh millennium and around the Fayoum Oasis in the late sixth millennium could have had as much influence, if not more, on the development of Egyptian civilization than those of Nabta Playa.

Whether the people of Nabta Playa played a major part in the development of early Egyptian civilization or not, the settlement certainly represents a major Neolithic site and an important window into the development of civilization in North Africa. Unfortunately, in 2007, the site of Nabta Playa was vandalized and a number of the stones were knocked over. Some of the stones were also stolen. No one knows for certain who is responsible for this moronic act, though personnel belonging to a United Nations force, known by its French acronym MINURSO, are known to have vandalized a number of sites in the Western Sahara, such as the decorated rock shelter at Lajuad. Why this takes place is anyone's guess, but some kind of security measures are surely called for at Nabta Playa before any more of this important site is mindlessly destroyed.

☒

Chapter 11

The World's Oldest Pyramid: The Step Pyramid at Saqqara (Egypt)

Step Pyramid of Djoser at Saqqara.

Located inside the vast necropolis of Saqqara, just south of Cairo and west of the ancient city of Memphis, the distinctive form of the Step Pyramid of Djoser rises up majestically from the desert plateau. On a clear day, the pyramid can be seen from Giza, just more than 10 miles to the north. The Step Pyramid is believed to have been created by one man, the polymath Imhotep ("the one who comes in peace"), considered to be the first engineer, architect, astronomer, and physician in history known by name. The structure dates back to the 27th century BC and is the most ancient of Egypt's 97 pyramids, and also the oldest yet discovered anywhere in the world.

Saqqara (or *Sakkara*; ancient Egyptians *kbhw-ntrw*—"libation of the deities") is situated close to the entrance of the Nile Delta on the west bank of the River Nile, and covers an area of around 4.3 miles by 0.9 miles. The site once served as the burial ground for Memphis, the Old Kingdom (27th–22nd centuries BC) capital of Egypt, and many of the kings of the First and Second Dynasty were buried there. The necropolis features a number of funerary monuments including decorated *mastabas* (rectangular tombs), rock-cut tombs, temples, courtyards, and pyramids. From the Middle Kingdom onward (c. 2040 BC), Thebes (in the modern town of Luxor) became the capital of Egypt, and royal funerary complexes were no longer built at Saqqara. However, the site retained its importance as a necropolis for non-royal burials and religious ceremonies up until the Roman period, around 3,000 years after it was first built.

After Saqqara was abandoned, the Pyramid of Djoser lay untouched for centuries. Though European travelers partially explored the monument in the 17th century, it was not until the first half of the 19th century, after the much-publicized French invasion of Egypt led by Napoleon Bonaparte in 1798, that investigations into Saqqara's Step Pyramid began. In 1821, Prussian general Johann Heinrich Freiherr von Minutoli uncovered the access shaft leading underneath the pyramid's north side, and in 1837 British engineer John Shae Perring (1813–1869) located the subterranean galleries beneath the main structure. More detailed work on the Saqqara Pyramid Complex was to follow from 1842 to 1845, when pioneering Prussian Egyptologist Karl (or Carl) Richard Lepsius (1810–1884) carried out survey and excavations at the site.

However, the first organized archaeological research on the Saqqara Step Pyramid did not begin until the 1920s, with British Egyptologist Cecil Mallaby Firth (1878–1931), who was the Inspector of Antiquities at Saqqara from 1913 to 1931. French architect and Egyptologist Jean Phillipe Lauer (1902–2001) joined Firth in 1926 to advise him on restoration work at Djoser's Pyramid. Lauer would spend the rest of his long life of working for the Egyptian Antiquities Service, excavating and reconstituting the Step Pyramid complex.

Step pyramids were the earliest form of Egyptian pyramids, and the Saqqara structure is the first of these. The Saqqara Pyramid was originally constructed as a flat-roofed mastaba for the mummified body of the pharaoh Djoser, of the Third Dynasty of Egypt (reigned c. 2635–2610 BC), with the burial chambers concealed underground within a labyrinth of tunnels, thought by archaeologists to discourage grave robbers.

Jean Phillipe Lauer, the main excavator of the Saqqara Pyramid, believed that the building of the great monument was done in distinct stages. According to Lauer, the mastaba that originally covered the tomb (itself somewhat unusual for being square rather than rectangular) was the first stage (M1—Mastaba 1) in the Pyramid's construction, followed by M2, which involved the enlargement of this structure on all sides, and M3, with enlargement of its eastern side only. The mastaba was then built up to form a four-stepped pyramidal-structure (P1—Pyramid 1) and then a six-stepped structure with a rectangular base oriented east-west (P2). The majority of rock for the construction of Djoser's Pyramid may have been obtained from the huge 2.460-by-131-foot trench that surrounds the Pyramid Complex. By the end of Djoser's 19-year reign, in 2610 BC (or 2648 BC, using a different chronology), the original mastaba structure had six stepped layers and had soared up to 204 feet high.

Djoser's Pyramid has a base of around 358 x 410 feet and contains around 11,668,000 cubic feet of clay and stone. It was once covered in fine polished white limestone, most of which has now disappeared, though a few blocks remain on the northern side of the pyramid. Standing on the flat desert plateau, this magnificent building must have been a dazzling site for miles around. This in fact may be a clue as to why the builders decided to transform the original mastaba structure into a lofty pyramid. In the opinion of Lauer it was Djoser's intention when planning the huge six-tiered structure to make the royal tomb visible from the Nile Delta.

The complex labyrinth of chambers and corridors, some of which were never completed, that make up Djoser's mortuary complex beneath the Pyramid are supposed to represent his palace in the Afterlife. This subterranean network is so complicated that it is extremely difficult to determine which tunnels belong to the original construction project and which are the work of later looters and explorers. It has been estimated that these tunnels run for around 3 1/2 miles beneath the Pyramid, connecting around 400 rooms. The burial vault of Djoser was located around 92 feet underground and was accessed by a vertical shaft, and, as with all Old Kingdom pyramids from this time onward (including the Great Pyramid at Giza), this was built into the north side of the structure. Djoser's burial vault consisted of four courses of well-dressed pink granite blocks from Aswan and measured around 5.2 by 9.5 feet in size. The single entrance to the chamber was sealed with a 3½-ton block of granite after the burial.

Northwest of the burial vault, in a small corridor that was later destroyed by looters, a wooden chest was discovered bearing Djoser's Horus name: Netjerikhet. The name Djoser was given to the Pharaoh much later, by New Kingdom visitors a thousand years or so after the building of the Pyramid. During the 1924–26 excavations inside the tomb chamber by Jean Phillipe Lauer, a damaged statue of Djoser was discovered. This painted limestone image of the Pharaoh is now in the Egyptian Museum at Cairo, and represents the oldest-known life-sized Egyptian statue.

In one of the rooms around the burial chamber, known as the King's Apartment, the walls are decorated with rows of tiny blue faience tiles with raised bands of limestone, probably designed to imitate reed mats and tapestries covering the walls of the king's private apartments in his palace at Memphis. There are also limestone reliefs of the Pharaoh running or walking, performing the heb-sed rituals (rites to celebrate the continued rule of a king), and wearing the red crown and the white crown, the symbols of Lower and Upper Egypt, respectively.

An incredible find was made in galleries to the east of the central burial chamber, an area believed to have been constructed for the burial of the king's wives and children. In this section archaeologists discovered more than 40,000 exquisitely carved stone vases and dishes in a wide variety of materials, including alabaster, serpentine, quartz crystal, limestone, and slate. Some of these vessels were painted, and, fascinatingly, a number of them bore inscriptions of First and Second

Dynasty rulers predating Djoser, suggesting they were heirlooms. The question puzzling archaeologists is why this vast amount of stone vessels, presumably belonging to Djoser's ancestors, was placed in his mortuary complex. One explanation, put forward by Jean Phillipe Lauer, is that the stone vessels came originally from the furnishings of Early Dynastic (31st to 27th centuries BC) royal tombs, later destroyed by Peribsen, a king of Egypt's Second Dynasty (c. 2775–c. 2650 BC). Lauer believed that Djoser may have wanted to give the objects a respectful final resting place inside his mortuary complex.

The Pyramid of Djoser is not an isolated building, but stands in a 37-acre religious complex enclosed by a wall of white Tura limestone once 34 feet high and 5,397 feet in length. This vast complex contained courtyards, temples, chapels, terraces, stairways, and tombs. Perhaps the most interesting of the components in the Pyramid Complex is the South Tomb, located on the southwestern corner of the complex. The Tomb demonstrates a number of features that replicate those of the substructure of the Step Pyramid, including a descending passageway, a shaft leading to a vault made of pink granite, chambers tiled with blue faience, and a room decorated with niche reliefs of the king. Interestingly, the granite vault, which measures about 5.2 x 5.2 feet, with a height of around 4.3 feet, is too small to hold a human burial, so perhaps it was meant to function as a cenotaph or as a place for the king's ka, or spirit, in the afterlife. Cecil Firth believed that the South Tomb functioned as a provisional tomb for Djoser, in the unfortunate event that he died before his royal burial complex was completed. Bearing in mind its design and position within the Step Pyramid complex, the South Tomb may also be interpreted as the precursor to the satellite pyramids of later Dynasties.

According to tradition, the Step Pyramid of Djoser was built by Imhotep—doctor, scribe, sage, astrologer, vizier, and high priest of the sun god, Ra, at Heliopolis. Despite the fact that Imhotep was a historical figure, little is known of his life, though we do know that he was one of the few commoners to be given divine status, when he was deified c. 525 BC, about 2,000 years after his death. Although stone walls and floors were known during Egypt's Early Dynastic (Archaic) Period (3100–2600 BC), a building of the size of Djoser's Pyramid constructed entirely from stone had never before been attempted in Egypt. In fact, the Step Pyramid was an architectural revolution in many ways. It is at Saqqara that we first see an Egyptian monumental royal tomb in the form of a pyramid. Djoser's Pyramid also represents the first large scale use of limestone as a building material. Prior to this the most common material used for large buildings had been mud brick. The change from building in mud brick to stone on such a monumental scale has significant social implications, not least the huge number of man hours required, organization of work forces, and access to resources. This suggests that the royal government had attained a greater level of power than at any time previously in Egypt's history. The building of such a vast monument as the Step Pyramid may also signify political stability in the country at the beginning of the Old Kingdom period.

In recognition of the Step Pyramid of Djoser's worldwide historical importance, UNESCO designated it a World Heritage Site in 1979. Unfortunately, the centuries have taken their toll on Djoser's great monument. It is not only the outer limestone casing that has disappeared, but in some parts the core masonry too. Deep cracks have spread throughout the walls and ceilings of the underground corridors, and parts of the queen's tunnels, located underneath the pyramid's main shaft, have collapsed. The structure has been deemed unsafe to visitors and has been closed to the public for some time.

Due to the fact that new monuments are constantly being discovered in Egypt the amount of time and resources available for existing structures is limited. However, in 2007, Egypt's Supreme Council of Antiquities (SCA) announced a new restoration project to be carried out by Egyptian engineers and archaeologists in three phases, with a budget of LE25 million ($4,547,348). In 2009, during this restoration work in the underground passageways of the pyramid, archaeologists discovered limestone blocks bearing the names of King Djoser's daughters, wooden instruments and statues, bone fragments, and the remains of a mummy. In light of these intriguing discoveries, one wonders what else awaits the archaeologist in the 3 1/2 miles of underground passageways beneath Djoser's Step Pyramid.

⌛

Chapter 12

Great Zimbabwe
(South Africa)

The Conical Tower inside the Great Enclosure at Great Zimbabwe.

Overview of Great Zimbabwe.

Great Zimbabwe is located on a plateau, 3,000 feet above sea level, in the watershed between the Zambezi and the Limpopo rivers, 17 miles beyond the southeastern town of Masvingo, in South Africa. Undulating across the landscape like a giant serpent, the extraordinary complex of residential and ceremonial enclosures was once home to some 12,000 to 20,000 people, and in its heyday was an important trading center. Ancient tales say that the vast ruins of Great Zimbabwe are all that remain of the capital of the once-great Queen of Sheba. Further stories link the site with the Egyptians, the Phoenicians, and even the legendary Christian king Prester John. But who really constructed the massive stone walls, which cover a staggering 1,800 acres of Zimbabwe? And why was the city abandoned in such a hurry?

The word *Zimbabwe* derives from the name for the ruins, coming either from *Dzimba dza mabwe*, meaning "great houses of stone" in the ChiKaranga dialect of the Shona language, or *dzimba woye*, meaning "venerated houses" in the Zezuru dialect of the Shona language. Shona is the name given to a Bantu people of Zimbabwe and southern Mozambique.

Great Zimbabwe was not a unique site; there are more than 150 ruins of the same architectural type in Zimbabwe. It is, however, the largest and most complex, meaning it was probably also the most important. The city complex of Great Zimbabwe can be divided up into three separate distinct architectural groups, known as the Hill Complex, the Valley Complex, and the famous Great Enclosure. The structures that comprise the city were made from rectangular granite blocks, placed carefully on top of each other without the use of mortar. Each layer of stone was recessed slightly more than the previous one to give an extremely stable inward sloping structure. Some of the walls are an incredible 20 feet thick and 40 feet high. The stone used was quarried from the nearby granite hills, and was probably utilized because it was easily split along fracture planes, which resulted in transportable cube-shaped blocks that were ideal for stacking without the necessity of using mortar.

The most impressive monument within the Great Zimbabwe complex, the Great Enclosure, represents the largest single ancient structure south of the Sahara. The oval-shaped Great Enclosure is more than 800 feet long, with walls as high as 36 feet, and encircles a complex of more than 300 smaller stone structures and an enigmatic 14th-century monument known as the Conical Tower. This mysterious building is 33 feet in height and 16 feet in diameter, and is thought to have been perhaps a royal residence or even a giant phallus symbol. In 2002, Richard Wade, an astronomer from the Nkwe Ridge Observatory Institute near Pretoria, put forward the opinion that parts of Great Zimbabwe functioned as a kind of giant primitive observatory, and that the Conical Tower lined up precisely with a supernova known to have exploded in the constellation of Vela 700 to 800 years ago. Wade therefore suggests that there was a correlation between the construction of the large tower and a spectacular event in the heavens at the time. Could the Conical Tower have been built to observe this exploding star? Intriguingly, an oral legend told by the Sena people of Zimbabwe says that their ancestors migrated from the north by following a particularly bright star in the southern skies. Perhaps this star was the supernova.

Researchers believe, based on finds of plastered altars and eight carved soapstone birds (which probably represent the spirits of former rulers), that the Hill Complex at Great Zimbabwe functioned as the city's royal and religious center. These birds, which incorporate human elements in their features, such as five-toed feet for claws, are on average 16 inches tall and were found atop 3-feet-high columns. The Zimbabwe Bird has now become a national symbol adorning the flag of Zimbabwe. The buildings on this steep-sided hill, which rises 262 feet above the valley floor, are the oldest on the site, with the remains of *daga* houses contained inside the towering walls. *Daga* houses were constructed of mud and brick, and, although most of the structures have long since eroded, some of them may once have been as grand as the stone buildings which survive at the site.

Only a very small portion of the overall population of Great Zimbabwe, probably 200–300 people, seem to have lived within its great stone enclosures. Whether the massive walls of these structures were built to defend the elite of Zimbabwean society is a much-discussed point among experts on the site. The walls, however, display no defensible features, with simple entrances that could be easily overcome by sustained attack. Finds of weapons at Great Zimbabwe are also minimal. This would suggest that the towering walls were constructed both to demonstrate the authority of the royal families who lived within them and to separate the elite from the common people outside.

Located between the Hill Complex and the Great Enclosure, the Valley Complex was the last part of the site to be constructed, and appears to have been used by the common citizens of Great Zimbabwe. The Valley area contains around a dozen enclosures, many surrounded by stone walls, which contain the remnants of a large number of daga houses.

The first Europeans to mention the vast remains of Great Zimbabwe were Portuguese traders in the early 16th century, who had heard about a fabled inland fortress city when they were establishing colonies in the South African countries of Angola and Mozambique. In his work *Décadas da Ásia* ("Decades of Asia"), a history of the Portuguese in India and Asia, the first volume of which appeared in 1552, Portuguese historian João de Barros described "a square fortress, masonry within and without, built of stones of marvelous size, and there appears to be no mortar joining them." De Barros never saw the mysterious African monument himself, but believed it to be Axuma, one of the cities associated with the fabled Queen of Sheba. Other Portuguese chroniclers linked the semi-mythical city in the interior of Africa with the biblical Ophir, from where King Solomon was said to have received a cargo of gold, silver, precious stones, ivory, sandalwood, apes, and peacocks. In his epic poem "Paradise Lost" (1667), English poet John Milton locates the fabulous city of Ophir in the area around the Congo and Angola (south-central Africa). Such wildly romantic notions about the origins and history of Great Zimbabwe persisted well into the 19th century. On September 5, 1871, local Karanga tribesmen led a German geologist named Carl Mauch to the site. When he saw the magnificent stone ruins, Mauch, like all Europeans before him, was unable to believe them to be the work of indigenous African people. Instead Mauch, obsessed by a biblical non-native explanation for the site, was of the bizarre opinion that the Hill Complex was a copy of Solomon's Temple on Mount Moriah, and that the buildings in the Valley Complex were modeled after the palace where the Queen of Sheba resided when she visited Solomon.

Mauch's explanations for the Great Zimbabwe structures appealed to English businessman and politician Cecil Rhodes, who gave his name to Rhodesia, as Zimbabwe was known in colonial times (1888–1965). Rhodes's British South Africa Company (BSAC) sponsored an investigation into the site, hiring J. Theodore Bent, an antiquarian who had worked in Greece and Asia Minor, for the job. In his work *The Ruined Cities of Mashonaland*, published in 1891 (Mashonaland is a region in northern Zimbabwe), Bent stated that the remains had been constructed either by the Phoenicians or the Arabs. He came to this erroneous conclusion despite the fact that the artifacts he recovered from his hugely destructive excavations, which included pottery, spindle whorls, iron, bronze, and copper spearheads, axes, adzes, hoes, and gold-working equipment, were almost identical to objects used by the local Karanga, one of the clans of the Shona people.

Things were to get even worse for Great Zimbabwe when the BSAC appointed Richard Nicklin Hall, a local journalist and author of *The Ancient Ruins of Rhodesia*, as custodian of the site. In his search for evidence of the white origins of the monuments, Hall's "archaeological" investigations destroyed layer upon layer of vital archaeological material without a second thought, imposing huge restrictions on all future work at Great Zimbabwe. Hall was soon fired from his position and the BSAC appointed an archaeologist of a very different type, David Randall-MacIver, to the position. Randall-MacIver, who had worked at Abydos in Egypt with the renowned Egyptologist Flinders Petrie, soon concluded that the remains of the mud structures and great stone walls were without doubt of African origin. In his *Medieval Rhodesia* (1906) Randall-MacIver rubbished the contemporary fantasy that the ruins at Great Zimbabwe were built by a vanished ancient white civilization, stating that they were African and dated from around the 14th century. This view was confirmed by further archaeological study at the site from 1928 to 1929 by English archaeologist Gertrude Caton-Thompson, and later radiocarbon dates that placed the oldest remains at the site in the 1200s.

Unfortunately, this was not to be the end of the racial prejudice surrounding the origins of Great Zimbabwe. In the 1960 and '70s the site became a powerful symbol for the African Nationalist movement, so much so that the white government of Rhodesia began a program of censorship of all materials related to Great Zimbabwe. Guidebooks, museum displays, school textbooks, radio programs, newspapers, and films mentioning the African origins of the site were all affected by government suppression. Fortunately, all of this ended with the achievement of majority rule for Zimbabwe in 1980.

On present evidence, although the first farmers had settled in the area by the fourth century AD, the origins of the Great Zimbabwe site itself only go back to the 11th century AD, when Bantu-speaking ancestors of the Shona people established a village on the hilltop. Archaeological work on the site has determined that the Hill Complex was not built until some time later, around AD 1250. The rulers of the village acquired considerable wealth from cattle, which were able to graze on the lush grasslands of the Zimbabwe plateau. However, around 1267 gold was discovered and mined on the plateau, which led to the establishment of the village as a major trading center. Other local resources that helped in the development of the village were iron, copper, and tin (the latter a highly valued commodity essential in making bronze). The ideal location of the site close to the gold mines and within reach of numerous African and Arab trading posts on the coast of the Indian Ocean meant that Great Zimbabwe expanded rapidly over the next few decades to become a powerful city as trade grew.

The site became an important part of a trade network that extended all the way to China, as illustrated by finds of Chinese pottery within the ruins. Other finds that show the extent of Zimbabwean trade include Arabian coins, glass beads from Syria, and ceramics from Persia. The city's increased wealth from trade led a substantial increase in population, between 10,000 and 20,000 at its height, and to the planning and building of more elaborate structures; the Great Enclosure, for example, was begun in the early 14th century, with its outer wall added almost 100 years later. The buildings in the Valley Complex were the last to be added to the city, during the early 15th century. Just a decade or two later, though, the center of trade began to shift northward along the Zambezi River, perhaps due to the near exhaustion of the Great Zimbabwe's gold supply. It is also believed that the population of Great Zimbabwe grew to such an unmanageable size that the region's agricultural resources and grazing land were used up, forcing the population to move elsewhere. Drought and disease have also been put forward as the reasons why, by the 16th century, the once-great city was largely abandoned.

Emerging from the collapse of Great Zimbabwe the *Mutapa* ("conquered lands") dynasty (c1450–1629) were a Shona-speaking kingdom of Karanga people and the ancestors of the modern Shona. The kingdom of the *Mutapa* was centered to the north at the new hub of the trading network, which by then included the Portuguese, who had begun to gain control of South Africa's east coast around 1505.

More than four centuries after the collapse, when Mauch arrived at the once Great Zimbabwe, he found the ruins inhabited by local Karanga people, who knew nothing of the site's history. Great Zimbabwe has since become a national monument and in 1986 was designated a World Heritage Site. Unfortunately, despite its huge historical and cultural importance, Great Zimbabwe has received precious little government funding in order to facilitate the scientific preservation of its remaining structures and any further archaeological investigations at the site.

Newport's Mystery Tower
(United States)

The Newport Tower.

*The 17th-century
Chesterton Windmill,
Warwickshire, England.*

The Newport Tower is a circular stone structure located in Touro Park, Newport, Rhode Island, in the New England region of the United States. Also known as "Mystery Tower," the structure has a reputation as one of the country's biggest architectural mysteries, and numerous theories have been put forward to explain its origins and functions. The conventional wisdom that the tower was built in Colonial times (1492–1763) has been challenged by independent researchers who have speculated that the Tower is several centuries older, and could have been constructed by the Norse, the Chinese, the Portuguese, or (of course) the Knights Templar. Is there any solid evidence for such speculation?

The two-story Tower is built of rough stone slabs bonded together by lime mortar. It is supported by eight cylindrical columns forming stone arches, and now measures about 26 feet in height with a diameter of about 23 feet, though it was originally somewhat higher. The Tower is not exactly circular in plan: Its diameter from southeast to northwest measures 22 feet, 2 inches; from east to west the diameter lengthens to 23 feet, 3 inches. This 11-inch difference has been the cause of much speculation as to whether it was deliberate, and would thus suggest that the Tower was not intended to be precisely circular, or caused by a flaw in the design of the structure. The remains of white plaster on parts of the outer wall show that the building was once covered in a smooth coating of this material. Located just above the arches are irregular beam slots that once held square wooden beams to support the floor of an internal chamber (the main room of the structure). This level of the Tower also has four windows, seven small niches, six diagonally spaced holes (which probably held wooden steps), and a fireplace built into the east wall. The upper level of the Tower is evidenced by four beam slots and three very small windows.

The Newport Tower is known locally as the "Old Stone Mill," reflecting the prevailing theory of most historians that it was built as a windmill in the mid-17th century, probably by the governor of Rhode Island, Benedict Arnold (1615–78), great grandfather of the infamous American Revolution General Benedict Arnold. The main evidence for the Tower's origin as a Colonial windmill is that it is recorded in the governor's 1677 will as his "Stone built windmill." Later records show that the Newport Tower was used during the American Revolution

(1775–83) as a watchtower by the Americans and as a powder magazine by the British. However, there have been many objections to the theory that the Tower was built as a windmill, including that Arnold's will does not actually state that he built the structure himself—only that it was located on his land. In his article "Newport's Mystery Tower" on his *Unexplained Earth* Website (*www.unexplainedearth.com/newport.php*), Chris Maier describes a number of objections to the mill theory.

Meier notes that a number of the Tower's structural features are unsuitable for a windmill. One such feature is the basic eight-pillar design of the building, where the arches support the weighty stone mass of the main structure. Surely a solid wall construction would have been more suitable? Another is the rather significant 11-inch variance in the diameter of the tower, noted previously. What would seem the most obvious design flaw with the Tower if it was intended to be used as a windmill is the presence of the fireplace built into the second floor of the structure. As flour dust is notoriously explosive, wasn't this was taking an extraordinary risk? Critics of the windmill hypothesis, including Chris Maier, also point out that around the time of the supposed construction of the Tower the colonists were engaged in a bloody conflict with Native Americans known as King Philip's War (1675–76). If the colonists were preoccupied with the dangers of Native American attack, Maier and others hypothesize, they surely would not have had the time or resources to undertake such a project as a stone windmill.

If we for the moment dismiss the idea the Newport Tower was constructed as a windmill by Benedict Arnold, then who built it and why? Researchers who disagree with a Colonial date for the Tower are unanimous in supporting a pre-Columbian origin, though their opinions on the actual builders differ wildly. The most widely accepted "alternative" theory for the Newport Tower is that it was constructed by Norse explorers. In 1837, in his *Antiquitates Americanae*, Danish antiquarian Carl Christian Rafn proposed that the Vikings had explored North America centuries before the voyages of Christopher Columbus and John Cabot. He suggested that the Newport Tower was originally part of an early Norse settlement. Rafn's ideas about a Norse origin for the Tower became so popular that American poet Henry Wadsworth Longfellow (1807–82) mentioned it in his ballad "The Skeleton in Armor."

More than a century later, Boston-born archaeologist and historian Philip Ainsworth Means echoed Rafn in his 1942 book, *The Newport Tower*, in which he supported the idea of a long-term Norse settlement in North America with an important 12th-/13th-century church at Newport—that is, Newport Tower. Means believed that Arnold had simply converted the old church building to a windmill.

In 1946, four years after the publication of Means's book, a claimed runic inscription was discovered on one of the stones of the west side of the Tower. Runes were a system of writing utilized by the Vikings, though they had been in use by early Germanic tribes in northern Europe from the first or second century AD. Five runic symbols were identified on the stone and in one interpretation they read "HNKRS," signifying the Old Norse word for stool, meaning the seat of a bishop's church. The inscription also included a date: 1010. So was the Newport Tower an early Norse church after all? A major problem with the supposed "runes" at Newport is that they appear more like faint random scratches than the deep deliberate grooves that constitute Viking rune carving. One has to make a considerable effort to interpret the scratches on the stone as an intentional genuine inscription, so the "runic" evidence for Norse presence at Newport should perhaps be regarded as dubious at best.

One problem with a Norse origin for the Newport Tower is the lack of any Norse artifacts found in or around the Tower, despite several excavations having taken place there. This contrasts notably with finds from L'Anse aux Meadows, Newfoundland, Canada, the only accepted Norse site on the American continent. Excavations at the L'Anse aux Meadows settlement site have discovered, among other things, the remains of three timber-and-sod longhouses, a possible charcoal kiln, and the remnants of a small iron smithy, as well as 11th-century Norse artifacts of iron, bronze, stone, and bone, including a soapstone, spindle whorl, and copper alloy ring-headed pin. It would be reasonable to expect something similar at Newport Tower if it had been indeed built by the Norse.

In his 2002 book, *1421: The Year China Discovered the World*, author Gavin Menzies claims that from 1421 to 1423, during the Ming Dynasty, Chinese ships explored the world before Europeans. Menzies believes that the Newport Tower was built by Chinese explorers in the

15th century as a lighthouse. He claims that the tower has many design elements in common with Chinese observatories and lighthouses, specifically the lighthouse at the port of Zaiton (Quanzhou) in Fujian province in southern China. However, this five-story octagonal structure was not built as a lighthouse at all, but as a Buddhist pagoda; its use as a navigational landmark (usually by putting lamps in the windows at night) was secondary. Incidentally, the Zaiton "lighthouse" also bears no resemblance whatsoever to the Newport Tower.

Yet another theory as to the origin of the Newport Tower was put forward in the early 20th century by Edmund Burke Delabarre (1863–1945), a researcher and professor of psychology at Brown University, Providence, Rhode Island. Delaberre proposed that the Tower was built as a signaling beacon by Portuguese navigator Miguel Corte-Real, whom he claimed was shipwrecked in the area in 1501 or 1502. Further support for the Portuguese theory was added in 1948 by Herbert Pell, U.S. ambassador to Portugal. In an article entitled "The Old Stone Mill of Newport" (*Rhode Island History 7, no. 4*, October 1948: 105–19), Pell noted a resemblance between the Newport Tower and the round church (rotunda or *charola*) at the Castle of Tomar, 85 miles northeast of Lisbon, Portugal, built by the Knights Templar around 1160. But, again, if the Portuguese built Newport Tower, why did they not leave a single artifact behind? Indeed, this is the problem with all Pre-Colonial theories for the construction of the Newport Tower: the lack of physical evidence.

Excavations at the Newport Tower in 1948 by the Society for American Archaeology, led by Hugh Hencken of Harvard, and in 2006 and 2007 by the Chronognostic Research Foundation (CRF), a non-profit Arizona corporation, found no artifacts dating back earlier than the 17th century. Although this absence of evidence does not completely rule out an earlier date for the building, the lack of even a single Pre-Colonial builder's tool or fragment of pottery makes a Colonial date the most logical. In 1993 radiocarbon dating tests were carried out by Danish researchers Dr. Hogne Junger of the University of Helsingfors and Jørgen D. Siemonsen on the mortar used in the Tower. The results showed that the Tower was probably built in the middle of the 17th century—again, Colonial times—though the error margin does not completely rule out a 16th-century date.

A collection of the theories to explain the origins and function of any mysterious ancient building would not be complete without the inclusion of one from the astronomical angle. So here it is, courtesy of University of Rhode Island physics and astronomy professor William Penhallow. After studying the windows in the Tower in 1998, Penhallow found a number of astronomical alignments. His research found that the three largest windows appeared to be linked to the sun and the moon. Thus the position of these celestial bodies could have been charted and used to determine for example the vernal and autumnal equinoxes (March 21st and September 21st) and also the solstices (June 21st and December 21st). One of the inferences from such work is that, by calculating these dates, the builder would then be able to work out the proper timing for planting and harvesting crops, and the dates for various holidays and feasts. One would have thought, however, that there must surely have been easier ways of calculating equinoxes and solstices than building complicated stone towers. Nevertheless, in a recent article on their Website (*www.chronognostic.org/over_touro_park.html*) the CRF suggested that the astronomical alignments at the site may be extremely relevant, and that the Tower was probably built as an observatory.

A significant element in the theory that the Newport Tower functioned as an observatory is its resemblance to a structure known as Chesterton Windmill. This two-story circular stone building, set on six pillars linked by semi-circular arches, is located in south Warwickshire, in the English Midlands. Chesterton Mill was built in 1632–33 and bears an uncanny resemblance to the Newport Tower. Some researchers, among them English engineer and historian Rex Wailes (1901–86), and Suzanne Carlson, president of the New England Antiquities Research Association, believe that Chesterton Mill was originally built as an observatory and later converted to a mill. If this theory is true, bearing in mind the similarities between the Newport and Chesterton structures, it would certainly lend some credence to the observatory hypothesis. Unfortunately for proponents of this theory, recent research on the Chesterton Windmill (see "History of the Chesterton Windmill" in the Bibliography) has discovered some of the original building accounts for the windmill, which record the names of several of the craftsmen who worked on the structure, how much they were paid, and records of payments for sailcloths.

So despite the objections raised earlier in this chapter, could the Newport Tower be a Colonial windmill after all? One of the main objections to the windmill theory was the inclusion of a fireplace in the structure of the Tower. However, this is a far from unique feature in windmills; there are numerous examples from Europe and even one from America. Other windmills with fireplaces include the Upholland Windmill, Lancashire, northwest England, where the fireplace is on the second floor, and the Bradwell Windmill, in Milton Keynes, southeast England, built in 1805, with a small fireplace on the ground floor. Incidentally, the doors and windows of the Upholland Windmill are aligned to the cardinal points of the compass—more scope for an observatory theory here surely? Much closer to home is the Old Powder House at the Nathan Tufts Park in Somerville, Massachusetts. This stone-built structure was constructed in 1703 or 1704 as a windmill by John Maillet, but from the mid-18th century was used as a powder magazine. The Old Powder House is around 15 feet in diameter and 30 feet high, and originally had three interior levels with heavy timber floors, a fireplace, and a chimney.

Due to the Newport Tower's close resemblance to the Chesterton Windmill, Arnold or whoever designed the structure could well have seen and been influenced by the Warwickshire example. In fact a contemporary of Arnold, John Hull, had seen Arnold's windmill in 1665 and notes in his diary that the governor had built the tower in the style of a windmill he had seen back home in England (*Diaries of John Hull*, 1847, Transactions of the American Antiquarian Society, pp. 208, 213, 218). If Arnold did build the Newport Tower as a windmill, he may have done so to replace the wooden-built windmill of a man named Peter Easton that is known to have blown down in a hurricane in August 1675. Of course this is not conclusive proof that Benedict Arnold built the Newport Tower as a windmill in the mid-17th century, but the "windmill theory" is the only one with any material evidence to back it up. It also ties in well with the date of the first settlement of Rhode Island by Europeans, when in 1636 Roger Williams and a group of followers arrived from the Massachusetts Bay Colony. In the end, the riddle of Newport's Mystery Tower can only really be solved by a full survey and excavation in and around the area of the structure, a task that the CRF have already tentatively begun.

Chapter 14

The Abandonment of Mesa Verde (United States)

Cliff dwellings at Mesa Verde.

Mesa Verde National Park is located in Montezuma County, in the southwestern corner of Colorado. The park occupies just more than 52,000 acres of the Colorado Plateau and is an area full of diverse and unique geological features. However, the main attractions of Mesa Verde (Spanish for "Green Tableland") are its 4,000 or so historic ruins, the most impressive of which are the 600 or so spectacular cliff dwellings carved into the sandstone cliffs beneath the mesa. These structures are the remains of homes and villages built by the ancient Pueblo people known as the *Anasazi* (Navajo for "Ancient Ones" or "Ancient Enemy"), or Ancient Pueblo People. These people are thought to be ancestors of the modern Pueblo Indians. For about 700 years from around the middle of the first millennium AD the Anasazi flourished in this area, eventually building their stone villages in the shelter of the canyon walls at Mesa Verde. But around AD 1300 they abandoned the region, never to return. What happened to the Anasazi, and why did they leave Mesa Verde so suddenly?

The culture known as the Anasazi emerged around 1200 BC in the Four Corners area (a region of the Southwest named for the only point in the United States that is on the boundaries of four states: Arizona, Colorado, New Mexico, and Utah). The Anasazi probably evolved from nomadic bands that hunted game and gathered wild plants in the Four Corners area, and lived in temporary dwellings. From around 200 BC, the culture began to depend increasingly on growing domesticated crops such as corn, beans, and squash-crops, and constructed more permanent dwellings. These Anasazi lodges, known as "pithouses," were shallow excavations in the ground, sometimes lined with rocks, covered by a roof built of mud-plastered timber and brush. By AD 500, the early Anasazi peoples were living in farming villages, though they still supplemented their agricultural produce by hunting rabbits and deer, and gathering wild plants. During this period, named by archaeologists Basketmaker III (c. AD 500–750) after the elaborate and finely woven basketry they produced, the Anasazi began making pottery, and the bow and arrow replaced the more primitive atlati (spear thrower). According to archaeological classification of the Anasazi culture, the Basketmaker I period refers to the era before 1200 BC, and Basketmaker II (divided into Early and Late) covers the period from c. 1200 BC to c. AD 500.

It was also around the middle of the first millennium that the Anasazi moved into Mesa Verde, settling mainly on the mesa tops, though they occasionally built in the cliff recesses. Somewhere around AD 750, at the beginning of the period known as Pueblo I (AD 750–900), the Anasazi began building their structures not in the form of pithouses, but on the surface of the ground as long rows of contiguous rooms with the jacal-style walls (walls of adjoining upright poles plastered with mud or an adobe clay). Pithouses were still built, though they may have served as meeting places or ceremonial chambers rather than houses.

In this sense they were perhaps the forerunners of the "kivas" of later times. (*Kiva* is a Hopi word for a ceremonial room or chamber.) These kivas were sunken rooms used by the Pueblo people for ritual activities and clan gatherings, and there was normally one kiva for each five or six rooms used as residences.

By the end of the first millennium, within the Pueblo II period (AD 900–1150), the people of Mesa Verde had made considerable progress in architecture and were constructing finely crafted two- or three-story masonry pueblos (villages) with 50 or more rooms and large circular semi-subterranean kivas (known as "great kivas"). The years from AD 1100 to 1300 are known as Mesa Verde's Classic Period and coincide roughly with the Pueblo III (AD 1150–1350) era. At this time, the people of Mesa Verde were part of a vigorous civilization and numbered several thousand, with perhaps as many as 100,000 Anasazi occupying the Four Corners region. The period is characterized at Mesa Verde by finely built compact multi-roomed villages built into the cliffs, perhaps as a defensive measure. The majority of these cliff dwellings were built and lived in for a period of about a hundred years, up until around AD 1300. The largest and best-known of these is known as Cliff Palace, which has 150 identified rooms and 23 kivas.

Craftsmanship at Mesa Verde also reached its height at this time, with sophisticated working in basketry, leatherwork, jewelry, pottery, tools, and weapons. Seashells from the Pacific coast discovered at the site are a sign of trade links between far-flung communities connected by a complicated network of trails.

However, despite the success of their civilization, some time around AD 1250 the Anasazi began to leave Mesa Verde, and by AD 1300 the site was completely abandoned. It is popularly assumed that archaeologists and historians do not know why this happened or where the Anasazi went. But the Anasazi did not in fact vanish, as is often thought to be the case; they simply migrated. When the population of Mesa Verde left the region, they headed south into present-day New Mexico and Arizona, and joined what are now Hopi and Zuni communities and Pueblo villages along the Río Grande. Indeed, a number of clans of present-day Native American tribes in the area trace their ancestry back to the cliff-dwelling Anasazi of the Colorado plateau.

Mesa Verde was not alone, but was one of a number of major Anasazi centers abandoned in the 13th and 14th centuries, including Chaco Canyon in northwestern New Mexico, a major center of Puebloan culture between AD 850 and 1250, and various cliff-dwelling sites in Kayenta, the largest of the Anasazi regions, which spreads out over northern Arizona, and into southern Utah and southwestern Colorado. By AD 1400 the majority of the Anasazi had migrated to the Southwest, where evidence of their presence can still be seen in New Mexico and Arizona in the form of classic late Mesa Verde-style settlements.

One difficulty with studying the Anasazi is that they had no written language, so we are ignorant of their spiritual views, songs, dances, and oral traditions, and the reason why they were forced to leave Mesa Verde. It is certainly true that no single cause seems to explain the abandonment. More likely, there were a number of contributing factors. One of these factors may have been the unstable climate of the area during the Pueblo III period, which resulted in a severe drought lasting from around AD 1275 to 1300, and would have caused serious crop failure. However, some archaeologists, such as Dr. Eric Blinman of the Office of Archaeological Studies of the Museum of New Mexico in Santa Fe, remain unconvinced that the drought alone would have been enough to persuade thousands of Anasazi to abandon their homes and flee. There are records of previous droughts in the area that the Anasazi seem to have survived, and recent studies have shown that the evacuation started began before the drought set in.

Nevertheless, if the population had already been weakened by other factors, then the timing of this drought would fit with the date of the abandonment of Mesa Verde. One of these factors may well originate in the success of the Anasazi culture, which was primarily based on agriculture. After hundreds of years of intensive land use, both for agriculture and hunting and gathering, local resources may have become exhausted and left the Anasazi vulnerable to the severe climate changes of the thirteenth century. As the population increased, the Anasazi no longer possessed the resources to support it.

An alternative suggestion is that the Anasazi were driven out by other tribes, perhaps the nomadic Utes or Navajos, though there is no evidence that these or any other groups were in the area during the 13th and 14th centuries AD. Warfare of a kind, however, may have been involved. If the previously mentioned stress on the environment led to competition for the available resources, then this may have caused conflict and warfare between the various clans of the Anasazi. In this light the 1997 excavations supervised by University of North Carolina archaeologist Brian Billman at Cowboy Wash, a group of nine archaeological sites around 12 miles west of Mesa Verde, may be relevant. The excavations at one of the sites, a dwelling believed to have been occupied between the years AD 1125 and 1150, recovered more than 1,000 human bones and bone fragments, including shoulder blades, skulls, vertebrae, ribs, arm bones, hand and foot bones, and teeth. The majority of these bones had been broken. Studies showed the remains represented at least five people: three adult males, one adult female, and an 11-year-old child. All the bones showed evidence of dismemberment and butchery, which suggested to the archaeologists who examined them that cannibalism was practiced by the Anasazi at the Cowboy Wash sites. Billman's conclusion is that, as resources became increasingly scarce, neighboring groups were using cannibalism as a "terrorist strategy" to scare away competitors for these resources. Other researchers, such as archaeologist Kurt Dongoske, are not convinced of Billman's conclusions regarding the Cowboy Wash bones, and believe they could just as easily be the result of ritual killings as cannibalism.

Sand Canyon Pueblo is an Anasazi site located about 20 miles west of Mesa Verde and was excavated by Kristin A. Kuckelman of the Crow Canyon Archaeological Center in Cortez, Colorado. The settlement was first occupied around the late AD 1240s or early 1250s and lasted until approximately AD 1280. The site contained around 420 rooms, 90 kivas, and 14 towers. Sand Canyon Pueblo was burned and abandoned around AD 1285, after a merciless attack where villagers were scalped, dismembered, and perhaps even eaten. Scientific analysis of the remains of 44 people found at the site has shown that the attackers were not outsiders but local, probably neighboring Pueblo people.

Although these signs of violence in the Mesa Verde region are suggestive of intersite warfare at some level, there is no similar evidence from the Mesa Verde site itself. However, piles of bones of men, women, and children that were discovered at the site and that were thought to have been destroyed during "ritualistic activity" may possibly have another explanation. The attacks at the nearby sites of Cowboy Wash and Sand Canyon Pueblo are evidence that severe strain on resources led to violence and cannibalism in the area, and thus the possibility of a similar situation at Mesa Verde should not be discounted.

The rapidity of the abandonment of Mesa Verde has suggested to some archaeologists that the inhabitants were perhaps attracted elsewhere. Researchers have suggested that a new evangelical-like religion may have swept through the region to the south of Mesa Verde that exerted some kind of pull on the Anasazi. In the absence of Anasazi writings, there is no way to prove or disprove this hypothesis, though it is possible that there was a change in the spiritual beliefs of the population, perhaps caused by a collapse in their religious and political infrastructure around the end of the 13th century.

In June 1906, President Theodore Roosevelt signed the bill that created Mesa Verde National Park, the first park established in the United States to preserve cultural heritage. On September 8, 1978, the National Park was designated a World Cultural Heritage Site by UNESCO due to its "outstanding archaeological remains and importance in preserving the global heritage of mankind."

⌛

Chapter 15

Tenochtitlan
(Mexico)

*Model of Tenochtitlan at the National Museum of Anthropology in
Mexico City.*

Now buried beneath the huge modern metropolis of Mexico City,
Tenochtitlan was once the capital city of the Aztec empire. The city
was founded in AD 1325, in an inhospitable location on an island in the
marshy bottom of Lake Texcoco in the Valley of Mexico. By the early
16th century, when it was ruled by the legendary Motecuhzoma II (aka
Montezuma), Tenochtitlan had expanded rapidly to become the largest,
most populous, and most powerful city in Central America, and one of

the largest cities in the world at the time. All that changed with the arrival of Spanish under Cortez in 1519. The city, including the wondrous Templo Mayor pyramid, was practically razed to the ground by Cortez and his troops, and over the centuries became covered by the vast urban sprawl that was to become modern Mexico City. It is only fairly recently, through careful archaeological investigations, that we have begun to build up a picture of the once magnificent Aztec city of Tenochtitlan.

The collection of ethnic groups of central Mexico who spoke the Nahuatl language and dominated large parts of Mesoamerica from the 14th to the 16th centuries is known to us as the Aztec. However, it is more accurate to speak of them as a tribe of the Mexica, who at the time of the Spanish invasion called themselves either "Tenochca" or "Toltec." The Aztecs were the last great pre-Columbian civilization of Mesoamerica, and began to develop their empire around AD 1200 in the Valley of Mexico, with their capital city of Tenochtitlan built upon raised islets in Lake Texcoco. The Aztec Empire was based on a political coalition that has become known as the "Triple Alliance." This alliance consisted of the Mexica of Tenochtitlan and the tribes of two other city-states: the Acolhua of Texcoco, and the Tepaneca of Tlacopan. The Triple Alliance came to dominate most of Mexico for around a century, between AD 1430 and 1521, extending its power from the Gulf of Mexico to the Pacific Ocean.

The founding of the Aztec capital Tenochtitlan was the result of an ancient prophecy. According to this prophecy, the location of the future city would be signaled by the sight of an eagle perched on a cactus and eating a snake. Despite the drawbacks of building their new city in an unpleasant swamp, the Aztec interpreted the sign to begin construction on this spot. This graphic vision of the eagle and the snake is now emblazoned on the Mexican flag.

Tenochtitlan was founded in AD 1325, and was constantly being enlarged as the Empire flourished. The city, which soon grew to become the dominant city in Mesoamerica, developed into a sophisticated center that included towering pyramids, the Emperor's palace, streets, canals spanned by wide bridges, floating gardens for growing crops (known as *chinampas*), aqueducts, and a ball court. Spanish conquistador Bernal Díaz del Castillo described the cities of the Aztec in *The Conquest of New Spain* (pp.190–91):

When we saw so many cities and villages built in the water and other great towns on dry land we were amazed and said that it was like the enchantments...on account of the great towers and cues and buildings rising from the water, and all built of masonry. And some of our soldiers even asked whether the things that we saw were not a dream?... I do not know how to describe it, seeing things as we did that had never been heard of or seen before, not even dreamed about.

The heart of the city of Tenochtitlan was the Sacred Precinct, a walled religious and ceremonial area that covered about 35 acres, and that could hold an estimated 8,000 people within its precincts. At its height the Sacred Precinct was home to an estimated 78 buildings, the most important of which were the Templo Mayor, the Ball Court, the *Calmecac* (priest's school), and the temples dedicated to Quetzalcoatl, Tezcatlipoca, and the Sun. The high masonry wall that surrounded the precinct was called *coatepantli* ("serpent wall") due to it being decorated with representations of serpents. The main building within the Sacred Precinct was the Templo Mayor (Spanish—"Great/Main Temple"), the symbolic center not only of the Aztec capital city, but also of their universe. The pyramid-shaped stone Temple was begun in 1390, but not completed until 1487, when, in order to commemorate its completion, thousands of people were sacrificed over a four-day period. The temple once stood around 200 feet high and contained two shrines on its summit, one dedicated to Huitzilopochtli (god of war and sun) and an adjacent shrine dedicated to Tlaloc (god of rain and fertility).

Excavations from 1978 to 1997 at the Templo Mayor uncovered a series of more than 80 separate offering deposits, which had been placed under floors or below stairs at each stage of the Temple's construction. These offerings, which originated from all corners of the Aztec Empire, included statues of gods; two identical, life-sized clay statues of Aztec warriors dressed in eagle costumes; masks; precious stones; jewelry; coral; sea shells; human remains; skeletons of jaguars and alligators; and a stone eagle symbolizing the god Huitzilopochtli, which was hollowed out at the center to receive the hearts of sacrificial victims. The most common form of Aztec human sacrifice took place on an altar close to the summit of the Pyramid. The victim, who was usually an enemy warrior captured in battle, was placed on his back on a sacrificial slab of the same volcanic stone that had been used to build the Pyramid. The priest then cut into the victim's abdomen with an obsidian knife and tore out the heart. The body was then usually hurled down the Temple's steps.

One of the most fascinating discoveries from the Templo Mayor was a large carved round stone, 11 feet in diameter, around 12 inches thick, and weighing 8 1/2 tons. The 15th-century stone depicted the severed limbs of the Aztec moon goddess Coyolxauhqui ("She who is adorned with Golden Bells"). The carving reflects the story of the goddess, who, according to Aztec mythology, was killed and dismembered by her brother Huitzilopochtli (the Sun god) because she had slain their mother. The Aztecs re-created this myth when they sacrificed prisoners to Coyolxauhqui, by cutting off their heads, removing their hearts, and throwing the bodies down Coyolxauhqui's temple steps. It is said that it was the appalling site of such bloody human sacrifice that contributed to the Spanish desire to destroy the Aztec capital.

When Spanish conquistador Hernán Cortez arrived in Tenochtitlan on November 8, 1519, the city contained a population of between 150,000 and 200,000 people living within an area of 5 square miles, making it one of the largest cities in the world at the time. Though the initial meeting between Cortez and the last elected ruler of the Aztecs Moctezuma II (reigned AD 1502–1520) was peaceful, the Spanish were nervous about being so vastly outnumbered, and Moctezuma was soon taken hostage and confined in the Axayáctal palace. Although there is a legend that the Aztecs initially believed Cortez was the feathered serpent deity Quetzalcoatl, who was supposed to return to Mexico the same year that Cortez landed, this story is false and originated during the conquest rather than with any genuine Aztec prophesy.

It was not the strength of the Spanish army alone that overran the Aztecs, but mainly a combination of the European diseases brought over by the conquerors, which decimated Central America, and Spanish alliance with the Texcocans, the Chalca, and the Tepanecs— all previously subjugated by the Aztecs. Although the next two years saw much fierce Aztec resistance to the Spanish invasion and numerous battles between the two sides, the siege at Tenochtitlan in the summer of 1521 finally decided the fate of the Aztec Empire. Cortez's relentless three-month-long offensive against the Aztec capital, making use of warships and cutting off supplies to the city, effectively ended Aztec resistance, and a large part of the population died from hunger and smallpox. The city finally fell on August 13, 1521. Almost all the Aztec nobility had died during the siege, and although Cuauhtemoc, last emperor of the Aztecs, survived, he was later executed for allegedly plotting to kill Cortez. About 450–860 Spanish soldiers and 20,000 Tlaxcalan warriors were killed during the siege, whereas 100,000 Aztec warriors had died fighting or from disease or starvation. With the destruction of their capital city, the once-great Aztec Empire was no more.

After the fall of Tenochtitlan, the Spaniards and their indigenous allies looted and burned the city until almost no trace of its former grandeur remained. The Spanish were to construct a new capital over the ruins of Tenochtitlan, erecting Catholic churches over the old Aztec temples, and rebuilding and taking over the imperial palaces for themselves. The new city was eventually renamed Mexico City, and Cortez claimed it for Spain. A year later, in 1522, he became governor and captain-general of New Spain. So complete was the Spanish annihilation of all remnants of Aztec culture in the city that it would be hundreds of years before any traces of the mighty Tenochtitlan were discovered.

Remnants of Aztec buildings and artifacts turned up periodically during building work in Mexico City from the late 18th century onward. The most fascinating discovery was that of the magnificent Aztec Calendar Stone or Sun Stone, which was found in 1790 underneath the Zocalo (Main Square) of the city. The ancient Aztec name for this huge monolith is *Cuauhxicalli* ("Eagle Bowl"). The massive disc-shaped stone measures 12 feet in diameter, is 3 feet thick, and weighs 25 tons. The stone, which dates to 1479, was made from basalt and is a carving of the Aztec calendar, which consists of a 365-day calendar cycle and a 260-day ritual cycle. Together, these two cycles formed a 52-year "century." The Stone is also said to tell the history of the Aztec people and prophesize the future. The magnificent Aztec Sun Stone is now kept in the National Museum of Anthropology and History in Mexico City.

Despite such important finds, it was not until the investigations of Leopoldo Batres at the end of the 19th century that the first official archaeological dig took place in Mexico City. In 1913, during the turbulent times of the Mexican Revolution, archaeologist Manuel Gamio was excavating just north of the 16th-century cathedral when he came upon the southwestern corner of the great Temple of Tenochtitlan. Although Gamio's excavation revealed that the Spanish had destroyed the Templo Mayor, inside it he discovered earlier smaller pyramids that the Spanish had failed to find.

As the 20th century progressed, the ancient Aztec capital beneath Mexico City slowly revealed itself, usually in the form of small chance finds made during construction work (such as the building of the Metro system in the 1960s and 70s) and a limited amount of excavation. For example, in 1948, Hugo Moedano and Elma Estrada Balmori, excavating in the Templo Mayor, discovered a platform containing serpent heads and offerings, and in 1966, Eduardo Contreras and Jorge Angula discovered a chest containing Aztec offerings.

In 1978, Mexico City electrical workers digging to the northwest of the cathedral and close to the Zocalo chanced upon an elaborately carved monolithic stone block. The stone turned out to be the famous Coyolxauhqui stone described previously in this chapter. Subsequent excavations in the same area directed by archaeologist Eduardo Matos Moctezuma on behalf of the Mexican government uncovered the remains of the Templo Mayor. The excavations, under the heading the Templo Mayor Project, continued until 1997, and have been responsible for the discovery of evidence for each separate building stage of the Great Temple, and also for a variety of smaller temples and palaces within the surrounding Sacred Precinct. Besides these architectural wonders, a bewildering array of more than 7,000 objects, mostly offerings, were found within the structure of the Temple.

Excavations continue today, slowly revealing the great Aztec capital of Tenochtitlan, which lurks beneath the modern concrete streets and squares that make up the heart of modern Mexico City.

Unexplained

Artifacts

⧗

Chapter 16

The Stone of Destiny
(Ireland/Scotland)

A replica of the Stone of Scone at Scone Palace.

The sacred Stone of Destiny, also known as the Stone of Scone, the *Lia Fáil*, the Coronation Stone, and the Stone of Fate, is a controversial ancient object long associated with the inauguration of kings. In fact, there are actually two contenders for the authentic Stone of Destiny. The first, the Lia Fáil (Irish—"stone of Fál"), stands upright on the windswept Hill of Tara, County Meath, Ireland; the other resides in the coronation chair at Westminster Abbey, London. These stones are surrounded by legend and associated with numerous conflicting theories for their origins. The stories connected with the Stone of Destiny bring in a huge cast of antique characters including the Picts, ancient Kings of Spain, the daughter of a pharaoh, the Tuatha de Danaan of Irish myth, the biblical Jacob, and the Knights Templar. Has the real Stone of Destiny ever been found? And if so, where is it today?

The Lia Fáil appears in the the *Lebor Gabála Érenn (The Book of the Taking of Ireland)*, known in English as "The Book of Invasions" or "The Book of Conquests." Compiled in the 11th century, the *Lebor Gabála Érenn* is a collection of poems and prose narratives dealing with the mythical history of Ireland. The book mentions the semi-divine Tuatha de Danaan ("peoples of the goddess Danu") bringing the Lia Fáil to Tara from Falias in Scotland. The Stone, one of four magical items that gave the Tuatha de Danaan victory in battle, was able to state whether the King about to be crowned on it was a rightful ruler of Ireland.

A legend recorded in the *Scalacronica*, a chronicle written in Anglo-Norman French by knight Sir Thomas Gray of Heaton in 1355, declares that Simon Brec (youngest son of the king of Spain) "brought with him a stone on which the Kings of Spain were wont to be crowned." This stone was brought to the "Royal Palace" (Tara). In the *Processus* of Scottish lawyer Baldred Bisset, written in 1301, "the daughter of Pharaoh, King of Egypt" arrives in Ireland accompanied by an army and a large fleet. Joining forces with the Irish she sails to Scotland, taking with her "the royal seat," which the King of England "with other insignia of the Kingdom of Scotland, carried with him, by violence, to England." According to this legend, the pharaoh's daughter's name was Scotta—who gave her name to the country Scotland.

Thomas Pennant, in his *Tour in Scotland and Voyage to the Hebrides* (1776), recounts the popular myth that the stone in the bottom of a chair in the abbey of Scone (in the Perth and Kinross area of Scotland) had originally been used by the biblical Jacob as his pillow when he was at Bethel, and had the famous dream of the ladder to heaven. According to this legend, the stone was later taken to Spain, "where it was used as a seat of justice by Gethalus, contemporary with Moses," before it finally ended up at Scone.

Genesis 28:22 (King James Version) was perhaps the inspiration for this story: "And this stone, which I have set for a pillar, shall be

God's house: and of all that thou shalt give me I will surely give the tenth unto thee."

The stone standing on the Hill of Tara (Irish *Teamhair na Rí*, "Hill of the Kings") is a 3.3-foot-high granular limestone megalith, half of which is concealed below the surface. Known as the Lia Fáil, it is blatantly phallic in shape. Tara constitutes one of the most important archaeological complexes in Ireland, and it is from here that 142 High Kings of Ireland are said to have ruled the land. The Hill of Tara comprises 25 visible ancient monuments, including a Neolithic passage grave known as the Mound of the Hostages, dating back to around 3350 BC; an Iron Age ringfort (fortified settlement) called the Rath of the Synods (second–fourth centuries AD); and another Iron Age fort: the Royal Enclosure, also known as the Fort of the Kings.

The Lia Fáil stands to the south of the Mound of the Hostages, in the middle of the King's Seat, one of two linked ringforts, the other being Cormac's House. The Stone has been moved several times over the years, it was relocated to its present position to mark the mass grave of the 400 United Irish rebels who fell at the battle of Tara on May 26, 1798. The Lia Fáil was supposed to have been used as a magical coronation stone for all the kings of Ireland, and, when the rightful king of the country stood upon it, it would roar three times in approval. According to some stories, this stone was taken from Tara to Scone, by an Irish prince, Fergus, who later became King of Scotland in the fifth/sixth century AD (in some versions, the ninth century), where it remained until the end of the 13th century, when King Edward I of England took it to be set up at Westminster Abbey.

However, archaeologists believe that the Lia Fáil originally stood in front of the entrance to the Mound of the Hostages, and like the two pillar-shaped stones that stand in front of the eastern and western passages at the passage grave of Knowth, a few miles away; it may have been contemporary with the tomb. If the Lia Fáil is part of the 5,300-year-old Mound of the Hostages, it would presumably never have left the Hill of Tara, so at some time in the distant past tradition has confused the Lia Fail with Scottish Coronation Stone, and associated both with the Stone of Destiny.

The Coronation Stone, now contained in a space under the seat of the Coronation Chair in Westminster Abbey, is a rectangular block of coarse-grained reddish-grey sandstone, decorated with a single Latin Cross. It measures 26 inches long by 16 inches wide, is 10 1/2 inches deep, and weighs approximately 336 pounds. There is an iron ring attached to each end of the stone, presumably intended to make transport easier. The Coronation Stone is believed to be one in the same as the Stone of Scone, originally kept at the late-12th-century Scone Abbey. Geological examination of the Stone has shown that it is "lower Old Red Sandstone" and was quarried in the area of Scone. The origins of this royal stone are obscure, but it may have been brought in the ninth century from Antrim in present-day Northern Ireland to Argyll, in western Scotland, and then to Scone by Kenneth MacAlpin, the 36th King of Dalriada. Dalriada was a Gaelic kingdom originating at least as far back as the fifth century AD, which extended on both sides of the North Channel, encompassing the western seaboard of Scotland and County Antrim on the Northern Irish coast.

The Stone was used for centuries in the coronation of Scottish monarchs, including Alexander III in the year 1249 and John Balliol in 1292. Coronations took place on Moot Hill, an ancient mound next to the Abbey. In 1296, English King Edward I conquered Scotland and, having already stolen the Scottish Regalia from Edinburgh, removed the Coronation Stone from Scone Abbey. Edward took the stone to Westminster Abbey, where it was fitted into a specially constructed oak chair, known as St. Edward's Chair, on which most subsequent English monarchs have been crowned.

On Christmas Day, 1950, a group of four Scottish students (Ian Hamilton, Gavin Vernon, Kay Matheson, and Alan Stuart) broke into Westminster Abby and stole the Coronation Stone. The students were members of the Scottish Covenant Association, an organization whose main goal was to gain public support for Scottish independence from England. In the process of removing the Stone from the Abbey it was broken into two pieces. The students eventually got the Stone to Scotland, where they arranged to have it repaired by a professional stonemason. In April 1951, it was left on the altar of Arbroath Abbey, in the royal burgh of Arbroath, Angus. The London Police were informed of the Stone's location, and it was returned to Westminster. The strange story of Ian Hamilton and company was made into a British-Canadian movie in 2008 called *The Stone of Destiny*, written and directed by Charles Martin Smith.

On November 15, 1996, amid much ceremony, the Stone was returned to Scotland, where it is now kept at Edinburgh Castle, until it is needed again for future coronation ceremonies at Westminster Abbey.

A further curious incident involving the Stone of Scone occurred in 1999, when a group of modern Knights Templar offered the new Scottish Parliament what they claimed was the original Stone. Apparently it was the last wish of Dr. John MacKay Nimmo, a Chevalier with the Knights Templar of Scotland and a Church of Scotland minister, that after his death the Stone be given to the Scottish Parliament. When he died in 1999, his widow, Jean, contacted the Templars, and they made the request to the Scottish Parliament for her. If this was the real Coronation Stone, from where did Nimmo get it? The Knights Templar claimed that they had acquired the Stone from the Scottish students in 1950. Allegedly, copies of the Stone were apparently made by Robert Gray, the Glasgow stonemason who had repaired it, so what was returned to Westminster was in fact a replica made by Gray.

As if this wasn't enough, in 2008, the First Minister of Scotland, Alex Salmond, spoke out about the Stone. Salmond believes that the monks at Scone Abbey fooled the English into thinking that they had stolen the Coronation Stone when in fact they had taken a replica. The Minister claims that the sandstone block formerly at Westminster Abbey and now in Edinburgh is almost certainly not the original Coronation Stone. Salmond thinks that the original stone could have been a fragment of meteorite and cites one medieval chronicler who describes it as a shiny, black, circular object with carved symbols—certainly not the same as an oblong piece of Perthshire sandstone.

Alex Salmond is not the first to express the belief that Edward I did not take the original Stone from Scone Abbey. Many researchers believe that the rough sandstone block that resided for so long in Westminster Abbey was, due to its appearance and proportions, more likely to have been used in building, rather than as a coronation stone. For centuries there have been tales that the monks at the Abbey hid the real Stone in the River Tay (or buried it on Dunsinane Hill or in a nearby cave on Moncrieff Hill) before Edward I and his army arrived. In his book *The Story of Scotland* (Routledge & Kegan Paul, 1987), Nigel Tranter expressed the belief that the "True Stone" was originally hidden by the Abbot of Scone, and later entrusted to the care of Angus Og MacDonald, Lord of the Isles, by Robert the Bruce (1274–1329). Angus Og afterward hid the Stone in his native Hebrides (a large group of Islands off the west coast of Scotland), where the stone remains to this day.

There are a couple of objections to the theory that King Edward I did not take the genuine Stone of Scone. If the original was still in Scotland, why was it never used again for coronations after the English invasion (at the coronation of Robert the Bruce on Moot Hill on March 25, 1306, for example)? Furthermore, if the monks were able to hide the Stone, and give Edward I a copy, why were the Scottish Regalia not also hidden away? Despite this, we do know that copies of the stone exist; there is one on Moot Hill at Scone Palace, for example. There is even one theory that this supposed replica is in fact the original Stone of Scone, and it has been hiding in plain sight for 60 years. Without scientific testing, however, the debate as to the whereabouts of the real Coronation Stone will always continue, despite the likelihood that the original is now firmly ensconced in Edinburgh Castle. But is this the Stone of Destiny? Perhaps we will never know. There was certainly never any connection between the prehistoric Lia Fail at Tara and the symbol of medieval Scottish Kingship, the Stone of Scone.

🕰

Chapter 17

The Mystery of the Ogham Stones
(Ireland/United Kingdom)

Oghman stone in the grounds of Ratass Church in Tralee, County Kerry, Ireland.

Dating back to around AD 300, the Ogham script is the earliest form of writing in Irish and one of the earliest in the British Isles. Inscriptions in Ogham were carved on the edges of standing stones, which are found mainly in Ireland, Scotland, and Wales, although there are a few examples from England. The precise origin of Ogham is shrouded in mystery, though there are various opinions about where it came from. Theories have been put forward that Ogham derives from the runic alphabet of Scandinavia, that it comes from northern Italy, and that it was originally invented by Gaulish druids as a secret system of hand signals. All of these hypotheses have their supporters, but where did Ogham really originate and what was it used for?

Ogham inscriptions are essentially notches and incisions made on the corner edge, or occasionally on the face, of either already-ancient standing stones or an especially quarried slab of stone. There is literary evidence for Ogham inscriptions on wood as well as stone, though any wood examples have unfortunately long since vanished. The "letters" of the Ogham alphabet consist of one to five perpendicular or angled strokes meeting or crossing a center line (known as a foundation-line). Ogham contains 20 letters—probably adapted from the Latin alphabet—divided into four groups, each containing five letters. The inscriptions were carved and read vertically from bottom to top, and occasionally right to left. The language of the inscriptions is mainly Primitive Irish and Old Irish, although a few examples in Scotland, such as the Lunnasting stone (from Lunnasting, Shetland), may be in the Pictish language (spoken until around the ninth century AD in northern and central Scotland). Later examples, especially from Wales and England, contain parallel inscriptions in both Ogham and Latin.

Ogham is sometimes referred to as the Celtic Tree Language or Alphabet, perhaps because each letter was supposed to have been named after familiar trees, or, according to some researchers (poet Robert Graves, for example), the names of 20 trees sacred to the druids. However, although a few letters were named after trees, this theory probably originated because the letters themselves are known in Irish as *feda* ("trees") or *nin* ("forking branches"), because of their shape.

There are more than 400 surviving Ogham inscriptions on stone monuments distributed throughout the British Isles, mainly dating from the fourth to sixth centuries AD. The majority of these inscriptions are found in the south and west of Ireland, though there are around 50 examples known from Wales, with others scattered throughout the west of England, Scotland, and the Isle of Man—in other words, the Celtic fringes of the British Isles. There are no examples of Ogham from Continental Europe, and certainly no genuine Ogham inscriptions in the United States, despite the claims of zoology professor Barry Fell in the 1970s. A large and important collection of Ogham Stones is on display in "The Stone corridor" in the North Wing of the Quadrangle at University College Cork (UCC), southern Ireland. These 28 stones were collected by Irish antiquarian Abraham Abell (1783–1851) and were put on display in the University in 1861.

Ogham inscriptions are very brief, and consist mainly of personal names and details. The inscriptions utilize a series of formula words, typically describing the person's ancestry or tribal affiliation. Ogham stones seem to have been erected as memorials to the dead or perhaps grave markers, although archaeologists have discovered no associated burials beneath or around them. However, many of the stones have been moved from their original positions, so the lack of evidence for associated burials is not completely reliable. Another possibility is that Ogham stones were used as tribal boundary markers.

One Ogham stone discovered at Castell Dwyran in modern Carmarthenshire, southwest Wales, commemorates "Vortiporius," a sixth-century king of Dyfed (an ancient kingdom covering modern southwest Wales). This stone contains the only Ogham inscription ever discovered with the name of an identifiable individual.

What is probably the tallest Ogham stone anywhere can be found at Ballycrovane, County Cork. The impressive 17-feet-high stone stands on a knoll in the Beara peninsula with spectacular views over the coast. The faded inscription reads "*MAQI-DECCEDDAS AVI TURANIAS*" ("Of the son of Deich descendant of Torainn"), and was added when the stone was already standing. Because the area is peppered with a number of Early to Middle Bronze Age (c. 2200–1500 BC) stone circles and standing stones, the stone would have been erected at least two thousand years before it was inscribed in Ogham.

A rare find of an Ogham stone a considerable distance from the main western British distribution was made in 1893 at the walled

Roman town of Calleva Atrebatum ("The town in the woods of the Atrebates tribe"), modern Silchester, Hampshire, southern England. The stone, a small greensand baluster column, was unearthed during excavations of a well belonging to a large Roman town house. The incomplete inscription, carved on the face rather than the edge of the stone, reads "*TEBICATO[S]/[MAQ]I MUCO[I--]*", which translates as "(The something) of Tebicatus, son of the tribe of N." The name, as was usual in Ogham, is in the genitive case, implying ownership, which would make the missing word possibly *memorial* or *stone*. The word may also be *land*,which would imply that the stone may have been inscribed to mark the ownership of the townhouse within which it was found, perhaps by an immigrant from Ireland during the fourth or early fifth century AD.

Beginning in the sixth century AD, Old Irish was written using the Roman alphabet, and Ogham gradually disappeared, though it was occasionally used for notes in manuscripts right up until the 16th century. A stone in the graveyard in Ahenny, County Tipperary, south-central Ireland, has an English inscription that reads: "Beneath this sepulchral tomb lie the remains of Mary Dempsey who departed this life January the 4th 1802 aged 17 years." The grave stone also bears an Ogham inscription reading in Irish *Fa an lig so na lu ata Mari ni Dhimusao mballi na gCranibh* ("Under this stone lies Mary Dempsy from Ballycranna'"). Although the Ahenny Stone was at one time held up as proof that knowledge of the Ogham alphabet survived among the country people of Ireland up until the early 19th century, it is more likely that the inscription was the result of a revival of interest, influenced by publication of descriptions of Ogham.

Perhaps the most controversial aspect of the Ogham script is its origin. Even the meaning of the word *Ogham* is disputed. One hypothesis is that the word comes from the Irish *og-úaim*—"point-seam"—referring to the ridge or groove made by the point of a sharp weapon. Ogham is said to be named after Ogmios, the Irish God of literature and eloquence, the son of De Dagda, and the champion of the semi-divine Tuatha de Danaan of Irish mythology. According to Irish legend, such as found in the 11th-century *Lebor Gabála Érenn* ("The Book of the Taking of Ireland") and the 12th-century or earlier *Auraicept na n-Éces* ("Scholars' Primer"), the Ogham alphabet was discovered after the fall of the Tower of Babel, along with those of Hebrew, Greek, and Latin, by the legendary Scythian king, Fenius Farsa (Farsaidh). The names Farsa gave to the Ogham letters were said to be those of his 25 chief scholars.

In the 1920s Irish archaeologist Robert Alexander Stewart Macalister (1870–1950) put forward the theory that Ogham was originated in Cisalpine Gaul (part of modern northern Italy) around 600 BC by Gaulish druids as a secret system of hand signals. Macalister believed that Ogham was inspired by a form of the Greek alphabet brought by Greek colonists to Northern Italy in the seventh century BC. After years of painstaking study of Ogham letters, however, subsequent scholars have unanimously rejected this theory, finding no connection between the Ogham alphabet and the form of the Greek alphabet put forward by Macalister. A related hypothesis is that the Ogham alphabet was created as a cipher by the druids, and used to encode and thus protect certain arcane knowledge from the authorities of Roman Britain, or perhaps even from the uninitiated among their own people, without writing it down. The problem is that so little is known about the druids and what language they used to record their knowledge, that it is impossible to link them with the Ogham alphabet. Researchers Carney and MacNeill have proposed a similar cipher theory where Ogham was invented as a cryptic alphabet by Irish scholars as secret means of communication against the Romans when there was a threat of a Roman invasion of Ireland.

In the late 1960s Klaus Düwel, and more recently Runologist/ occultist Stephen Flowers (*The Book of Ogham*, 1992, published under the name "Edred Thorson"), have claimed a close relationship between Ogham and the Germanic runic alphabet. However, at the time of the earliest Ogham inscriptions—the 4th century AD—runes were not very widespread even in continental Europe. Consequently, although there are similarities between the two alphabets, no solid links have yet been proven and it now seems likely that Ogham and runes were developed independently of each other.

The difficulty of determining the origins of Ogham is that there is no evidence for its development and introduction, indicating that such evidence was recorded on perishable material, probably wood, or even that it was never recorded at all. Even the most widely accepted interpretation of Ogham as an expression of the Irish language through the Latin alphabet, has been challenged, as the highest concentration of Ogham inscriptions are in the south and west of Ireland, where Roman influence was probably minimal. However, although the Romans never invaded Ireland, by the fourth century AD when Ogham first appeared, they had occupied Great Britain for around three centuries, so there must have been considerable contact and cultural exchange through trade and raiding during this time. Indeed Saint Patrick's (c. 387–493) arrival in Ireland was the result of his capture by Irish raiders in Britain, who took him across the Irish Sea as a slave. Another link between Ogham and Latin is that the Ogham alphabet contains letters not used in the Irish language (q, v, and z) but that are found in Latin.

The actual form that Ogham letters take, the strokes and notches, has made it difficult for scholars to work out the parent alphabet from which Ogham derives. Celtic scholar J. Vendryes put forward the intriguing theory that the forms of Ogham letters derived from notched wooden tally sticks used to count sheep, cattle, or grain, and that perhaps even functioned as rudimentary calendars. Unfortunately, without more evidence, ideally from Ogham Stones found in reliable archaeological contexts like that at Silchester, we cannot be sure about the origins of Ogham. Nevertheless, the fact that the main distribution of inscribed Ogham stones occurs in southern and western Ireland, makes it likely that the alphabet was devised in that area, some time prior to the earliest Ogham inscriptions in the fourth century AD. This date contradicts theories that posit Ogham as a Christian development, possibly by Irish monks, and would make the invention of Ogham in Ireland pre-Christian, as the earliest date for a Christian community in the country is around AD 400.

⧗

The Coligny Calendar and the Druids (France)

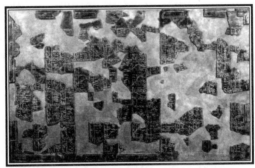

View of the re-assembled Coligny Tablet.

The Coligny Calendar, or Coligny Tablet as it is sometimes known, is an ancient Gaulish Celtic solar/lunar ritual calendar that was unearthed in Coligny, France, at the end of the 19th century. The Calendar is a fascinating discovery not only for the light it casts on pre-Christian astronomical and mathematical achievements in Northern Europe, but also in terms of early Celtic rituals and festivals such as Samhain (the origin of the modern Halloween), and on the now-extinct Gaulish version of the Celtic language. More controversially, some researchers have pushed back the origin of the Calendar to the age of the megalithic passage tombs of Ireland, more than 5,000 years ago.

In November 1897, in Ain, east-central France, a Monsieur Roux made an extraordinary discovery. In a field north of Coligny, he found the buried remains of a bronze statue of a youthful male figure (later interpreted as the Roman war god, Mars), and a pile of 153 bronze fragments contained in a kind of basket. When the bronze pieces were examined more closely, it was discovered that many of them bore text written in Latin inscription capitals, in the Gaulish language, and the objects were soon recognized as the remains of an ancient recording device, probably a calendar.

After reconstruction, researchers found that the fragments made up about 45 percent of what had once been a bronze tablet approximately 5 feet wide and 3 ½ feet in height. The Coligny Tablet, as it became known, appeared to be a five-year calendar, with the information arranged into 16 vertical columns with 62 months distributed over a five-year span. This cycle was composed of three years, each containing 12 lunar months (of 29 or 30 days), and two years having 13 lunar months. Two intercalary months were inserted over the five-year period to make the lunar calendar correspond to the solar year, making the Tablet in effect a lunisolar calendar. The fact that the Coligny Tablet is a lunar calendar makes it somewhat unique, as the majority of other inscribed public calendars from the ancient Mediterranean world are solar.

The remains of a calendar of almost identical type to the Coligny example, though only preserved in eight small fragments, were found in 1807 in a lake near the neighboring village of Villards d'Heria. Interestingly, this village contains a large Gallo-Roman complex, which includes temples, a theater, baths, and an aqueduct. The fragments of this calendar are now preserved in the *Musée d'Archéologie du Jura* (Museum of the Archaeology of the Jura region) in the town of Lons-le-Saunier, eastern France.

Research into the calendars of Coligny and Villards d'Heria has resulted in some general principles being ascribed to Celtic calendars, though there is debate among scholars as to the real merit of these principles. The common Celtic lunar year appears to have contained either 354 or 355 days, and the Continental (as opposed to British) Celtic calendar year seems to have began with *Samonios,* usually thought to correspond to Old Irish *Samhain,* and thus making the year start in autumn. However, not all researchers agree with this interpretation, as in the ancient Gaulish language *Samon* means "summer," which would indicate that the Celtic year may have began at the summer solstice, rather than in the autumn. An entry inscribed on the Coligny Calendar reading

"*TRINVX[tion] SAMO[nii] SINDIV*" ("three-nights of Samonios to-day") would suggest that the Samhain festival lasted for three nights.

On the Coligny Calendar there are 12 named months. Months of 30 days were marked *Mat(os)* ("lucky"); months of 29 days were marked *Anm(atos)* ("unlucky"). Each month is divided into two halves of approximately two weeks in length, one "light" and the other "dark." There is a reference to the same division in Julius Caesar's work *The Gallic Wars*, where he mentions that in Gaul (France) the days, months, and years start with a dark half followed by a light half. Scholars disagree whether the start of the Celtic month was at the new moon or the full moon. On the Coligny Calendar, the division of the two parts of the month is marked by the word *Atenoux*, which probably means "renewing," which would suggest that the month would begin at the new moon and atenoux would indicate the renewal or the full moon.

From the information in Caesar and on the Calendar it can be deduced that the basic unit of the Celtic calendar was the fortnight or half-month, a fact given some support by elements in Celtic folklore. The following table, from *The Celtic Tradition* by Caitlin Matthews (Element Books, 1994*),* sets out the Celtic year with the author's interpretation of the names of the months and their modern meaning:

Month	Period	Meaning
Samonios	Oct/Nov	Seed-fall
Dumannios	Nov/Dec	The Darkest Depths
Riuros	Dec/Jan	Cold-time
Anagantios	Jan/Feb	Stay-home-time
Ogronios	Feb/Mar	Time of Ice
Cutios	Mar/Apr	Time of Winds
Giamonios	Apr/May	Shoots-show
Simivisionios	May/Jun	Time of Brightness
Equos	Jun/Jul	Horse-time
Elembiuos	Jul/Aug	Claim-time
Edrinios	Aug/Sep	Arbitration-time
Cantios	Sep/Oct	Song-time

Some researchers have claimed that Beltane, a Gaelic festival that takes place on the first day of May (*Giammonios* full moon on the Calendar), and Lughnasadh (*Elembivios* full moon), a Gaelic festival that traditionally occurs on the first of August, are marked on the Coligny Calendar by small sigils, though this opinion has not found widespread acceptance among scholars.

There has been much debate about the date of the Coligny Calendar. Although the initial date estimated for the object was around the first century BC, more recent estimates, based on the style of lettering used and the type of artifacts that were discovered along with the Calendar, put it somewhere between the late second century and early third century AD. This date is long after the Roman general Julius Caesar had conquered Gaul in 55 BC, though it does not mean that the calendrical system the object uses was not in use for decades or even centuries before.

The fragmentary nature of the Calendar when it was discovered has persuaded some researchers that the Romans smashed it to pieces during their suppression of druidic practices. French archaeologist J. Monard, who studied the Coligny inscriptions for many years, believed the Calendar was made by Gallic druids in an attempt to preserve the ancient Celtic system of timekeeping, and was probably destroyed by the Roman authorities wishing to enforce the Julian calendar throughout the entire Roman Empire. However, this would necessarily place the creation of the Calendar around the turn of the first century AD, at least two centuries before the accepted date. It is perhaps more likely that, during the third century AD, Roman Christians attempting to wipe out all traces of paganism in Gaul destroyed the Tablet and the statue of Mars discovered along with it. The fragmentary remains of the calendar and statue seem to have been hidden in the field at Coligny by someone (the druids, in the opinion of some researchers) for safekeeping, but where were these objects originally? The most likely explanation is that both the calendar and the bronze statue were originally located at a religious site of some kind, possibly the temple at the nearby Gallo-Roman site of Villards d'Heria.

If the calendrical system used on the Coligny Tablet had already been in use for some time before it was inscribed on the Calendar, the question remains: how far back into prehistory can it be traced?

According to Martin Brennan, author of *The Stones of Time: Calendars, Sundials, and Stone Chambers of Ancient Ireland* (Inner Traditions, 1994), the origin of the Coligny Calendar could date back to around 3200 BC. Brennan believes that one of the engraved megaliths (kerbstone 15) at the passage tomb of Knowth in County Meath, north of Dublin, Ireland, represents a lunar calendar using the same general principles as the Coligny Calendar. The decorated stone, with its seemingly random collection of engraved spirals, wheels, zigzags, and wavy lines, apparently shows all 29 phases of the moon, and, in Brennan's opinion, represents sophisticated lunar timekeeping as far back as the Neolithic period. In fact, Brennan goes even further than this, stating that the Neolithic passage graves and standing stones of Ireland were constructed as sophisticated calendrical devices, though the question remains why these people would have gone to such extraordinary lengths to keep time. Perhaps Brennan's theory is a case of projecting the modern obsession with timekeeping and technology back onto cultures that had motives and beliefs we could never even begin to comprehend.

About 60 linguistic forms are shown on the Coligny Calendar, although many of the words are abbreviated, with the result that they have been extremely difficult to interpret. Nevertheless, the Calendar has been a vital source for words in the Gaulish language—not only the names for months, but also, for example, their words for "lucky," "unlucky," and "sense, understanding." The latter word is written "CIALLOS" on the Coligny Calendar, and is the name of the additional month inserted to calibrate the moon and sun cycles, indicating the "sense" of adding the extra month.

Gaulish is the Continental branch of Celtic ("Insular Celtic"— refers to British Celtic), in many respects a similar language to Latin. The Calendar remains today the longest text in the extinct Gaulish language, though a number of inscriptions in Gaulish have been found throughout the area of Roman Gaul, a territory that stretched beyond the borders of modern France into parts of modern Belgium, Germany, Switzerland, and northern Italy. Recent research by Dr. Peter Forster, a geneticist from the University of Cambridge in England, and Dr. Alfred Toth, of the University of Zurich, using the Coligny Calendar along with other Celtic inscriptions, have attempted to reconstruct the history of the Celtic language as part of their work on the development of the Indo-European language tree. Perhaps the two researchers' most controversial conclusion is that the traditional date of 600 BC for the arrival of speakers of the Celtic language, based on archaeological evidence, is far too late. Basing their conclusions on DNA sequencing and phylogenetic (relating to or based on evolutionary development or history) network methods the researchers' suggested new date is 3200 BC, during the Middle Neolithic period. This is the date at which Forster and Toth calculate that the continental and British versions of Celtic (of which Gaulish is an example) diverged. If this theory were proved correct it would have a profound effect, not just on the study of Celtic languages, but on our interpretation of the prehistory of the whole of Europe. It must be added, however, that the proposed new date of 3200 BC does have a rather large error margin of plus or minus 1,500 years. Nevertheless, the fact that such groundbreaking research is possible, based in part on the Coligny Calendar, shows the importance and relevance of such artifacts in the understanding of our prehistoric past. The Coligny Calendar is now on display at the *Musee de la Civilisation Gallo-Romaine* (Museum of Gallo-Roman Civilization), Lyon, France.

Chapter 19

The Mystery of the Glozel Stones (France)

Glozel Tablet showing mysterious characters.

A chance discovery on an isolated hillside near Vichy, central France, in 1924 has become one of the most controversial archaeological mysteries of the last hundred years. The Glozel Stones, as they are collectively known, are a strange group of more than 3,000 objects: ceramic tablets, sculptures, decorated vases, bone objects, and engraved pebbles. The controversy stems partly from the fact that the objects have been dated to a wide variety of different periods, including the Upper Palaeolithic (c. 40,000–c. 10,000 years ago), Neolithic (up to c. 6,500 years ago), Iron Age (beginning c. 2,700 years ago), and Medieval. There have also been accusations that the entire group of artifacts, or at least some of them, are 20th-century fakes. The undeciphered script found on the ceramic tablets and some vases from Glozel has been variously identified as a previously unknown Neolithic language, ancient Iberian, Phoenician, and Iron Age Celtic. With all this apparently conflicting data, have modern scientific techniques brought us any nearer to solving the Glozel mystery, or is it one great hoax after all?

L'Affaire Glozel, as it is often known, began on March 1, 1924, when 17-year-old Émile Fradin, a farmer's son from the village of Glozel, was using a cow-drawn plow in one of the family's fields. One of the cows put her foot into a cavity in the ground and while Émile, aided by other members of his family, was attempting to free the animal he discovered a chamber with heavily vitrified brick walls. The family began digging and became so engrossed in their discovery that they continued for another week. What they found was a roughly oval feature containing a number of mysterious artifacts, including carved bones and pebbles, ceramic vases, inscribed clay tablets, and pieces of human bone, including a skull.

A local teacher named Adrienne Picandet visited the Fradin's farm toward the end of March and afterward notified the Minister of Education about the strange discoveries. The result was that on July 9th another local teacher, Clément Benoit, visited the Fradins on behalf of the Societé d'Emulation du Bourbonnais (Competitive Society of Bourbonnais). Clement returned on July 28th, accompanied by a man named Viple, and they began using pickaxes to break down the remaining walls of the pit, which they took with them when they left. Two weeks later the family received a letter from Viple identifying the strange pit as Gallo-Roman (the culture of what is now France and Belgium under Roman rule), like many ancient sites in the area. Viple also gave a suggested date of between c AD 100 and 400 for the finds.

The January 1925 issue of the *Bulletin de la Societé d'Emulation du Bourbonnais* carried a brief description of the unusual discoveries at the Glozel farm. This came to the attention of Antonin Morlet, a physician and amateur archaeologist living in Vichy. Intrigued by what he read, Morlet visited the farm on April 25th. After examining the finds Morlet was so impressed that he offered the family 200 francs to be allowed to complete the excavations of the pit. Over the next few weeks an agreement was reached: Dr. Morlet had the right to excavate the site and to publish his work there for a fee of 200 francs a year; the Fradin family would retain possession of the artifacts. A month later Morlet began his excavations at Glozel and before long had discovered clay tablets, idols, engraved stones, bone and flint tools, and a small amount of human bone. Morlet believed that the artifacts were Neolithic and quickly published a series of small booklets on the site, the first of which came out in September 1925 and was entitled "Nouvelle Station Néolithique" ("A New Neolithic Site").

The doctor's publications brought the Glozel site to the attention of the French academic community, who were incensed at Morlet's claims about the dating of the finds, and with the fact that an amateur archaeologist and a peasant farmer had published a book about the site. French archaeologists objected that the crudely made finds from Glozel bore no resemblance to known Neolithic objects from France and suggested that they were modern forgeries, probably crafted by Émile Fradin. Despite these objections, hoards of visitors continued to visit the site and, in June 1927, two oval-shaped tombs were discovered, each containing similar artifacts to those found in the original pit in what was by now christened le Champ des Morts ("The Field of the Dead").

The Fradins opened a small museum in a specially constructed room next to the farmhouse kitchen to display the more than 2,000 objects recovered from the site, charging four francs admission. In early November 1927, the International Commission arrived at Glozel and undertook a three-day excavation at the Fradin's site, uncovering two bone awls, a pebble engraved with a reindeer head and six "Glozelian" letters, a bisexual idol, two bone pendants, a schist ring, a tablet, and a clasp made of antler. All seemed well but, when the report of the International Commission was published in late December 1927, it stated that, although a few objects from Glozel such as the flint axes and some pieces of stoneware were genuine, everything else was a forgery. The "tombs" were recent and there was no trace of ancient fauna in the excavated soil.

However, a further group called the Committee of Studies was set up by archaeologists who believed in the authenticity of the Glozel site. The Committee of Studies excavated at Glozel between April 12 and April 14, 1928, during which time they discovered three engraved pebbles, one of which depicted a reindeer and three Glozelian signs, a fossilized bone pendant with Glozelian characters engraved on one side, a large piece of an inscribed tablet, a bone engraved with a goat and Glozelian signs, and a small clay lamp. After they had completed their work, the Committee of Studies declared that the finds were genuine and that they belonged to the Neolithic period.

The controversy was not so easily resolved. In February 1928, Felix Regnault, the president of the French Prehistoric Society, had paid a brief visit to the Fradins' museum. After he left he made a formal complaint that the whole site was a fraud, which led, on February 25th, to the police visiting the museum and confiscating three cases of artifacts. Gaston-Edmond Bayle, chief of the Criminal Records Office in Paris, analysed the tablets from the Fradins' museum. In May 1929, a 500-page report was published detailing the results. The report stated that the tablets had been manufactured in the last five years, and that Bayle had even discovered a fresh apple stem in one of them. As a result, on June 4, 1929, Émile was formally indicted for fraud and underwent regular interrogation while the case was being investigated. However, no direct evidence was ever produced against him, and two years later, in April 1931, the public prosecutor in the nearby town of Cusset, Mr. Antonin Besson, dismissed the case.

Seemingly undaunted by all the controversy, Dr. Morlet continued his excavations at Glozel, but, in September 1941, a new French law was passed, stating that no archaeological excavations could take place without government authorization, thus outlawing private excavation. With the work at Glozel finished, and Émile Fradin married and working his land, the controversy seemed to be over. In the 1950s Dr. Morlet attempted to get some of the bone from Glozel dated using carbon-14 dating, but he was unsuccessful and died in 1965 with his theories regarding the site not authenticated.

However, in 1974 extensive tests were carried out on ceramics from Glozel by Van Mejdahl, Hugh McKerrell, Henri François, and Guy Portal, using the newly developed Thermoluminescence (TL) dating.

The results appeared in the British journal *Antiquity* in 1974 (McKerrell et al). By 1979, 27 artifacts from Glozel had been dated using TL with the dates falling into three groups: an early period from between c. 300 BC to AD 300 (Late Iron Age or "Celtic" and Roman Gaul), c. 13th century AD (medieval), and a recent period. The dates renewed the controversy and woke the sleeping giant of l'Affaire Glozel once more. In 1983 the French Ministry of Culture decided to investigate Glozel and other sites in the area, and spent a week at Glozel digging five test holes in the Field of the Dead. Although the Ministry never published a full report of their work at Glozel, a 13-page résumé appeared in 1995, suggesting that the site was medieval, possibly containing a few Iron Age objects, but was probably supplemented by forgeries. The absence of "Glozelian" objects from the nearby sites of Chez Guerrier, Puy Ravel, and Le Cluzel, which were also examined by the Ministry in 1983, led them to believe that the "Neolithic" finds from the Field of the Dead were modern and had been planted at the site.

This was still not the end of the Glozel Affair. Further tests on objects from Glozel in 1984 at Oxford, in the UK, using carbon-14 analyses dated a piece of charcoal from the site to between the 11th and 13th centuries AD, and a fragment of an ivory ring to the 15th century. In 1995 Alice and Sam Gerard, together with Robert Liris, tested bone tubes from Glozel at the University of Arizona using carbon-14 and produced dates in the 13th century. These dates would suggest that Glozel was medieval, but what about the most widely discussed artifacts from the site—the mysterious inscribed ceramic tablets and stones?

Tests on the engraved stones, which contain Upper Palaeolithic type illustrations of reindeer, have shown that the engravings were made with steel tools, which indicates a modern date (hence a forgery). The ceramic tablets from Glozel, of which there are about 100, bear inscriptions of on average six or seven lines. The symbols on the tablets have not been deciphered, though the wildest of these claims—that they are represent a previously undiscovered Neolithic alphabet—can be dismissed, as the writing has been identified as contemporary with the development of the Latin alphabet. There have been suggestions that some of the inscriptions resemble Phoenician writing, which is true, but some of the tablets containing Phoenician-like characters are also inscribed with modern Latin characters, putting the genuine antiquity of the objects into serious question. At least 133 "Glozelian" symbols have so far been identified, too many for Phoenician or any authentic alphabetic writing system, though that does not mean that the language is a modern invention. Swiss researcher Hans-Rudolph Hitz has suggested that Glozel was a kind of sacred writing school, visited by speakers of a "Celtic" language. He thus identifies the inscriptions on the tablets as written in a local Gaulish language or dialect, dating them to the Iron Age, between the third century BC and the first century AD. One theory to explain the inscribed bones, which bear similar characters to the tablets but date from a later period (probably medieval), is that they contain copies of the writing used in the Iron Age. As the combination of characters on these later bone examples is meaningless, though, it could suggest that the medieval authors had no understanding of the language they were using.

What does all this massive confusion of dates and artifacts from Glozel mean? What kind of site was it? About the only thing most researchers can agree on, taking into consideration the nature of the finds and high proportion of medieval dates recovered from Glozel, is that the oval feature initially discovered by the Fradin family is a 12th- or 13th-century glass kiln that was later re-used for human burial. Beyond this all is conjecture.

For some, the entire Glozel affair is a hoax. The engravings on bone and stone are amateurish and clumsy attempts to reproduce Upper Paleolithic artwork, and the inscriptions on the tablets are no more than random symbols taken from examples of Greek, Phoenician, and Latin scripts and artlessly jumbled together. Furthermore, the Glozel artifacts as a whole are without convincing parallel elsewhere, and no certain Iron Age or Gallo-Roman artifacts (pottery, coins, jewelry) have ever been recovered from the site. Nevertheless, despite these serious objections, the TL and C14 dates from the site still remain an enigma. In her book, *Glozel: Bones of Contention* (2005), Alice Gerard has suggested that some of the Glozel finds could represent hastily constructed ritual objects for use in a mysterious local cult, with the medieval artifacts signifying its continued existence or perhaps a revival of it.

Émile Fradin protested his innocence throughout his entire life, and insisted that the finds from Field of the Dead represented a genuine Neolithic settlement. In the 1990s, Professor René Germain, of the University of Saint-Etienne, France, established an international group of scholars called CIER, with the intention of providing proof for the authenticity of Glozel. This research group has organized a series of yearly conferences, each focusing on a different aspect of the Glozel site. Unfortunately, commendable as the intentions of CIER may be, it is clear that, without further excavation in the Field of the Dead, the puzzle of Glozel will never be solved.

🕰

Chapter 20

The Puzzle of the Golden Hats (Central Europe)

Berlin Golden Hat.

A group of ancient conical gold foil vessels from sites in Switzerland, Germany, and France are among the most baffling archaeological finds anywhere in the world. There are four known examples of these enigmatic objects: the Golden Hat of Schifferstadt, near Speyer, southwest Germany; the Avanton Gold Cone, from near Poitiers, western France; the Golden Cone of Ezelsdorf-Buch, near Nuremberg; and the Berlin Gold Hat. Many theories have attempted to explain these beautiful "Golden Hats." Were they parts of Bronze Age suits of armor, wizard's hats, ceremonial vases, or perhaps even ritual calendars? Recent research by historians at Berlin's Museum of Pre- and Early History has cast some fascinating new light on the possible function of these objects.

The so-called Golden Hat of Schifferstadt was the first of these objects to be discovered, during agricultural work in a field 0.62 miles north of Schifferstadt on April 29, 1835. This well-preserved, cone-shaped "hat" is 11.6 inches in height, with a diameter of 18 centimeters at its widest part and a weight of about 0.77 pounds. The object is hammered from a single sheet of thin gold, the composition of which is 86.37 percent gold, 13 percent silver, 0.56 percent copper, and 0.07 percent tin. The surface is subdivided into horizontal ornamental bands, applied using the repoussé technique (hammering and pressing designs in relief). These decorated zones bear systematically stamped disk and circle motifs surrounded by concentric circles.

When the Golden Hat of Schifferstadt was discovered it was standing upright in a rectangular pit about 2 feet below ground with three bronze axes leaning against it. These associated axes date the Golden Hat somewhere between the 15th and the 13th centuries BC (the Middle to Late Bronze Age), and the assemblage has the appearance of a ritual deposit. Throughout the years, Bronze Age pottery fragments and animal bone have been picked up in the surrounding fields, which suggests the presence of a settlement, on the edge of which the Golden Hat and its associated metal work were placed. The Golden Hat of Schifferstadt is now on display in the Historisches Museum der Pfalz in Speyer.

The Avanton Gold Cone was discovered in 1844, in a field near the village of Avanton, about 7 1/2 miles north of the city of Poitiers. The object seems to have been damaged, as it has no flanged "brim" like the other Golden Hats. The Avanton Cone is 1.8 feet in height and weighs 0.63 pounds. Like the other "hats," its ornamentation is divided up into horizontal bands, in this case decorated with concentric circles of varying diameters. It has been dated to c. 1000–900 BC (the Late Bronze Age), and is now exhibited in the Musée d'Archéologie Nationale at Saint-Germain-en-Laye, near Paris.

The Golden Hat of Ezelsdorf-Buch was found in 1953 while clearing tree stumps between the villages of Ezelsdorf (Franconia) and Buch (Bavaria) in Southern Germany. The "hat" was apparently discovered just more than 3 inches below the surface but unfortunately was not immediately recognized for what it was. Consequently, the object was hacked into several pieces by the workmen's tools and disregarded before a shower of rain revealed that the metal pieces were in fact gold. George Raschke of the German National Museum in Nuremberg, who was able to reconstruct the object, rescued the pieces afterward, though it was not until the 1990s that the gold pieces were recognized as one of the "Golden Hats."

The reconstructed Hat from Ezelsdorf-Buch is the tallest of all the Golden Hats at around 2.9 feet high, and weighs about 0.73 pounds. Toward its bottom the object, bronze rings, two of which were recovered by George Raschke after the object had been damaged, reinforced the object. Like the other Golden Hats, the Ezelsdorf-Buch example is hammered from a single piece of gold alloy, composed of gold (88.3 percent), silver (11 percent), copper (0.59 percent), and tin (0.086 percent). Its average thickness is a mere 0.03 of an inch, and it has been calculated that the quantity of gold used in its manufacture is about equal to the size of a matchbox.

The surface of the whole length of the Golden Hat of Ezelsdorf-Buch is divided into horizontal bands and rows of symbols (a total of 154 rows in all) created using the repoussé technique. As with the other Golden Hats, the majority of these symbols are concentric circles, though there are three unusual motifs present: small horizontal ovals that resemble eyes (also present in the Schifferstadt and Berlin Hats), miniature eight-spoked wheels, and small cones. The tip of the Ezelsdorf-Buch Cone is decorated with a 10-point star. Researchers have deduced that such complex decoration would have required 20 different decorative punches, a comb, and cylindrical stamps (or decorated wheels). The Golden Cone of Ezelsdorf-Buch, which has been dated to c. 1000–900 BC, is currently on display at the German National Museum in Nuremberg.

The final example, which has become known as the Berlin Gold Hat, is the best preserved of all the four Gold Hats. The Berlin Hat was purchased in 1996 by the Berlin Museum für Vor- und Frühgeschichte (Museum of Prehistory and Early History). Its provenance is uncertain, though it may have come from a 1950s/1960s Swiss private collection, and was probably originally found in either Swabia (part of southwest Germany) or Switzerland.

The Gold Hat is 2.4 feet in height and weighs 1.08 pounds, with an average thickness of only 0.02 inches. The long slender cone was hammered from a single piece of gold alloy that consists of 87.7 percent gold, 9.8 percent silver, 0.4 percent copper, and 0.1 percent tin. As with the Golden Hat of Ezelsdorf-Buch the Berlin Gold Hat is reinforced at its bottom by a ring of sheet bronze.

The Berlin Hat is decorated with 21 horizontal ornamental bands and rows of symbols along its entire length. The symbols consist of predominantly buckle and circle motifs surrounded by concentric circles, though one distinct band consists of recumbent crescents on top of an eye-shaped symbol. As with the Ezelsdorf-Buch example, the point of the cone is decorated with a star, in this case eight-pointed. A minimum of 17 separate tools were used to achieve the complex design system on the Berlin Gold Hat, probably fourteen separate stamps and three cylindrical-stamps. The Berlin Gold Hat has been dated stylistically to c. 1000–800 BC and is now one of the star attractions in the Bronze Age collection of the Museum für Vor- und Frühgeschichte, Berlin.

These four enigmatic Golden Hats should not be viewed in isolation but against the cultural background of the end of the Middle Bronze Age and Late Bronze Age in Central Europe. An archaeological term called the *Urnfield culture* has been used to describe this period, roughly from 1300 to 750 BC, in this area of Europe, though the culture gradually spread through Italy, France, Spain, and Scandinavia. The name "Urnfield culture" derives from the custom of placing the cremated bones of the dead in urns, which were then buried in pits in fields. These burials ranged from the simple to the elaborate, emphasizing the social stratification of the culture. The more extravagant burials were usually accompanied by weapons and jewelry, often deliberately bent or broken before deposition. The most interesting of these burials are the dozen or so wagon-burials of four-wheeled wagons with bronze fittings known mainly from Germany and Switzerland.

There are, however, few real parallels for the Golden Hats. Perhaps the closest are the Late Bronze Age gold leaf crowns or hats from Leiro beach (Rianxo, A Coruña) on the Atlantic coast of Galicia, Spain, and the golden bowls from Axtroki (Guipúzcoa) in northern Spain. The latter are now on display in the National Archaeological Museum in Madrid. There are also certain parallels between the Golden Hats and depictions of hats or crowns on stone slabs in the King's Grave (*Kungagraven, Kiviksgrave*) near Kivik in the southeastern part of the Swedish province of Skåne. The King's Grave is the remains of a rather grand Nordic Bronze Age double burial dating to around 1000 BC, similar in date to the German Golden Hats. The Mold Gold Cape, a sheet-gold object from Flintshire in North Wales has similar decoration to the Golden Hats, though it is considerably older, dating to between 1900 BC and 1600 BC.

The possible functions of the mysterious Golden Hats have been debated for decades. Questions of why they were constructed and who used them are made all the more difficult to answer by the fact that we only have four known examples, although it is entirely possible that others exist in private collections. Due to the amount of time and effort that went into the manufacture of the Golden Hats, as well as the value of the raw material, it is reasonable to suppose that the objects were used by an elite group from the society that made them. One theory is that the Golden Hats were not worn as hats at all but were used as ceremonial libation vessels. A more-popular hypothesis is that priests wore the Golden Hats at religious ceremonies—almost literally "wizards' hats." The diameters and shapes of the objects, roughly equivalent to those of a human skull, would support such a function. The gold foil hats would have been too fragile to be worn in the form they were discovered, so presumably they functioned as the external covering of a head-dress composed of organic material. An alternative to this theory is that the Hats were placed on top of tall wooden posts that are a prominent feature of many Bronze Age ritual sites in Central and Northern Europe.

A recent hypothesis to explain the Golden Hats is that they served astronomical/calendrical functions. In 2002, historians at the Berlin

Museum of Prehistory and Early History carried out detailed research into the Berlin Gold Hat. The director of the Museum, Wilfried Menghin, and his research team believe that the 1,739 sun and half-moon symbols decorating surface of the object represent a system corresponding to the "Metonic cycle" discovered by Greek astronomer Meton of Athens in 432 BC. In effect, this would make the Berlin Gold Hat a lunisolar calendar. In the opinion of Menghin, the symbols on the Hat illustrate that the astronomer-priests of Late Bronze Age societies were able to calculate the movements of the sun and the moon in advance, thus giving them the ability to accurately predict the correct time for sowing, planting, and harvesting crops, and also for religious festivals. The possession of this mysterious astronomical knowledge would give the priests who used, and perhaps also wore, these Hats, a considerable mystique and influence over the rest of their society.

Comparisons have been made between the Berlin Gold Hat and the Nebra Sky Disk, a bronze disk of around 30 centimeters diameter, inlaid with gold symbols representing the moon, stars, and perhaps the sun. The Nebra Sky Disk certainly seems to be an ancient astronomical device of some kind, and also originates in Germany (the state of Saxony-Anhalt). Like the Mold Cape, it is considerably older than the Golden Hats, dating to around 1600 BC. Of course the Golden Hats may have performed dual functions: as a religious emblem of the priest's rank or position in society, and as practical lunisolar calendars. On the other hand, perhaps the Hats served more as an illustration of the astronomical knowledge possessed by the priests rather than as usable calendrical devices.

One problem with assigning an astronomical or any other definite function to the Golden Hats is that they are practically unique; there are so few of them that there is just not enough material to work with. Furthermore, none of the objects were discovered in modern archaeological excavations; thus, apart from the Golden Hat of Schifferstadt, the Hats lack a meaningful archaeological context. The only way to get to the bottom of the mystery of the Golden Hats would be through the discovery of further examples in datable contexts from archaeological excavations. Until then the Golden Hats, though they represent an immense technical achievement on the part of the Late Bronze Age cultures of Central Europe, must remain a tantalizing enigma.

⊠

Chapter 21

Paleolithic Venus Figurines (Europe/Western Asia)

The Venus of Brassempouy.

Venus Figurines are a class of distinctive portable artifacts dating back to the Upper Paleolithic Period (roughly between 40,000 and 10,000 years ago). Early-20th-century prehistorians, believing that the figurines depicted an ancient model of beauty, named the objects

Venus Figurines in reference to the Roman goddess of beauty. The figurines were fashioned mainly in the form of stylized representations of females with large breasts and buttocks, and are found over a vast area of Europe and parts of western Asia. The most famous Venus Figurine, and the best-known early image of a human, is the "Venus of Willendorf" found near the town of Willendorf, Austria. Recently, however, a remarkable carved ivory Venus Figurine was discovered in Hohle Fels Cave in Germany, which is thought to be the oldest sculpture of a human figure ever found. What was the function of these unique artifacts, and why do they show such a marked degree of similarity over such a wide geographical area and time period?

The most notable and common type of Venus Figurines are small three-dimensional sculptures of voluptuous women, ranging in height from 1.2 inches to more than 15 inches, and carved from a wide range of materials including serpentine, schist, limestone, hematite, lignite, calcite, steatite, fired clay, ivory, bone, and antler. There are also carved plaques showing similar representations, and figurines that show apparently pre-pubescent females. Furthermore, although females are the most commonly depicted, there are also representations of men, children, and animals.

The sizes and proportions of the Venus Figurines vary, though the majority follow certain artistic conventions: large breasts and stomach, wide hips and swollen thighs—all probably intended to depict pregnancy. Facial features are usually absent, as are arms, hands, and feet, and the heads are relatively small. A few examples have what appears to be braided hair (such as the Venus of Brassempouy and the Venus of Willendorf), and others have been discovered with traces of red ochre on them. Venus Figurines were manufactured over a vast period of time, from around 33,000 BC up until around 11,000 BC. The figurines have been discovered from the French Pyrenees to the Siberian plains, mostly from cave and rock shelter sites.

Perhaps the most recognizable of all Venus Figurines was discovered in 1908 by archaeologist Josef Szombathy in a Palaeolithic site about 100 feet above the Danube River, near the town of Willendorf in Lower Austria. The Venus of Willendorf (also known as "The Woman of Willendorf") is 4.4 inches in height and was carved from a fine porous oolitic limestone not local to the region, indicating that either the stone or the finished object originated elsewhere. When the figurine was found it was covered with a thick layer of red ochre. A study of the stratigraphic sequence of the archaeological layers at the site where it was found indicates a date for the Venus of Willendorf of around 24,000–22,000 BC. The figure is of a woman with a large stomach, large breasts and thighs, and an emphasized vulva. She has no facial features and has what appears to be either braided or plaited hair, although this has also been interpreted as a woven hat or cap. Either way, it was done deliberately to hide the face. The statue also has no feet and appears to have been designed not to stand on its own. The enigmatic Venus of Willendorf is now part of the collection of the Naturhistorisches Museum in Vienna.

A rather different example of a Venus Figurine was one of a number discovered at the Grotte du Pape ("The Pope's Cave"), a cave or rock shelter near the village of Brassempouy, Aquitaine, southwestern France, in 1892. The Venus of Brassempouy, or La Dame à la capuche ("The Lady in the Hood") as she is also known, is the name given to the surviving head and neck of a mammoth ivory carving about 1.4 inches high, 0.9 inches deep, and 0.7 inches wide. The sculpture, which is about 25,000 years old, is presumed to be that of a woman and represents one of the earliest-known realistic representations of a human face. The Venus is elegantly carved with a triangular face, forehead, nose, and brows carved in relief, but without a mouth. Her expression seems calm, almost serene. Like the Venus of Willendorf, La Dame à la capuche is depicted with what is either braided hair or wearing a wig or a hood.

Another example, the Venus of Dolní Věstonice, was discovered in 1922 at Dolni Vestonice, a complex of Upper Paleolithic habitation sites on the slopes of the Pavlov Hills, near the town of Brno, Moravia, Czech Republic. This fired clay figurine, fashioned around 27,000 years ago, is the oldest-known baked clay figurine in the world. It measures 4.5 inches tall and 1.7 inches at its widest point, and exhibits the usual exaggerated hips and breasts. Dolni Vestonice is also the site of the earliest-known potter's kiln, and a fascinating triple burial discovered in 1986, from around the same date as the figurine. The burial consisted of a shallow grave containing the bodies of three teenagers—two males and a female. The males had been healthy and had died in the prime of life, but examination of the female skeleton discovered that she had suffered from spinal scoliosis, had an asymmetrical skull, and an underdeveloped right leg, all suggesting she had been seriously crippled in life. She had died aged between 17 and 20. The male skulls were adorned with necklaces of arctic fox teeth, wolf teeth, and ivory beads, and red ocher powder had been sprinkled around each skull and between the legs of the female.

The bodies themselves were arranged in very unusual positions, with the female placed in the grave first, lying on her back. One of the males was interred to the left, with his head facing toward the girl and his arms reaching toward some red ochre located between her legs. The third body had been interred to the right of the girl, face down on his belly, but with his left arm linked with hers. What the explanation could be for this enigmatic burial is difficult to fathom, but as the odds of three young people dying at the same time at Dolni Vestonice must be fairly remote, murder or even ritual sacrifice have been suggested.

The oldest Venus Figurine known to exist was discovered during excavations in 2008 at the Upper Paleolithic cave site of Hohle Fels, in the Swabian Jura of southwestern Germany. The 2.4-inch-tall figurine was produced at least 35,000 years ago, making it the oldest-known example of figurative art from anywhere in the world. The artifact was found in six fragments in an area strewn with flint knapping debris, worked bone and ivory, bones of horse, reindeer, cave bear, mammoth, and ibex, as well as burnt bone. Excavations at the site by Professor Nicholas J. Conard, of the University of Tubingen, Baden-Württemberg, Germany, also discovered other figurines, including a horse's head, a water bird, and a half-human/half-lion figurine, all dated to about 30,000–33,000 years ago. A bird-bone flute unearthed in this incredible cave was carved around 35,000 years ago, making it the oldest handcrafted musical instrument yet discovered.

The Hohle Fels Venus shares many of the "classic" features of many of the later Venus Figurines: a short and squat form with broad shoulders and wide hips, large breasts, and exaggerated buttocks and genitalia. The sculpture was fashioned without a head, like some other examples of Venus figurines, but it does have a carved ring where the head should be, suggesting that it was worn as a pendant. In the opinion of Professor Conard, the various incised lines and markings that cover much of the surface of the figure may represent clothing. One intriguing possibility that has been suggested is that Neanderthals, rather than anatomically modern humans (*Homo sapiens*), crafted the artifacts at the Hohle Fels site. However, although Neanderthals were still living in Europe around 30,000–35,000 years ago, and frequented the Hohle Fels cave, the archaeological layers in which the Venus Figurine and other carvings were found is characteristic of modern humans rather than Neanderthals.

A wide variety of interpretations regarding what Venus Figurines were meant to represent exist. These explanations range from children's educational material to fertility goddesses, self-portraits of women, or even men's sex toys. The steatopygia (extreme accumulation of fat in and around the buttocks) exhibited by many of the figurines has led some researchers, such as French archaeologist Edouard Piette (1827–1906), to suggest that the figurines are actual physical representations of members of the Palaeolithic hunting tribes who made them. In the modern world steatopygia is common only among the females of certain African tribes, notably the Khoikhoi ("Hottentots"), San (Bushwomen), and Pygmies. Steatopygia is also a genetic characteristic of the Khoisan peoples of Southern Africa. Venus Figurines are even sometimes referred to as "steatopygian Venus" Figures. However, these figurines do not in fact strictly qualify as steatopygian, as they exhibit an angle of approximately 120 degrees between back and buttocks, while steatopygia is diagnosed at an angle of about 90 degrees. Furthermore, the fact that many of Venus Figurines do not have features that could in any way be interpreted as steatopygian would suggest that the theory is at best unproven.

A few decades ago the most popular theory to explain Venus Figurines was that they were representations of a worldwide mother-goddess cult. The belief, put forward by Lithuanian-American archaeologist Marija Gimbutas, among others, that Stone Age peoples worshipped the Earth mother as a universal deity has been largely discredited now; it is entirely speculative and cannot be scientifically evaluated. The clearly emphasized sexual attributes of the Palaeolithic Venuses would suggest that they may be amulets connected with fertility magic. A related theory is that the figurines were intended to depict pregnancy or childbirth, or even represent the entire female life cycle.

In Palaeolithic, pre-agricultural, hunter-gatherer societies, who lived in a harsh ice-age environment where the population did not have easy or quick access to a food supply, the Venus Figurines may have suggested a desire for abundancy and security, though as noted, not all examples were rotund or had exaggerated feminine feature. The fact that Venus Figurines are found over such a wide geographical area indicates that there was a shared understanding among the Palaeolithic hunter-gatherer tribes of Europe and western Asia of a particular aspect of womanhood or a certain type of woman. However, like the vast majority of examples of prehistoric art, we can only guess at the cultural meaning and significance of the Venus Figurines to our remote Ice Age ancestors.

⧖

Chapter 22

The Uluburun Shipwreck
(Turkey)

Life-size replica of the Lulburun ship, Bodrum Museum of Underwater Archaeology (Bodrum, Turkey).

Discovered off the southern coast of Turkey in the 1980s, the Uluburun Wreck is the oldest-known shipwreck in the world. Dating back around 3,300 years, the ship carried a cargo of incredible richness and diversity that included Egyptian scarabs, copper ingots from Cyprus, Mycenaean pottery from Greece, Canaanite jars, lamps, and bowls, ebony logs from Egypt, an Italian sword, elephant tusks, gold, silver, faience, and amber from Northern Europe. There have been suggestions that this wealthy cargo was a gift or offering from Egypt's Queen Nefertiti, wife of the Egyptian Pharaoh Akhenaten, or that it was a Phoenician trading ship or, because of the amount of raw material found aboard, some kind of itinerant smithy or tinker. Where was the ship going when it sank? And what can the more-than-15,000 artifacts found aboard tell us about trade in the ancient world?

The Uluburun Wreck was discovered by accident in 1982 by Mehmet Çakir, a Turkish sponge diver. The wreck was located about 164 feet down, 6 miles off the southern coast of Turkey, near Kas. Because of the great depth of water, investigation of the wreck proved difficult, and excavation time for each diver had to be limited to 15 to 20 minutes per dive, twice per day. The excavation of the Uluburun Wreck, which took place between 1984 and 1994, was directed by George Bass and Cemal Pulak of the Institute of Nautical Archaeology, and recorded 11,000 hours of diving and careful recovery of often extremely delicate artifacts. Unfortunately, very little of the ship itself remained due to the area's strong currents, which prevented the wood from being immersed in the marine silts essential for the preservation of ship timbers in submarine environments. Nevertheless, the archaeologists did find fragments of oars, as well as hull planks preserved under a large stone anchor, and other timbers underneath rows of copper ingots. These timbers indicated that the ship was about 50 feet in length and 16 feet wide. The hull of the vessel was made of cedar wood of edge-joined planks, a construction technique also known from later Phoenician, Greek, and Roman ships. When it sank, the ship was carrying about 20 tons of cargo.

The huge cargo of the ship included both raw materials and finished goods, which has been attributed to 12 different Bronze Age cultures. The archaeologists were able to map the distribution of the objects on the sea bed and reconstruct the wreck, allowing them to differentiate between the ship's cargo and the crew's personal effects. A concentration of artifacts in the stern of the vessel, which the excavators believe were the personal possessions of the crew (including a ship's lamp, weights, a cylinder seal, scarabs, and a macehead), indicated that some type of cabin was located in that part of the ship.

The majority of the ship's cargo was a diverse and rich collection of raw materials, the most impressive of which were 10 tons of Cypriot copper in the form of 500 individual ingots. The majority of these ingots were flat and rectangular, with four handles, and are known as "oxhide" ingots due to their shape, which allowed them to be easily transported on the backs of horses or mules. Each of these ingots weighed from 55 to 60 pounds and represents a common form of transporting copper in the ancient world. Chemical analysis of the copper (using lead-Isotope tests) determined that it originated from Cyprus, which was the main supplier of copper to the ancient Syrian port city of Ugarit, a hugely important Mediterranean trading center during the Late Bronze Age (16th–13th centuries BC). The ship was also carrying 40 ingots (weighing a ton) of pure tin, which contained a minimal amount of led. The tin ingots represent the largest source of tin ever found from the Bronze Age, although its exact origin is still unknown, but it may have originated in the port of Tartessos (Tarshish), in southern Spain, or perhaps in Afghanistan. This large shipment of copper and tin would have been the raw material for making bronze.

The Uluburun Wreck also yielded up the earliest-known intact ingots of glass: 175 of these discoid shaped objects, in cobalt blue, turquoise, and one in lavender, were discovered and would have been used for faience or glass inlay. An Egyptian origin has been suggested for these ingots, and parallels have been drawn with cylindrical vessels thought to be ingot moulds from Tell el-Amarna, the heretic pharaoh Akhenaten's city, located some 365 miles south of Cairo. These ingot molds are of the same dimensions as the Uluburun ingots. Another interesting raw material discovered in the wreck was around a ton of terebinth resin, contained in an estimated 130 Canaanite amphora, the largest amount of this material ever discovered in antiquity. This yellowish, semi-fluid, aromatic resin comes from the *Pistacia* tree, and was used in the manufacture of perfumed oil and incense, and probably also for dying cloth.

Other exotic raw materials found in the Uluburun Wreck were logs of Egyptian ebony, for furniture; elephant ivory and hippopotamus ivory, for furniture, inlay, and plaques; ostrich eggshells and tortoise shells (modified to function as sound-boxes for stringed musical instruments), and murex seashells, possibly for incense and known to have been used later by the Phoenicians, who extracted a red dye from them. Large quantities of scrap gold and silver were also found in the wreck.

A number of Egyptian objects of gold, electrum, silver, and stone were discovered among the ship's cargo. One of these items, an electrum ring, had been cut in half with a chisel and was probably part of the scrap metal hoard discovered in the wreck. Five Egyptian scarabs, perhaps used as charms or talismans, or as seals, were found in the ship's cabin area and were presumably the property of one or more members of the ship's crew. One unique find was a gold scarab bearing the cartouche of Queen Nefertiti, the beautiful wife of the Eighteenth Dynasty Egyptian Pharaoh Akhenaten (died 1336 BC or 1334 BC). It is the only known scarab of the famous Egyptian queen, and, as the inscription on it is rather worn, it had probably been in use as jewelry or a good luck charm for some time.

A large amount of jewelry was also found in the wreck, including Canaanite bracelets and gold pendants, two duck-shaped ivory cosmetics containers, a trumpet carved from a hippopotamus incisor into the shape of a ram's horn, seashell rings, and beads of gold, agate, carnelian, quartz, faience, ostrich eggshell, and amber. The five amber beads are the first ever found outside of Greece that have been positively identified as originating in the Baltic Sea area (Northern Europe). Baltic amber is found throughout the Eastern Mediterranean, with the earliest example coming from graves in the Greek citadel of Mycenae (c. 1700 BC) and further finds coming from as far south as Egypt (18th dynasty, c. 1570 BC), indicating the wide extent of the trading network in operation at the time. The array of bronze weaponry from the Uluburun Wreck also indicates the far-reaching nature of this trade. The weapons discovered included six spearheads of European-type, which resemble examples from the Eastern Alps and Italy, arrowheads, daggers, Italian swords, and a rare stone ceremonial scepter-mace, from Bulgaria or the Carpathian Basin.

Among the most astonishing and unique finds from the Uluburun Wreck were two wooden writing boards (known as a *diptych*), which represent what is probably the world's earliest book. The writing tablet/

book consists of a pair of boxwood leaves joined with an ivory hinge, the inner faces of the leaves have slightly recessed surfaces to hold beeswax for writing. The writing would have been done with a stylus on this wax surface, but unfortunately thousands of years under water has removed whatever was recorded in the book. The excavators have concluded that the object may have been the captain's logbook, and George Bass has commented that it matches the writing tablet described by Homer in the *Iliad*.

The ship was not only carrying raw materials and luxury goods, but also a wide range of much more functional objects. These items included fish hooks, fish spears, lead net weights (all indicating fishing from on board the ship), pottery, a collection of bronze tools, sickles, drills, drill bits, chisels, axes, oil lamps, and at least 24 stone anchors. Several sets of pan-balance weights made of stone, lead, and bronze indicate the presence of merchants on board the ship when it went down. Traces of food were also found in the wreck, in the form of fish bones, olive pits, and the remains of acorns, almonds, pine nuts, figs, grapes, black cumin, sumac, coriander, safflower, pomegranate, wheat, and barley.

Only very few of the objects found in the Uluburun Wreck can help in dating the ship. One of the cylinder seals found in the probable cabin area of the ship was likely of Syrian origin and dated to the 18th century BC. The fact that this object was an heirloom is indicated by the dates of the Egyptian scarabs, which range from the Second Intermediate Period (1785–1567 BC) to the late 18th or early 19th Dynasty (late 13th century BC). These dates show that, like the Syrian seal, some of these scarabs were already hundreds of years old when the ship went down. The latest of these Egyptian scarabs, however, would indicate a date for the wreck in the late 13th century BC, as would the Mycenaean pottery and the gold seal of Nefertiti.

In an attempt to provide an absolute date for the Uluburun ship, seven wood samples taken from the keel-plank, planking, and cedar logs were sent to Peter Kuniholm of Cornell University, New York, for dendrochronological (tree ring analysis) dating. The results of the analysis gave a date of between 1318 BC and 1305 BC, suggesting that ship sank not during the rule of Nefertiti (who lived c. 1370–c. 1330 BC), but some years later.

The Uluburun Wreck is a rarity in terms of both the amount and vast range of the goods on board. As such, it has few if any parallels in the ancient world. However, a wreck discovered in 1954 in roughly the same area as the Uluburun find does provide some interesting parallels. The wreck, from Cape Gelidonya, near Finike, Turkey, was of a Phoenician merchant ship dating from about 1200 BC. The ship was about 40 feet in length and was carrying a cargo of Cypriot copper ingots, several hundred broken tools, including axes, adzes, picks, hoes, shovels (obviously collected for scrap), some of which had Cypriot signs scratched onto them, and Syrian oil lamps. The items on board this vessel would suggest that the captain or head merchant of the ship was a traveling tinker, who manufactured bronze tools and weapons to order from scrap metal, and copper and tin ingots he collected. Could the Uluburun vessel then be interpreted in the same way as that from Cape Gelidonya? Bearing in mind the amount of scrap metal on board the Uluburun ship, the answer to this question must be in the positive, though the vessel may well have had additional functions. To help us understand what these functions may have been, it is necessary to work out the possible origin and destination of the Uluburun ship.

Examination of the anchors discovered aboard the Uluburun vessel has shown that they were manufactured from rock found along the Carmel Coast in modern Israel. As mentioned, much of the raw material is from Cyprus, and there is a significant amount of Canaanite (from modern-day Israel, and parts of Lebanon, Syria, and Jordan) material (the oil lamps used on board, for example). Mycenaean Greeks seem to have been on board the ship, given the presence of personal items such as a pair of lentoid seals and amber beads manufactured in the Mycenaean style, as well as the writing tablet, swords, spear heads, and curved knives. Perhaps these objects suggest that the ship was bound for a port in Greece?

Because the vessel was carrying such a luxurious and expensive cargo it may represent royal gifts or tribute, perhaps involving Egyptian pharaohs, as mentioned in records kept by Late Bronze Age Egyptian and other Near Eastern rulers. A recent study of mice and rat bones discovered among the cargo found that the port of Ugarit was one of the vessel's last stops before sinking. Indeed, bearing in mind the fact that Ugarit was a great international emporium at this time, the ship may well have originated there. The Egyptian raw materials and finished items could indicate that the vessel's ultimate destination was the Nile River, an important center of trade in the Late Bronze Age, probably via southern Anatolia and the Aegean, a conventional course around the eastern Mediterranean at that time.

The importance of the Uluburun Wreck, in terms of the light it casts on commercial trade in antiquity, cannot be overestimated. The vast array of goods originating in so many different ancient cultures is testament to the fact that more than 3,300 years ago these cultures were mixing commercially and probably socially. Finds from the Uluburun Wreck are currently on display at the Bodrum Museum of Underwater Archaeology in Turkey, along with a wooden model of the vessel. Beginning in 2004, a team called the 360° Research Group began work on a full-scale navigable reconstruction of the Uluburun ship in the coastal town of Urla, İzmir. The completed vessel, christened *Uluburun II*, was officially launched in March 2005. On October 28, 2006, another replica, *Uluburun III*, was deliberately sunk, complete with fake cargo in Hidayet Bay near the original wreck site at Kas. One hopes that the examination of this modern wreck will add considerably to our understanding of the Uluburun vessel and consequently to our knowledge of ancient trade in the Mediterranean.

Chapter 23

The Iron Pillar of Delhi (India)

The Iron Pillar of Delhi.

The Iron Pillar stands in the courtyard of the 12th-century Quwwat-ul-Islam mosque, inside the Qutab complex of monuments and buildings at Mehrauli, close to Delhi, India. One of the world's most enigmatic structures this 24-foot-high tapered pillar was probably constructed during the reign of the emperor Chandragupta II Vikramaditya (AD 375–413) of the Gupta dynasty that ruled northern India from AD 320 to AD 540. Until around the end of the 19th century, the Pillar was the heaviest-known piece of wrought iron anywhere in the world, and is still today the largest hand-forged block of iron known from antiquity. The most controversial aspect of the pillar, the oldest of a number of such monuments dotted throughout India, is that it has remained virtually free from rust, despite having stood for around 1,600 years exposed to the elements.

The Delhi Pillar is more properly known as the *Singh Stambh* ("Lion Pillar"), and, although sometimes called the "Asoka (Ashoka) Pillar," this latter title is not entirely accurate. The pillars of Ashoka are a series of carved stone columns spread throughout the northern Indian subcontinent, erected during the reign of Emperor Ashoka in the third century BC, several centuries earlier than the Iron Pillar. The Delhi Pillar has a generally smooth and highly polished surface, though the lower, underground part was deliberately made rough for a better grip when the monument was standing. The structure measures 24.2 feet in height, with a diameter of 16.4 inches at its bottom and 13.4 inches at its top. It has an estimated weight of more than 6 tons. The Pillar is crowned by a decorative bell capital below a platform that once held a carved Ashoka Chakra Emblem. The body of the Pillar contains several inscriptions, the oldest and longest of which is in Sanskrit and explains that the structure was erected as a standard to honor the Hindu god Vishnu, and in praise of the memory of the Gupta King Chandra, who has been identified as Chandragupta II.

The Pillar does not stand in its original location. It is believed to have been brought to the area of Mehrauli from Udayagiri (Sanskrit—"sunrise hills"), 31 miles east of Bhopal, central India, in AD 1233 by Shams-ud-din Iltutmish, Sultan of Delhi at the time. Udayagiri is the site of a number of important Jaina and Buddhist rock-cut caves containing inscriptions, some of which date back more than 2,000 years. Professor R. Balasubramaniam of the Indian Institute of Technology,

Kanpur (IIT Kanpur) believes that the Pillar almost certainly served an important astronomical function at Udayagiri based on the site's location on the Tropic of Cancer. Balasubramaniam has theorized that the Pillar was erected at the entrance of the Udayagiri, cave complex, in front of Cave 7. He proposes that the structure was aligned with the cardinal directions so that in the early morning of the summer solstice it cast its shadow along a specially excavated passageway toward a panel depicting the god Anantasayin Vishnu in Cave 13. However, it is not certain that the Pillar was brought to Mehrauli in AD 1233 by Shams-ud-din Iltutmish. One of the inscriptions on the Delhi Iron Pillar was made by King Anang Pal, the Tomar king who according to legend founded Delhi, and has the date AD 1052 attached. If this inscription is to be taken at face value, it is also possible that 1052 is the date when the monument was transported to its current location, and that it was Tomar King Anang Pal who arranged it. However, a recent suggested redating of Anang Pal's reign to 1130–1145 casts serious doubt on the historical accuracy of this inscription.

The Pillar has generated widespread attention and controversy among archaeologists, historians, "alternative historians," and metallurgists. Much of the debate and often fantastical theorizing about the iron Pillar is based on its resistance to corrosion despite standing for 16 centuries. The original source for the irrational speculation about a fantastic age for the Pillar and the unsolvable mystery of its possibly "extraterrestrial" metals is Erich Von Daniken in his book *Chariots of the Gods* (1968). Von Daniken maintains that the Pillar was manufactured 4,000 years ago from some mysterious, unknown alloy. With the huge growth of the internet over the last decade or so, the Iron Pillar has been quoted as an "Out of Place Artifact" (OOPART): an object of historical, archaeological, or palaeontological interest seemingly found in an extremely unusual or ostensibly impossible context. Such objects apparently pose a serious challenge to the established facts of prehistory and history.

The existence of the rust-proof Iron Pillar of Mehrauli certainly raises some fascinating questions about technology in ancient India. Scientific studies of the Pillar began with Sir Rodert Hadfield, who published a paper on his research into the monument in the *Journal of Iron Steel Institute* in 1912. The results of almost a century of such investigations, the latest of which (by Professor Balasubramaniam) was published in 2005, have established that the Pillar is composed of 98 percent wrought iron of relatively pure quality. Tests have shown that the ancient Indians used forge welding (where two or more pieces of metal are heated and then hammered together) to manufacture the Pillar, utilizing a unique iron-making process where the iron ore was reduced to steel by mixing it with charcoal. This technique is different from modern blast furnaces, which use limestone instead of charcoal, and produce molten slag and pig iron that is later converted into steel. In the modern iron-making process, most phosphorous is carried away by the slag, but the ancient Indian technique results in a high phosphorous content.

It is the presence of this phosphorous, along with the alternate wet and dry environment of Delhi, that Professor Balasubramaniam believes have been crucial in preventing widespread rust on the Iron Pillar. According to Balasubramaniam and metallurgists at Kanpur IIT, a thin layer of a compound of iron, oxygen, and hydrogen, which they term *misawite*, has protected the cast iron pillar from extensive rust. This protective film developed within three years of the erection of the pillar and has been increasing gradually since that time. However, contrary to popular knowledge about the corrosion-resistant Pillar, it does in fact rust (for example, in the region just below the decorative bell capital, though this is a very low amount of corrosion for the 1,600 years the object has been standing).

The sophistication of iron technology in ancient India resulted in major achievements in the forging of huge iron objects of which the Delhi Iron Pillar is only one example. Two other ancient Indian iron pillars, at the Mookambika temple in the Kodachadri Hills, in the southern state of Karnataka, and at Dhar in the state of Madhya Pradesh, central India, will be discussed later. Also worthy of note are the iron beams used in the construction of a number of the ninth- to 13th-century temples located in the Indian state of Orissa on the east coast of India, along the Bay of Bengal, a major pilgrimage center for Hindus.

One of the earliest temples in this area utilizing iron beams is the exquisitely carved 11th-century Brahmeswar Temple. The Temple of Jagannath at Puri includes 239 huge wrought iron beams, the largest of which is more than 17 feet long. In contrast to the Delhi Pillar, however, the beams at the Temple of Jagannath are severely corroded due to the structure's proximity to the salt air of the sea coast. The best-known example of iron use in the Orissa Temples is the 13th-century Sun Temple at Konark. The temple, a World Heritage Site, was designed in the form of the huge chariot of the sun god Surya (Arka) drawn by seven horses. Indian legends tell of a magnetic lodestone on the top of the Sun temple, which would attract vessels passing through the Konark Sea, resulting in them being smashed to pieces on the coast. Whether these wrecks were due to the effect of the lodestone on the ships' compasses is not clear, though the legend could be a confused memory of the 29 massive iron beams (the largest of which was 25 feet in length) used in the construction of the Sun Temple.

The colossal wrought iron pillar at Dhar has received considerably less attention than that at Delhi. Unfortunately, the Dhar pillar has suffered considerably from the ravages of time and conquest, and now lies in three pieces on concrete supports, outside the Lat Masjid (Pillar Mosque), built by the governor of the Malwa province Dilawar Khan in 1405. Local tradition maintains that the pillar was constructed during the reign of King Bhoja (AD 1010–1053), though there is no inscription on the object to date it or identify its builder. The huge monument weighs more than 7 tons, and has a length of 44 feet and an average width of about 10 inches. Tests by Professor Balasubramaniam and colleagues have shown that the microstructure of the Dhar Pillar is characteristic of ancient Indian iron, and, like the Delhi Pillar, exhibits considerable resistance to rust due to the presence of a relatively high amount of phosphorus.

The third iron pillar is located at the Mookambika temple, an important monument visited by pilgrims from all over India. The temple is located close to the Arabian Sea, about 90 miles from Mangalore, in the state of Karanata. In Indian legend, the Mookambika temple is associated with the killing of the dumb (*mookasura*) demon by the Goddess Shri Mookambika, and local lore has it that the iron pillar is the top of the trident with which the Mother Goddess nailed down the evil demon into the earth. This pillar, popularly referred to as the *Dwaja-Sthamba* (flag-staff) of the Mookambika temple is little known to the public, perhaps due to the relative inaccessibility of the forested area around Kodachadri village. Though not as imposing as the pillars at Delhi and Dhar, the Mookambika temple pillar has an impressive total height of around 46 feet (allowing for portions hidden under its modern platform and below the earth), with an estimated weight of 0.5 tonnes. There has been minimal scientific study of this pillar, so exactly when and by whom it was erected remain a mystery, though preliminary tests by Professor T.R. Anantharaman have revealed that the iron used in its manufacture is definitely not modern and, like the other ancient iron pillars of India, it exhibits high corrosion resistance.

The Iron Pillar of Delhi represents a graphic testimony to the advanced state of metalworking technology in ancient India. It was not an isolated example of this ancient technology, as India's other lesser-known Iron pillars and iron beams used in the temples of Orissa testify. Though we do not know the function of the Delhi monument for certain, it fits in well with ancient commemorative columns known from India, such as the Ashoka Pillars, often known as "kirtistambhas" (pillars/towers of fame) or "jayastambhas" (pillars/towers of victory). The Pillar currently stands on a recently built cement platform and is surrounded by iron fencing, erected around the structure in 1997 due to the popularity of a local tradition. This tradition was that anyone who could stand with his back to the Pillar and encircle it with their arms would have good luck. The results of years of this popular practice are evident in the form of white patches on the lower portion of the pillar. Although the good-luck-bringing "pillar-hugging" is now at an end, the still-mysterious Iron Pillar at Delhi continues to fascinate, and it remains one of Delhi's prime tourist attractions.

⧖

Chapter 24

The Dendera Lamps
(Egypt)

The Dendera Light in one of the crypts of the Hathor Temple.

Double representation of the Dendera Light in one of the crypts of the Hathor Temple.

The Dendera Temple complex, located about 37 miles north of Luxor on the west bank of the Nile, is one of the best-preserved collections of ancient monuments in Egypt. Contained inside the complex is the superb Temple of Hathor, founded in 54 BC by Cleopatra's father, Ptolemy XII. On the walls of one of the crypts underneath this temple are a series of relief carvings sometimes known as the "Dendera Light" or the "Dendera Lamps" because of their resemblance to light bulbs. Some "alternative historians" have interpreted these carvings to mean that the ancient Egyptians developed electric lights and were thus as technologically advanced as we are today. Is there any evidence to back up such an extreme claim, or can the reliefs in the Temple of Hathor be interpreted in another way?

The vast Dendera (Ancient Egyptian—*Iunet* or *Tantere*) Temple complex covers an area of 430,560 square feet and is surrounded by a high mud brick enclosure wall. The complex belongs mainly to the Ptolemaic (between 305 BC and 30 BC) and to the Roman period (between 30 BC and AD 395), though the buildings replaced much older temples on the same sites. The Dendera complex contains a range of monuments including the Hathor Temple, a temple of the birth of Isis, a sacred lake, various chapels, Roman kiosks, and a Christian church. The earliest-surviving building on the site is the *Mammisi*, a large granite shrine built by Nectanebo II, Egypt's last native pharaoh, who ruled from 360 BC to 343 BC.

The main temple at Dendera is the magnificent Temple of Hathor, which in its present form was mostly constructed over a period of around 30 years, from 54 to 20 BC, during the reigns of Ptolemy XII and his daughter, Queen Cleopatra VII. Along with the Ptolemaic Temple of Horus at Edfu, located about 68 miles south of Luxor, this Temple is the most completely preserved in Egypt. On the Temple's outer wall there are finely carved reliefs showing both Cleopatra and her son by Julius Caesar, Caesarion (Ptolemy XV). The grand, elaborately decorated sandstone Temple of Hathor was dedicated to the cow-headed goddess Hathor, the consort of the falcon-god Horus, and goddess of love, motherhood, joy and music. The building contains a sanctuary, chapels, great halls, cult rooms, and subterranean crypts, and is completely enclosed by a 115-by-194-feet wall standing more than 40 feet in height. The imposing façade of the Temple has six massive columns with capitols representing Hathor with cow ears.

The famous Dendera Zodiac relief, the first-known representation of the stars in the form of a zodiac in Egypt, was found in the Temple of Hathor, adorning the ceiling of the Second Chapel of Osiris, one of the six rooftop chapels dedicated to the great Egyptian god of the underworld. The zodiac is now on display at the Musée du Louvre, Paris. Beneath the floors of Hathor's Temple cult chambers are 14 crypts, suites of rooms of three or sometimes four stories. These subterranean rooms were used to store cult equipment, archives, and magical emblems for the Temple's protection. The most important of the numerous statues kept in the crypts was a statue of the *Ba* of Hathor. The Ba was believed to be the being's personality and was depicted as a bird or a bird with a human head. Access to these crypts was gained from hidden trapdoors in the floor and secret sliding doors in the walls. Subterranean crypts were a common feature in Egyptian temples from the Late Period (beginning with the 26th Dynasty; 664–525 BC) onward. However, unlike crypts at other temples, eleven of those in the Hathor

Temple contain relief decoration. It is three of the relief carvings in the easternmost of the five crypts along the Temple's southern side that have caused some debate in fringe archaeology circles.

One of the controversial reliefs at Dendera shows Horus holding an elongated bulb-like object containing snakes, which is supported by a Djed pillar (symbol resembling a column with a broad base and capital divided by four parallel bars) with two human arms. A huge baboon-like demon holding two knives in his hands is depicted to the right.

Although Egyptologists interpret these images as representing lotus flowers spawning a snake, some researchers have other explanations for their meaning. In their 1996 book, *Das Licht der Pharaonen* ("The Light of the Pharaohs"), Austrian ancient astronaut theorists Peter Krassa and Reinhard Habeck conjecture that the snake inside the lotus flower represent light bulbs. They suggest that in the reliefs the snake represents the electric current, the lotus flower the socket of the bulb, the lotus stem the cable, and the Djed Pillar the isolator. Krassa and Habeck believe that due to the extreme darkness of the crypt some form of light would have been required, and as there are apparently no traces of soot in the room, this must have been an electrical lighting system.

No discussion of "alternative" explanations for ancient mysteries would be complete without the inclusion of the granddaddy of ancient astronaut theorists, Erich Von Daniken. In his book *The Eyes of the Sphinx: The Newest Evidence of Extraterrestrial Contact in Ancient Egypt* (1996), Von Daniken echoes the opinions of Krassa and Habeck that the Dendera Reliefs illustrate an ancient electric light bulb, cryptically adding that the image of the baboon is a warning that the electrical device could be dangerous if used incorrectly (!). He also states that the relief is located in a "secret chamber." In 1981, Viennese electrical engineer Walter Garn constructed a model based on the reliefs at the Temple of Hathor complete with Djed Column insulator, bulb, and twisting wire, which did indeed functional and emit light. So can we interpret these images as proof that ancient Egyptians used electricity to light their underground tombs and crypts, and were thus in possession of incredibly advanced technology thousands of years ago?

The first basic objection to the theory that these ancient reliefs show electric lamps is that an electric light bulb does not need an extra insulator (the Djed); the glass of the light bulb insulates the filament.

Secondly, no material evidence has ever been found, despite hundreds of years of investigations and excavations in Egypt—not a trace of associated artifacts or supporting technology, such as wires or power supplies that would be required to manipulate electricity. Thirdly, the assertion made by Krassa and Habeck that no traces of soot have ever been discovered in Egypt's thousands of underground tombs, pyramid shafts, and crypts is completely untrue. It is there in abundance on the burial chamber walls of the Red Pyramid of Dahshur, for example. In other cases, such as the walls of the passages in the Great Pyramid at Giza, for example, decoration was undertaken in daylight, before the ceiling and roof were installed. Furthermore, even a quick perusal of the Dendera Reliefs shows that they are in fact covered in soot; the original white color of the lime stone is still visible around the edges of the block.

Krassa and Habeck are also of the opinion that the objects in the Dendera Reliefs are shown in their natural proportions. German researcher Frank Dörnenburg has calculated that, if this is the case, then the "light bulbs" depicted would be 8.2 feet in length, with a maximum diameter of around 3.3 feet. Furthermore, if we apply this literal interpretation to the whole scene, it would follow that ancient Egyptian Djed pillars possessed human arms and giant baboons carried out surgery. The working reconstruction of the Dendera Lamp by Walter Garn, proves nothing. There are reasons why we use small light bulbs rather than huge 8.2-feet-long ones.

So how do we interpret the enigmatic reliefs in the crypts of the Temple of Hathor? Although it is not known exactly what the Djed Pillar represents, its hieroglyphic meaning is "enduring" or "stability," and sometimes "column." The Djed Pillar has also been interpreted as combination of the four pillars that the Egyptians believed supported the four corners of the earth, as a cedar tree with lopped branches, as the backbone of the god Osiris, and as a stylized sheaf of corn. It may have represented all of these things at various times in ancient Egyptian history. Many Egyptian pyramids and tombs display the Djed symbol in their decoration, including Snefru's Step Pyramid at Meidum, 62 miles south of Cairo, where the Djed pillars form columns supporting the sky, and in Djoser's Step Pyramid at Saqqara (see Chapter 9), where there are doorways surmounted with rows of Djed pillars supporting an arch above. Both of these structures date back to the 27th century BC.

Rather than being an illustration of ancient Egyptian electricity, the scene in the Dendera Reliefs is interpreted by Egyptologists as a depiction of a Djed pillar, and a lotus leaf and flower giving birth to a sacred snake inside it, in accordance with Egyptian mythology. In his work *Dendera et le Temple d'Hathor* (Cairo, 1969, pp. 60–61), French Egyptologist François Daumas (1915–1984) gives a description of the Dendera reliefs:

> In the last room, one sees, carefully carved on the Southern wall, a falcon with detailed feathers, preceded by a snake emerging from a lotus blossom within a boat. Whereas the whole of the temple is constructed of sandstone, to facilitate a relief of fine quality there was placed in the wall, at the level of the figures, a block of limestone suitable for very detailed work, and of this the artist took full and perfect advantage. These reliefs are cosmological representations. The snake that comes out of the lotus is equated with the shining deity Harsamtawy as he appears for the first time out of the primordial sea. He is again represented near the bottom of the crypt in the form of two snakes also coming forth, but this time wrapped in lotuses like protective envelopes.

Admittedly, we cannot explain every detail shown in the Dendera Reliefs. However, this does not mean we have to ascribe to them fantastical interpretations, entirely without a shred of evidence to back them up. The electric lamp theory for the reliefs seems to be based on nothing more than that the images look like modern light bulbs, and therefore ancient Egyptians must have possessed electricity. People often see what they want to see in ancient art, projecting their own values, obsessions, and meanings back onto ancient civilizations far removed from us in time and culture. One of the 21st century's major obsessions is with technology, which is why every ancient object or image that is imperfectly understood has to be an ancient machine of some kind that show that our ancestors "were just as advanced as we are today." This attitude tells us absolutely nothing about ancient cultures, buildings, and artifacts, but everything about ourselves. The Dendera Reliefs must be understood in terms of ancient Egyptian religion and not modern technology; the scenes depict a magical and not a technical process.

⏳

Chapter 25

The Oak Island Treasure
(Canada)

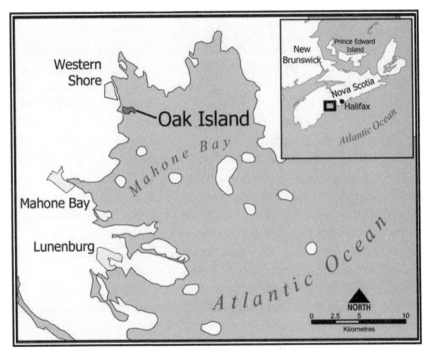

Oak Island, Nova Scotia.

The story of the Oak Island Treasure is a controversial and complex one. Investigations into the supposed home of the treasure, the "Oak Island Money Pit," Nova Scotia, Canada, have allegedly been taking place for more than 200 years, during which time various authors and researchers have circulated tales of the discovery of strange man-made artifacts, human bones, and booby-traps to protect the mysterious treasure. There have also been bizarre claims made connecting the Money Pit with the ancient Egyptians, Knights Templar, Marie Antoinette's jewels, pirate treasure, and lost Francis Bacon manuscripts. Is there any truth behind these stories, or are we dealing with a simple folk tale that has developed into "truth" after numerous re-tellings over the centuries?

Oak Island is one of around 360 small islands in Lunenberg County on the south shore of Nova Scotia, Canada. The tree-covered island is about 3/4 of a mile long and less than 1/2 mile wide at its widest point, and rises to a maximum of 35 feet above sea level.

The general outline of the story of the supposed discovery of the Oak Island Money Pit is as follows. Some time in 1795, 16-year-old Daniel McGinnis (or McInnis) stumbled upon a circular depression, 15 or 16 feet in diameter, in the ground in a clearing on the southeastern end of the island. There was an ancient tree close by with an old tackle block on one of its overhanging branches (in other accounts the tree bore the marks of unnatural scarring), which persuaded McGinnis, who had heard tales of Captain Kidd's buried treasure on the island, that there was something important buried in the vicinity. McGinnis went home and returned the next day with friends John Smith (in early accounts, Samuel Ball) and Anthony Vaughan. The boys began digging with picks and shovels, and a few feet below the surface discovered a layer of flagstones covering the hole. As they excavated deeper, they came upon a layer of logs 10 feet down, then another at 20 feet, and again at 30 feet, where they stopped digging. Unable to continue their excavations without further help, the boys returned home, planning to return later with more help.

It would be eight years before the boys were able to return to Oak Island again. This time they returned with The Onslow Company (owned by wealthy local businessman Simeon Lynds), a company with a large labor force formed for the sole purpose of retrieving what they believed was a vast treasure from the strange pit. Beginning in 1803 or 1804 (or 1810, in one version), the team continued where the previous excavation had left off and as before found oak platforms at exact intervals of 10 feet. Apart from the platforms, the team also found a layer of charcoal at the 40-feet level, at 50 feet a layer of putty, and at 60 feet a layer of what was identified as coconut fiber, even though the nearest source of coconuts was hundreds of miles away. At 90 feet the Company made a fascinating discovery: a large flat stone bearing a mysterious inscription. Unfortunately, in a rush to get to the treasure they believed lay beneath the stone the team discarded the important relic; apparently it later found its way into John Smith's fireplace and disappeared for good about 1919 (1912, in some accounts). No drawings were made of the stone at the time, and no photographs of it are known to exist. However, a note of the inscription was made at some time, which was later translated to read "Forty Feet Below Two Million Pounds Are Buried."

Digging below the stone the team hit something hard, but suddenly water began seeping into the pit and work had to be abandoned for the night. Unfortunately when they came back the next morning, the team found that the shaft was flooded with 60 feet of water, and all attempts at bailing out the pit with buckets failed. They had no choice but to temporarily abandon the project. The following year the Onslow Company returned and excavated a parallel shaft 100 feet down to connect with the original pit, but again the structure flooded, eventually caving in the walls of the new shaft. This disaster signaled the end of the Onslow Company's investigations on Oak Island. Some researchers believe that the Onslow Company had inadvertently triggered a booby trap, a 500-foot-long flood tunnel that had been dug by the shaft's designers leading from the pit to nearby Smith's Cove.

The supposed treasure inside the Money Pit lay forgotten for more than 40 years, until 1849, when another group, the Truro Company (said by some sources to have included Simeon Lynds and Anthony Vaughn), re-excavated the original shaft down to the 86-foot level, where it again flooded. The workers then set up a platform and used a hand-operated auger to drill into the bottom of the pit. In the cores of material recovered from the pit, the team discovered some "ancient"-looking wood and three links from a gold chain. Finding nothing else, the Truro Company stopped work on Oak Island in the fall of 1850.

Various other explorations followed throughout the 19th century, with very little result. The Oak Island Association, Oak Island Eldorado Company, and Oak Island Treasure Company all attempted and failed to find any trace of treasure at the site. The latter company did allegedly discover a fragment of parchment that bore two letters (which possibly read "ri"), but this has never been substantiated.

Investigations continued during the 20th century, with the digging of numerous bore-holes, shafts, and tunnels to try to locate the fabled treasure. The "Money Pit" also claimed its fair share of lives. In 1965 four men working on excavations of the site by the Restall family died after being overcome by swamp gas or engine fumes in a shaft near the beach. In 1966 Florida building contractor Dan Blankenship and Montreal businessman David Tobias teamed up and began an extensive drilling operation in the area of the Money Pit, sinking around 60 bore-holes in 1967. They managed to attract numerous investors, and in 1968 became Triton Alliance. In 1971, the Alliance lowered an underwater camera down a 235-foot shaft they had excavated, which recorded images of some blurred shapes, interpreted by Blankenship and Tobias as wooden chests and a human hand. A promised $10 million excavation of the site by Triton Alliance, however, never materialized, and the project collapsed.

Dan Blankenship did not give up on the Oak Island treasure, however. He became part owner of the island and in 2008 the first excavations at the supposed site of the Money Pit in 17 years got underway with Blankenship and his new partners, a group of oil barons known as the Michigan Group. The team is now collectively known as Oak Island Tours Inc. As nothing was reported in the press from the 2008 investigations, they presumably failed to discover anything during their first season, and further work planned for 2009 was held up as the company had not received a Treasure Trove License to proceed with work on Oak Island.

Stories of Oak Island's connections with Egyptians, Incas, and lizard beings notwithstanding, what, if anything, could be buried in the Money Pit? The original theory was that the Oak Island shaft contained pirate treasure, probably secreted there by Scottish sailor Captain Kidd. However, research into the life of Kidd has shown that he was never in Nova Scotia, and he was a privateer (that is, he was entitled by state to attack and rob enemy vessels during wartime) rather than a pirate in the traditional sense. Another theory, put forward by, among others, Steven Sora in his book, *The Lost Treasure of the Knights*

Templar: Solving the Oak Island Mystery (Destiny Books, 1999), is that the mysterious Knights Templar buried their fabulous treasure at the bottom of the Oak Island pit. The basic objection to this hypothesis is that there is no reliable evidence that Templar Knights ever visited North America, let alone Oak Island. Furthermore, if the Templars did deposit their treasure in the Money Pit, it would have to have been no later than 1500, probably somewhat earlier. If so, then after around 300 years there would certainly be no trace of the tree and its pulley device, which McGinnis came upon, or the indentation in the ground, or indeed the clearing itself.

In a 1953 article, "A History and Inquiry Into The Origin of The Money Pit" (*home.att.net/~mleary/oakislan.htm*), author Penn Leary put forward the idea that the lost manuscripts of Sir Francis Bacon were concealed in the Oak Island shaft. Sir Francis Bacon did have some connection with Canada: he and his associates formed the Newfoundland Colonization Company in 1607, and three years later Bacon sent John Guy to found a colony in Newfoundland. However, there is no evidence that Bacon ever traveled to Canada himself, and there is nothing to link him with Oak Island. Again, because Bacon died in 1626, and the Money Pit was not discovered until 1795, there is a similar problem with the chronology to the Templar theory. There is one serious problem with all theories of buried treasure in the Oak Island Money Pit, whether it be pirate treasure, loot from a wrecked Spanish galleon, or even (with the help of the French navy) Marie Antoinette's lost jewels: why would anyone concealing a treasure, presumably with the intention of coming back for it one day, leave such obvious markers as to the treasure's location? The pulley on the tree, the clearing, the indentation on the ground, and the cipher on the stone are surely clumsy errors for someone adept enough to design the intricate Money Pit.

Perhaps there is a far less sensational explanation for the Oak Island Pit. Researcher Joe Nickell has suggested that the pit was simply a natural sinkhole that McInnis and his friends, with thoughts of buried pirate treasure in their heads, mistook for something more exotic. The Island itself and the mainland opposite are full of such sinkholes, as well as natural underground caves. An uncannily similar "Money Pit" was discovered by accident in 1878. A farmer was plowing just 120 yards away from the original shaft on Oak Island, when the ground gave way underneath and her oxen disappeared into a 12-foot-deep sinkhole. In 1949, on the shore of Mahone Bay, close to Oak Island, workers excavating a well came upon flagstones at a depth of 2 feet. Digging down to a depth of 85 feet, they discovered sporadic layers of spruce and oak logs, and became excited at the thought of another Money Pit. However, further investigations showed that the feature was a natural sinkhole that had been filled up with storm debris, including logs and even coconuts, which had traveled hundreds of miles on ocean currents. (This would explain the coconut fiber discovered in the Money Pit.) As far as the "booby-trap" flooding system for the Money Pit is concerned, a two-week-long investigation in 1995 by the Woods Hole Oceanographic Institution found no direct connection from the Pit to the surrounding ocean, and concluded that the flooding there was an entirely natural phenomenon.

If the Money Pit is after all a natural feature, then what about the artifacts supposedly discovered inside it? First, the current location of these artifacts is unknown (if they still exist). Secondly, as such a vast amount of tunnels and shafts have been dug into the area, the artifacts from inside the pit could easily have been left over from previous work on the site rather than belonging to the original Money Pit deposit. The "cipher stone" allegedly discovered there by the Onslow Company in 1803/4 is almost certainly a hoax, possibly concocted by the Company to attract investors in order to continue the operation, as the group was said to have been running out of money at the time. However, there is no proof that the Onslow Company ever existed, so the whole story of the discovery of the stone may well be 20th-century fiction. Bear in mind that no description or illustration of the stone appeared until it appeared in the 1951 book *True Tales of Buried Treasure* by Edward Rowe Snow. Snow claimed to have been given the set of symbols by Reverend A.T. Kempton of Cambridge, Massachusetts, who, as there is no evidence for the existence of the cipher before this time, probably invented it himself.

As Richard Joltes points out in his comprehensive survey *History, Hoax, and Hype: The Oak Island Legend*, no contemporary sources for the Oak Island Money Pit exist at all. The first item published regarding the Oak Island Mystery dates to 1849, and is a note giving permission for treasure hunters to dig on the island. After this is an 1857 note by a traveler who visited the abandoned site and made comments on the rubbish he found there. The first accounts giving any detail of early investigations at the site were published in 1861 and 1863 in the *British Colonist* and *Liverpool Transcript* newspapers—well more than a half century after the events were supposed to have taken place. The initial discoverers did exist, however, though they were not boys. Both McInnis and Anthony Vaughn were in their mid-30s in 1795, and both owned land on the island.

The fact that the first note of anything regarding treasure on Oak Island appeared in 1849, the same year as the huge California gold strike, has persuaded Richard Joltes that the entire story may have begun as a scam to defraud investors. After the publication of the newspaper articles in the 1860s, the story got out of hand, feeding off its own legend and incorporating various pieces of classic treasure lore (a cipher stone, a stone covering the treasure's hiding place, the treasure always being just out of reach, the discovery of the site by children rather than adults) along the way. As Richard Joltes succinctly puts it, the Oak Island Money Pit then became a piece of "runaway folklore" with a mind of its own. Richard Joltes's theory certainly sounds feasible, though we will probably never know for sure. The area around the Money Pit has been practically obliterated by 150 years of drilling and digging, so much so that the location of McGinnis's supposed original find has probably been lost for good.

ENIGMATIC

PEOPLE

Chapter 26

Merlin the Magician (UK)

Merlin advising King Arthur in a Gustave Doré illustration.

The mysterious sorcerer of the tales of King Arthur and the Knights of the Round Table, Merlin is a legendary figure whose appeal is as strong in the 21st century as it was in the medieval period when the stories were first written down. However, Merlin was a much more complicated and enigmatic figure than the wizard of Arthurian myth. Medieval and earlier sources portray him as not only a wizard, but at various times a prophet, a bard, a teacher, and even a supernatural creature that could shape-shift at will. There are also indications that the legendary Merlin may have been based in part on two figures of the British Dark Ages, the Romano-British war leader Aurelius Ambrosius (Welsh—*Emrys Wledig*), and the sixth-century Welsh bard Myrddin Wyllt. What was the real character of literature's most famous wizard, and is there a historical person behind the legend of Merlin?

The main sources for the story of Merlin are two works by 12th-century British cleric Geoffrey of Monmouth. Both of these, *Historia regum Britanniae* ("History of the Kings of Britain"; c. 1138) and *Vita Merlin* ("Life of Merlin"; c. 1150), were written in Latin. Geoffrey's earlier work, *Prophetiae Merlini* ("Prophecies of Merlin"), begun in 1135, was later incorporated into his History of the Kings of Britain (as Book VII). Merlin first appears in Geoffrey's History as a boy living at the time of King Vortigern, a possibly historical fifth-century British chieftain. Vortigern was attempting to build a fortress as protection against his enemies, but every time the structure was completed it collapsed. The king's magicians informed him that in order for the fortress to stand he must sacrifice a boy with no father and sprinkle the foundation stones of the building with the boy's blood.

The king's messengers were immediately dispatched to find such a boy, and they eventually discovered Merlin, whose mother was the daughter of the king of Demetia (Dyfed, one of the ancient kingdoms of Wales). Merlin's mother told the king that the boy was fathered by a demon, in the form of an incubus, who visited her at night. (Merlin inherited his supernatural powers from this non-human origin.) When Merlin asked Vortigern why he was brought before him, the king told the boy that he was to be sacrificed so that the fortress would stand. Merlin dismissed this reasoning, telling the king and his magicians that they did not understand what it was that really hindered the building of the fortress.

I entreat your majesty would command your workmen to dig into the ground, and you will find a pond which causes the foundations to sink. This accordingly was done, and then presently they found a pond deep under ground, which had made it give way...Command the pond to be drained, and at the bottom you will see two hollow stones, and in them two dragons asleep. The king made no scruple of believing him, since he had found true what he said of the pond, and therefore ordered it to be drained: which done, he found as Merlin had said; and now was possessed with the greatest admiration of him.

(Geoffrey of Monmouth
History of the Kings of Britain
[Book VI, XVII –XIX])

As Merlin predicted, when the pond was drained two dragons rose out of the water and immediately began fighting each other. Merlin explained that the two dragons symbolize the Britons and the Saxons, and foretold the future of Britain, including the fall of Vortigern and the ultimate rise of Arthur to the kingship of Britain. This part of Geoffrey's *History* derives largely from the *Historia Brittonum* of ninth-century Welsh monk/historian Nennius. The only differences are that in Nennius's work the boy-prophet is named Ambrosius (Welsh— "Emrys Wledig") and that his father is stated to have been a Roman consul. Geoffrey also called Merlin "Ambrosius," which he seems to have taken from the semi-historic Aurelius Ambrosius, a war leader of the Romano-British who is said to have been victorious in an important battle against the Anglo-Saxons in the fifth century.

Geoffrey's *History* goes on to describe Merlin's rise to power, his construction of Stonehenge (which Geoffrey calls the "Giant's Dance") by magical means, and his arranging of the conception of Arthur. Merlin engineered Arthur's birth by using his magic to help King Uther Pendragon seduce Igraine, the duchess of Cornwall, who begets Arthur. Pendragon later married Igraine, making her queen and thus legitimizing Arthur's succession to the throne. Although Arthur and his heroic exploits were described in the *History*, Merlin's role ended with the conception of Arthur. In Geoffrey's account the wizard played no more part in Arthur's life, and we must look to other authors to continue the story of Merlin.

The *Prose Merlin*, which survives in a single manuscript text kept at Cambridge University Library, is a late medieval Arthurian work probably written around the middle of the 15th century. This work is a translation into English of the Merlin section of the *Old French Vulgate Cycle*, a group of related Arthurian works composed during the first half of the 13th century. The first five sections of the *Prose Merlin* are probably derived from the poem "Merlin" by Robert de Boron, a French poet of the late 12th to early 13th centuries. The rest of the work is believed to be based on a sequel to de Boron's poem written during the first half of the 13th century. De Boron's "Merlin" was part of his popular cycle of Arthurian Romances centered on the Holy Grail, though his work only survives in fragments and in these later prose versions.

In the *Prose Merlin*, we find many of the familiar elements in the story of Merlin that we know today. The Christian standpoint of the work is much in evidence, and great emphasis is laid on Merlin's demonic origin. Another aspect of the wizard presented in the *Prose Merlin* is his shape-shifting ability; Merlin used this power on many occasions to change himself into various people and animals. The *Prose Merlin* also introduces the motif of the sword in the stone (although it was originally an anvil), the Holy Grail, and the Round Table. Merlin was the designer and constructer of the Round Table, which he had modeled on the Grail Table fashioned by Joseph of Arimathea, which was itself a replica of the table used at the Last Supper. The Round Table was fashioned for Uther Pendragon, however, not King Arthur.

The Holy Grail appeared in the Arthurian tales when King Arthur fell sick and his knights fought among themselves, leading Britain into civil war. In order to reunite the kingdom, Merlin devised the quest for the Holy Grail, a sacred cup that, when drunk from, could cure all illnesses. Guided by Merlin, the Knight Sir Perceval eventually found the Grail, King Arthur recovered, and the country was once again united.

The *Prose Merlin* also introduced Merlin's seducer, known variously in this and other Medieval works as Nivaine, Nimue, or simply the Lady of the Lake. In one version, Nivaine was a mortal, the daughter of the king of Northumberland (northeast England). She was a wild-natured and cunning 15-year-old girl, very much like the Greek goddess of the hunt Artemis (Roman Diana). Merlin became infatuated by the girl, who swore she would never love him unless he taught her all his magic. Merlin agreed, unaware that Nivaine would use this magic against him, which she did by imprisoning him in a magical stone burial chamber, where he died. In other versions of the tale the enchanted prison was variously described as a cave, an oak tree, an invisible tower in the forest, and, in Malory's *Le Morte d'Arthur* (1485), a large rock. In the *Prose Merlin*, the wizard's seducer and lover Viviane confined Merlin in a prison of air, thus isolating him from all other contact and keeping him for herself.

When Geoffrey of Monmouth wrote of Merlin again in his *Life of Merlin*, a dozen years or so after the publication of his *History*, he described a very different character. The *Life of Merlin* told the story of Merlin's madness and its cure, and discussed the prophecies spoken by both Merlin and his sister, whom Geoffrey called Ganieda. It seems probable that, for this version of the life of the great wizard, Geoffrey was drawing on separate traditions and different sources, most notably tales of the sixth-century Welsh bard Myrddin Wyllt. Poet and seer Myrddin Wyllt ("Mad/Wild Merlin") is mentioned by name in a number of early Welsh poems: "Yr Afallennau" ("The Apple Trees"), "Oianau" ("The Greetings"), and "Ymddiddan Myrddin a Thaliesin" ("Dialogue of Myrddin and Taliesin"). These poems are preserved in the manuscript known as the *Black Book of Carmarthen*, written down c. 1250, but dating back centuries earlier. Another work, *The Red Book of Hergest*, believed to have been written sometime between 1375 and 1425, includes a poem called "Cyfoesi Myrddin ac ei Chwaer Gwenddydd" ("The Conversation of Myrddin and his Sister Gwenddydd"). In this poem we learned that Myrddin and Gwenddydd were twins and that Merlin's father was named Morfryn. According to the *Annales Cambriae* (*The Annals of Wales*), which dates from around AD 970, after the death of his king Gwenddolau in the Battle of Arfderydd in AD 573, Myrddin fled half-insane into the forests where he lived in trees with wild beasts, and in his madness acquired the gift of prophecy.

In all of these early Welsh poems, Myrddin has no association with Arthur at all, but seems to be the same character that a Scottish source (*The Life of St. Kentigern*) gives the name of "Lailoken" ("Llallogan" in Welsh) and an Irish story calls *"Suibhne Geilt" ("Mad Sweeney")*. Also known as the "Madman of Caledonia," Lailoken was a madman and prophet who lived in the forests of the ancient British Kingdom of Strathclyde, on the west coast of what is now Scotland. Similarly, in the Irish tale Suibhne Geilt was a king who went mad during the battle of Magh Rath (allegedly fought c. AD 642 in Moira, County Down, Northern Ireland) and afterward wandered all over Ireland.

Myrddin Wyllt is said to have prophesied his own death, which was destined to occur by the seemingly unlikely combination of falling, stabbing, and drowning. However, the prophesy was fulfilled when a group of shepherds pelted him with stones, driving him off the edge of a cliff and down the bank of the River Tweed, where he was impaled on a sharp stake left by fishermen, and fell into the river, where he died. According to a legend that dates back at least as far as the 15th century, Myrddin is buried at the root of a thorn tree near the River Tweed in the town of Drumelzier, southern Scotland, in the area where Lailoken was said to have wandered in his madness. The spot is now marked by a thorn tree planted in 1996 surrounded by a small fence; the tree bears a plaque stating that the original tree planted on "the Wizard Merlin's grave" was washed away by floods in 1928. It seems that no structures have ever stood on the site, though there are the remains of a Bronze Age (c. 2000–800 BC) burial cairn close by, the discovery of which may have inspired the tradition of a grave in the area.

In the mythology of many countries, including Ireland, the threefold death suffered by Myrddin usually applies to kings, heroes, and gods. There is also fascinating archaeological evidence for human sacrifice by threefold death in the form of bog bodies. These bog bodies, many of which date to the Iron Age (eighth century–first century AD), are well preserved human remains recovered from sphagnum bogs in Northern Europe, Britain, and Ireland. One of the most interesting and best-preserved of these bodies is known as Lindow Man, discovered in 1984 in a peat bog at Lindow Moss, Cheshire, northwest England. The remains were of a high-status male in his mid-20s, who had been ritually executed by being hit on the head, strangled, and having his throat cut. After suffering this threefold death he was deposited face-down into Lindow Moss. There have been speculations by some researchers, including Dr. Anne Ross and Don Robins, that Lindow Man was a high-status druid, possibly sacrificed during the feast of Beltane (May Day). Although there is no conclusive proof of this theory, the possible connection between the British sorcerer/madman and his threefold death and the ritualistic death of Lindow man, and other bog bodies, is a tantalizing one.

Myrddin/the "Madman of Caledonia" may well have been a historical character and is certainly a prime candidate for the prototype of the legendary wizard Merlin. However, the composite figure of Merlin we have today is the result of hundreds of years of development from many different sources and literary traditions. Nevertheless, the image of Merlin as the quintessential wise man and wizard is as pervading as ever—witness the success of the *Harry Potter* books and movies, for example—but there is also perhaps a darker side to the Merlin figure, as a half-mad prophet and keeper of arcane knowledge, knowledge that is destined to disappear with him when he suffers his threefold death or is imprisoned by the Lady of the Lake in her enchanted tower.

Chapter 27

Boudica
(England)

Statue of Boudica near Westminster Pier, London.

In stature she was very tall, in appearance most terrifying, in the glance of her eye most fierce, and her voice was harsh ; a great mass of the tawniest hair fell to her hips ; around her neck was a large golden necklace ; and she wore a tunic of divers colours over which a thick mantle was fastened with a brooch.

(Cassius Dio *History of Rome* [Book LXII.2])

Boudica was a queen of the Iceni tribe of Eastern Britain and is regarded as one of Britain's greatest heroines for her brave rebellion against the tyranny of Roman rule. Boudica's uprising was the most dangerous threat to its power that the Romans in Britain were ever to face, and a defeat could have altered the face of European history. Was Boudica the brave and heroic queen she is often painted as, or was there a much darker, even brutal side to her character? And what happened to her after the final bloody battle against the might of the Roman legions?

The Roman invasion of Britain under the Emperor Claudius I (10 BC– AD 54) began in AD 43, and Roman occupation of the country lasted until about AD 410. Roman politician and general Aulus Plautius, who became the first governor of the new province (in office from AD 43 to AD 47), led the invasion. But the Romans took decades to accomplish full rule over Britain and even then some parts of Scotland (and the whole of Ireland) never became part of the Roman Empire. At this time, during the mid-first century AD, Britain was split into various tribes ruled by tribal chiefs; there was no unified British/Celtic army to meet the Romans when they landed. One such tribe was the Iceni in the east of Britain, who inhabited an area corresponding roughly to the modern-day county of Norfolk, in East Anglia.

There is archaeological evidence for the sophistication of the Iceni in the form of exquisitely worked gold and silver torcs (a necklace, or similar ornament of a twisted narrow band of precious metal), brooches, bracelets, and coins. The silver coins made by the Iceni depict faces, horses, boars, and more abstract patterns; some even have writing on them—among the earliest writing so far discovered in Britain. A number of their coins are inscribed ECENI, which makes the Iceni the only coin-producing tribe to use their name on coins.

Our information for the career of Boudica comes from two Roman literary sources: senator and historian Tacitus (c. AD 56–c. 117) in his works *Agricola* (c. AD 98) and *The Annals* (c. AD 109), and Cassius Dio (c. AD 155–c229), a Roman historian and politician, in *The Rebellion of Boudicca* (c. AD 163). Sixth century British monk Gildas may also be referring to Boudicca in his surviving written work, *De Excidio et Conquestu Britanniae* ("On the Ruin and Conquest of Britain") when he describes "that deceitful lioness" who murdered Roman rulers in Britain during her uprising.

Tacitus is not only a vital contemporary source for Roman Britain, but he also had a personal connection in the form of his father-in-law and subject of his first work: the Roman general Gnaeus Julius Agricola. From AD 58 to AD 62 Agricola was a military tribune serving in Britain under Gaius Seutonius Paulinus, and he later became governor of Britain, from AD 77/78 to AD 84. Consequently Tacitus must have received important firsthand information from Agricola about the country during these periods. Tacitus gives the warrior queen of the Iceni the name Boudica (sometimes mistranslated as "Boadicea"), a Latinization of the Celtic word *bouda* meaning "victory," thus making her name equivalent to the modern Victoria.

Around 15 years after the Roman conquest of Britain, Boudica's husband, King Prasutagus, died. Prasutagus had probably submitted to Roman authority in 43 and kept his crown as a client-king. Such client-kings were a common and essential part of the Roman Empire; they would continue to rule in their native land as they had done before the coming of the legions, but under the government of the Romans, and paying taxes to Rome. As a part of this arrangement, Prasutagus named the Roman emperor as co-heir to his kingdom. On his death Prasutagus left a will dividing his large estates between his two daughters, Camorra and Tasca, and the Emperor Nero. Although British law allowed royal inheritance to be passed to daughters in the absence of male heir, Roman law only permitted inheritance through the male line. Consequently the Romans ignored the will of Prasutagus, deprived the local nobility of all their estates, and took over the Iceni kingdom. Outraged, Boudica resisted the Roman takeover; as a result she was publicly stripped and flogged, and her two teenage daughters were raped.

Seeking revenge for the insult, Boudica raised the Iceni and the neighboring tribe to the south, the Trinovantes, along with a number of other tribes in a planned revolt against Roman rule. The Trinovantes had reason to join the rebellion, as their tribal capital Camulodunum (modern Colchester) had been occupied by the Romans and converted into a military camp. Around AD 44, the Romans had also constructed a temple to the late emperor Claudius in Camulodunum, which had been paid for by heavy taxes imposed on the Iceni and their neighbors. At this time, in AD 60 or 61, the Roman governor

Seutonius was on campaign in north Wales with a large part of the Roman army. It was then that the British struck at their first target: the *colonia* of Camulodunum, practically undefended and left in the hands of a colony of Roman veterans. Probably viewing the town and its temple to the emperor Claudius as a symbol of hated Roman authority, Boudica and her vast hoard of allies, which, according to Cassius Dio, numbered 120,000 (though this figure included women, children, and the elderly), attacked and burned Camulodunum to the ground. Indeed the Britons attacked with such ferocity that the destruction layer from the fire is still visible below ground in the form of a thick layer of red soot known to archaeologists as Boudica's Destruction Horizon.

In response to the attack, the Ninth Hispanic Legion (*IX Hispana*) under Quintus Petilius Cerialis was sent to relieve the settlement. The Britons were too strong, and the Legion suffered a serious defeat. The entire infantry was wiped out; only the commander and some of his cavalry escaped. Boudica and her allies then marched southward to the largest town in Roman Britain, the commercial center of Londinium (London).

When news of the British rebellion reached Seutonius, he realized that the Romans did not have the manpower to defend Londinium and decided to sacrifice it in order to help preserve Roman rule in the island. Accordingly Seutonius ordered the abandonment of Londinium, though a large number of the inhabitants remained behind. Boudica and her hoards swept through the city, burning and slaughtering as they went. As at Camulodunum, a thick red layer of burned debris is the archaeological evidence of the destruction. According to Tacitus, the Britons took no prisoners and massacred the 25,000 inhabitants—Romans and their Romano-British allies alike—without mercy. Excavations in London show that very few buildings in Londinium survived the fire. Cassius Dio paints a lurid and probably unreliable picture of the brutality of Boudica and her allies, playing on the theme of the savagery of the "natives" versus the sophistication of their Roman conquerors:

> Those who were taken captive by the Britons were subjected to every known form of outrage. The worst and most bestial atrocity committed by their captors was the following. They hung up naked

the noblest and most distinguished women and then cut off their breasts and sewed them to their mouths, in order to make the victims appear to be eating them; afterwards they impaled the women on sharp skewers run lengthwise through the entire body. All this they did to the accompaniment of sacrifices, banquets, and wanton behaviour, not only in all their other sacred places, but particularly in the grove of Andate. This was their name for Victory, and they regarded her with most exceptional reverence.

(Cassius Dio *History of Rome*
[Book LXII.7])

From Londinium the Britons moved north to another major Roman city, Verulamium (the modern city of St. Albans, Hertfordshire). The city seems not to have been occupied by Roman military forces at the time of Boudica's attack, but by Romano-British allies of the Romans. As at Londinium, those who did not flee were slaughtered mercilessly, and the city was razed to the ground. An estimated total of 70,000–80,000 people were killed in the three cities attacked by Boudica. It is impossible to tell how many were Roman soldiers, though it is likely that the majority were Roman and Romano-British citizens.

Meanwhile, Seutonius had regrouped his legions, the *XIV Gemina* (Fourteenth Twin Legion) and detachments of the *XX Valeria Victrix* (Twentieth Valerian Victorious Legion), and various auxiliary troops, in all perhaps around 10,000 men. According to Dio Cassius, Boudica's rebel hoard by then numbered close to 230,000 (in reality it was probably closer to 100,000), but they were desperately short of food, as Seutonius had arranged the burning of Roman food stores, which the Britons had depended on taking. Seutonius and his army took a stand to check the onslaught of the Britons at an as-yet-unidentified location, probably along the Roman road known as Watling Street, somewhere in the West Midlands. Although heavily outnumbered, the discipline and training of the Roman army combined with their mechanized field artillery soon began to gain the upper hand.

According to Tacitus, Boudica urged on her troops from her chariot but the lack of maneuverability of the large British force, encumbered by their wagons, supplies, and pack animals, and their exhausted state from hunger, put them at a severe disadvantage, and they were soon overrun. If we are to believe Tacitus, 80,000 Britons were killed in the battle, while the Roman army lost only 400 men. We do not know what happened to Boudica. Tacitus wrote that, rather than submitting herself to capture by the Romans, she took poison. Dio Cassius says she fell ill and died, and that the Britons gave her a lavish funeral. The Boudican rebellion of AD 61–62 had caused such a crisis in Rome that the emperor Nero had considered withdrawing all Roman forces from Britain, but after Seutonius's victory the Romans strengthened their military presence in the island.

Two fascinating archaeological mysteries associated with Boudica's last days are the location of the final battle and the whereabouts of her burial. Because according to Tacitus more than 80,000 are supposed to have been killed in the British defeat, it would be natural to assume that at least some remnants of the battle—huge burial pits for both humans and animals, for example—have been discovered, but that is not the case. Even the exact location is uncertain. We know that Boudica and her vast army were moving north from Verulamium, and that Seutonius and his troops were probably moving south from north Wales along the Roman Watling Street (the modern A5). The movements of the two armies are by no means certain, but if they were traveling in these directions, then a meeting somewhere in the English West Midlands seems likely.

High Cross in Leicestershire, on the junction of the Roman roads of Watling Street and Fosse Way, Cuttle Mill, Paulerspury, near Towcester (Roman *Lactodorum*) in Northamptonshire, and *Manduessedum* (modern Mancetter), near the modern town of Atherstone in Warwickshire, have all been suggested. However, so far none of these locations are supported by archaeological discoveries, and the exact location of the fateful battle remains a mystery.

A number of suggestions have been made over the centuries as to the location of Boudica's grave. These include a burial mound in Parliament Hill Fields, London, traditionally known as "Boadicea's Grave"; the Neolithic/Bronze Age site of Stonehenge; and even under one of the platforms (platform 9 or 10, apparently) in London's Kings Cross station. The latter is, however, no more than an urban legend and seems to originate with Scottish journalist and folklorist Lewis Spence in his book *Boadicea—Warrior Queen of the Britons* (1937). King's Cross Station was built over the site of the village of Battle Bridge in

1851/2, associated by some (probably due to its name) with Boudica's last battle. However, the original name of the bridge was Bradford ("Broad Ford") Bridge; it was corrupted in the Tudor period (1485 to 1603) to Battle Bridge.

A recently proposed site for the tomb of Queen Boudica is in the Birmingham suburb of Kings Norton, next to the local McDonald's, no less. One of the many sensationalistic news articles (from the BBC news Website) that reported the discovery of the site was entitled "Is Boudicca Buried in Birmingham?" However, the piece mentions nothing to connect the first and second centuries AD Roman finds from near Parson's Hill, Kings Norton, with Boudica. Admittedly, the site is in the West Midlands and close to a Roman road (Ryknild Street) and fort (Metchley Roman fort, partly contained within the main campus of the University of Birmingham). Although the area could conceivably be added to the list of possible locations for the final battle between the Romans and Britons, there is no reason to assume that Boudica is buried in the vicinity.

Despite her brutal excesses in battle, Boudica remains a heroic figure, one who was, after all, fighting to defend her entire culture. If her revolt had been successful, the Romans may have been driven out of Britain forever, and the culture, language, and subsequent history of Britain, Europe, and even perhaps the world, may have been very different. In 1902, a bronze statue of Boudica by Thomas Thornycroft was erected on Westminster Bridge in London. This iconic statue perhaps sums up the contradictory nature of Boudica: the Iceni queen is depicted heroically, armed with a spear and riding in a chariot with scythed wheels drawn by two rearing horses. Behind her stretches the vast expanse of modern London, the descendent of the city she once razed to the ground.

⧖

Chapter 28

Nero and the Great Fire of Rome (Italy)

Marble portrait of Nero, first century AD, from the Palatine Hill, Rome.

Nero is perhaps the most infamous of all the Roman rulers. Emperor from AD 54 to 68, Nero's reign has been associated with extravagance, oppression, and brutality. Very few surviving sources give favorable impression of him. He is said to have had his mother, adoptive brother, and first wife, Octavia, executed, and, most famously of all, played his fiddle while Rome was burning to the ground. Some sources blame Nero himself for starting the Great Fire of Rome in AD 64, and then afterward blaming the Christians for the act. Is there any truth behind this story? And how reliable is the picture we have today of Nero as a deranged, sadistic tyrant?

Building up a detailed picture of Nero's life and reign is problematic, as no contemporary sources have survived. Details of the emperor's life are based mainly on the *Annals* 12–16 of Tacitus (AD c. 56–c117), Suetonius's *Life of Nero* (AD 110) and the *Roman History,* Books 61–63, of Dio Cassius (AD c. 150–c235).

Nero was born Lucius Domitius Ahenobarbus on December 15, AD 37, in Antium, near Rome, the son of Cnaeus Domitius Ahenobarbus, a member of an ancient noble family. Through his mother, Agrippina, he was a great-grandson and the only surviving male descendant of Caesar Augustus, the first Roman Emperor. When he was 2 years old, Nero and his mother were banished by his brother, the Emperor Caligula, to the Pontian Islands (off the west coast of Italy) on charges of treason. Nero's father died in AD 40, leaving him the sole responsibility of Agrippina. After the murder of Caligula in AD 41 and the installation of Claudius (Agrippina's uncle) as Emperor, Agrippina and Nero were recalled from exile.

Claudius's wife, Valeria Messalina, died in AD 48. The following year Agrippina persuaded the emperor to marry her and make Nero his adopted son and heir, at the expense of his natural son, Britannicus. From then onward, her son became known as Tiberius Claudius Nero Caesar. On October 13, AD 54, Claudius died, allegedly after eating some poison mushrooms given to him by Agrippina. The same day, Nero, only 16 years of age, succeeded to the throne.

The following year Nero married Claudius's daughter, Octavia, though he soon became involved with the beautiful Poppaea Sabina, wife of his friend Marcus Salvius Otho. Agrippina, as mother of the new emperor, was at first a woman of great importance in Rome, and her portrait even appeared on some coins next to her son's. However, Nero did not wish to share power with anyone, and soon had his mother moved to a separate house, away from the imperial residence and the corridors of Roman power.

A series of brutal assassinations allegedly arranged by Nero himself followed. In February AD 55, Britannicus died at a dinner party in the palace—probably poisoned by Nero, who viewed the son of Claudius as a constant threat to his power. In AD 59, Agripinna was clubbed and stabbed to death on Nero's orders. The emperor's marriage to Octavia had never been a happy one, and in AD 62 he divorced her and married Poppaea. Octavia was then banished to the island of Pandateria (modern Ventotene) on a false charge of adultery, probably on the insistence of the new empress, Poppaea. She was later executed and her severed head was sent back to Rome.

The early years of Nero's rule were, however, not known only for atrocities. Under the influence of his tutor and advisor, Seneca (c. 4 BC–AD 65), and Praetorian prefect (Roman official, responsible for the imperial guard and the administration of justice), Burrus (AD 1–62), Nero often followed a somewhat liberal policy. He allowed slaves to file complaints against their masters, frequently gave criminals clemency rather than sign their death warrants, banned capital punishment, helped cities that had suffered from disasters, and lowered taxes.

Nero also devoted himself to his long-held artistic and literary interests, organizing poetry competitions and singing to the harp, at first only for a private audience but later on, much to the alarm of the Senate, in public. As Nero was emperor, no one was allowed to leave the auditorium during his performances. Historian Suetonius mentioned women giving birth during Nero recitals, and men faking death in order to be carried out. Nero was also extravagant with public funds, embarking on ambitious and costly building projects, even planning, supposedly, to pull down a third of Rome in order to construct a series of palaces that would be known as Neropolis. In AD 62, Seneca retired from public affairs after facing embezzlement charges, and Burrus died from an unknown illness, to be replaced by the ruthlessly devoted Gaius Ofonius Tigellinus.

On the night of July 18, AD 64, one of the worst disasters ever to hit the city of Rome occurred. Beginning in the southeastern part of the Circus Maximus (a large, open-air venue used for public events) close to the Palatine and Caelian Hills, a great fire ignited. Fanned by summer winds, the blaze spread through the shops filled with flammable goods clustered in the area and rapidly onward, destroying a vast swathe of the ancient city. We have very little in the way of eyewitness reports of the catastrophe, but in *The Annals* (Book XV, Chapters 33–47), written around AD 116, Roman historian Tacitus (who was 9 at the time of the fire) describes the scene:

> The flames, which in full career overran the level districts first, then shot up to the heights, and sank again to harry the lower parts, kept ahead of all remedial measures, the mischief travelling fast, and the town being an easy prey owing to the narrow, twisting lanes and formless streets typical of old Rome. In addition, shrieking and terrified women; fugitives stricken or immature in years; men consulting their own safety or the safety of others, as they dragged the infirm along or paused to wait for them, combined by their dilatoriness or their haste to impede everything.

> (*Annals*, 15.38)

According to Tacitus, not until the fire had been raging for six days, was it brought under control, by demolishing numerous buildings and clearing a vast area of open land, thus leaving nothing to feed the fire. However, this was not to be the end of the terrible blaze:

> But fear had not yet been laid aside, nor had hope yet returned to the people, when the fire resumed its ravages; in the less congested parts of the city, however; so that, while the toll of human life was not so great, the destruction of temples and of porticoes dedicated to pleasure was on a wider scale.

> (*Annals*, 15.40)

After the flames finally subsided, a large part of the city had been destroyed, though accounts vary as to the extent of the damage. Tacitus writes that the fire completely destroyed four out of the 14 Roman districts and seriously damaged seven. Other accounts state that 10 districts were left in ruins by the fire (about 70 percent of the city).

Nero's palace, the *Domus Transitoria* on the Palatine Hill, the Temple of Jupiter Stator, and the hearth in the Temple of Vesta were all gone. Hundreds of people were dead, and thousands were left homeless. Although popular legend holds that Emperor Nero fiddled while Rome burned, there is in fact no truth behind this. First, violins were not invented until around the 1520s. Tacitus does repeat the story that during the fire Nero "mounted his private stage and, reflecting present disasters in ancient calamities, sang about the destruction of Troy" (*Annals*, 15.39), but he takes care to state that it was only a rumor. More significantly, at the time the fire started, Tacitus describes Nero as being 35 miles away at his summer palace in Antium (modern Anzio).

According to Tacitus, upon hearing news of the fire, Nero rushed to Rome and immediately organized a relief effort, which included a team of firefighters and food and shelter for the survivors of the blaze. The emperor also began an ambitious rebuilding project for the city, which included widening the roads, reducing the height of tenement blocks, and constructing a new villa complex for himself—the "Golden House" (*Domus Aurea*), which still survives today.

Nevertheless, despite his efforts to rebuild the city, rumors began to circulate in Rome that Nero had started the fire himself. Some of the population had received word of the emperor's supposed plans for Neropolis and believed that this was enough motivation for him to start the blaze and thus clear space in the city for his new project. Ancient sources carry conflicting accounts regarding whether the fire was started deliberately or was an accident. Suetonius and Cassius Dio point the finger at Nero as the culprit, burning the city in order to construct a new imperial palace; Tacitus says that Christians confessed to causing the blaze. If Nero had started the fire, it seems odd that he would have allowed it to destroy parts of his own palace, the Domus Transitoria. Modern archaeological work in Rome has also cast some doubt on the theory that Nero caused the blaze. Excavations have discovered that the fire began not on the site of Nero's future villa, the *Domus Aurea*, but 0.62 miles away on the other side of the Palatine Hill.

Nevertheless, after the catastrophe, a significant part of Rome's population still mistrusted Nero. Tacitus wrote that to deflect the blame from himself, even if the fire had been an accident, Nero needed a scapegoat, and this was to be an obscure religious sect called the Christians. According to Tacitus, Nero began by arresting a few members of the sect who, under torture, implicated others in the crime. Spreading word that the Christians had burned Rome, Nero created huge resentment against the sect, who were mercilessly hunted down and put to death. Tacitus noted that Christians were convicted "not so much of the crime of firing the city, as of hatred against mankind" and that they were "covered with the skins of beasts, [and]...torn by dogs and perished, or were nailed to crosses, or were doomed to the flames and burnt" (*Annals*, 15.40).

Some traditions also associate the executions of St. Peter, crucified upside down on the Vatican hill, and St. Paul, beheaded along the Via Ostiensis, with Nero's persecution of Christians after the Great Fire. Professor Gerhard Baudy, of the University of Konstanz, Germany, believes that Nero was correct in blaming the Christians for setting the blaze. His studies have shown that in the poor districts of Rome at the time of the fire Christians were circulating apocalyptic texts predicting that the city would be destroyed by a terrible inferno. Baudy claims that the Christians believed they were fulfilling divine prophesies and that the fire was part of a revolt to bring down the Roman Empire.

Not all ancient historians agree with Tacitus's account of Nero's relentless persecution of the Christians. Although Seutonius, who was born around AD 71, says that "punishment was inflicted on the Christians, a class of men given to a new and mischievous superstition" (*The Life of Nero*, 16.2.) by Nero, this was not at the time of the Great Fire. He mentions no persecution of the Christians after the fire at all, merely saying that Nero "made no effort, however, to find the authors; in fact, when some of them were reported to the senate by an informer, he forbade their being very severely punished" (*Life of Nero*, 39.2.).

With as many as 100 minor fires breaking out every day in ancient Rome during the summer months, perhaps the Great Fire of Rome was the fault neither of Nero or the Christians after all, but a result of the poorly constructed wooden tenement buildings that covered much of the city. These building certainly allowed the fire to spread more rapidly.

Meanwhile, Nero's rule as emperor soon began to crumble. In AD 65 he was alleged to have kicked his pregnant wife, Poppaea, to death, though it is just as likely that she died in childbirth. In AD 68, faced with a revolt from the Gallic and Spanish legions, along with the Praetorian Guards, Nero fled Rome. The senate declared him a public enemy and facing execution, on June 9, AD 68, he committed suicide with an iron blade. With the death of Nero, the Julio-Claudian dynasty finally came to an end.

Chapter 29

The Ida Fossil
(Germany)

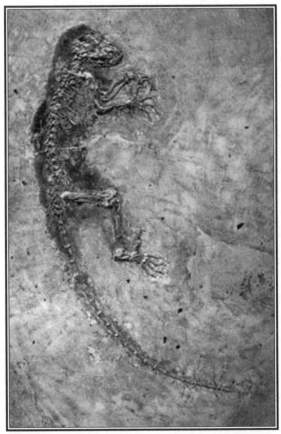

Main slab of the Darwinius masillae *holotype fossil.*

In May 2009, a fossil claimed by its discoverers to be a "missing link" was revealed to the world at a press conference at the American Museum of Natural History in New York. The event was highly publicized; the rock-star-like press conference even included a speech by Michael Bloomberg, the mayor of New York City. Amid all the hype and razzmatazz, though, is there any evidence that the controversial 47-million-year-old fossil, which has been nicknamed "Ida" (after the discoverer's young daughter), is really that long-sought Holy Grail of paleontology—the missing link in human evolution?

What has been dubbed "the greatest fossil discovery of all time" was found during an amateur excavation at the Messel Pit, an unused shale quarry in the district of Darmstadt-Dieburg, 22 miles southeast of Frankfurt, Germany. Once a volcanic lake, the Messel Pit is a treasure trove of extraordinarily well-preserved Eocene fossils from around 47 million years ago. The Eocene epoch, which lasted from approximately 55 to 35 million years ago, was a time in geological history significant for the emergence of many modern forms of mammals. Past discoveries at the Messel Pit include pygmy horses, large mice, primates, crocodiles, frogs, turtles, salamanders, more than 10,000 fossilized fish of various species, and large numbers of birds, as well as plants and insects. This vast array of excellently preserved fossils at Messel suggest that during the Eocene the lake periodically became a death trap for the surrounding fauna, spewing out huge amounts of poisonous volcanic gases that would have immediately suffocated anything in the vicinity. This extraordinary site was declared a UNESCO World Heritage Site on December 9, 1995.

In December 2006, paleontologist Dr. Jorn Hurum, of the University of Oslo's Natural History Museum, was approached by a German fossil dealer who offered to sell him the remains of a small, lemur-like juvenile female primate, measuring about 2 feet long (roughly the size of a small cat), for $1 million. Incredibly, the fossil was 95 percent complete, with only the left leg missing. Dr. Hurum was impressed and persuaded the Oslo museum to contribute half toward the purchase, with the rest of the sum to be provided if x-ray scans proved conclusively that the fossil was genuine. After tests had shown that the fossil was indeed authentic, Dr. Hurum bought the specimen for $750,000, and proceeded to assemble a team of scientists who worked in secret for two years to investigate it. This team included primate evolution expert Professor Philip Gingerich of the University of Michigan; Dr. Jens Franzen, former director of the Senckenberg Research Institute, Frankfurt; and Dr. Jörg Habersetzer, also of the Senckenberg Museum's Research Institute.

The scientists' findings shocked the scientific world. Dr. Hurum and his colleagues concluded from their research that the Ida fossil was on the human evolutionary line, the closest thing that humans can get to a direct ancestor. They classified the fossil as a member of the primate family *Notharctidae, subfamily Cercamoniinae*, implying that it was an important transitional form, possibly representing a missing link between the prosimian (lemurs and relatives) and simian (monkeys and apes) lineages of primates. They also identified Ida as belonging to a new species and gave her the formal scientific name *Darwinius masillae*, to celebrate both her place of origin and in honor of the bicentenary of the birth of Charles Darwin.

Dr. Hurum excitedly described Ida to the media as "like the Eighth Wonder of the World" and "our Mona Lisa." The team published their findings online in *PLoS ONE*, an open-access journal of the Public Library of Science on May 12, 2009, and a week later revealed their astonishing findings to the world at the New York press conference.

The scientists' research suggested that 47 million years ago Ida had been drinking from the Messel Lake when she was overcome by carbon dioxide fumes, became unconscious, and fell into the water. She quickly sank to the bottom, where she was covered in sediment, and over the millennia became fossilized. When Dr. Hurum and his colleagues examined the fossil they found it so well preserved that they could even discern traces of fur, as well as evidence of Ida's last meal of fruit and leaves in the preserved stomach contents. CT scans and x-ray images of the fossil revealed the presence of milk teeth and newly erupting permanent teeth, indicating that Ida was about 8 months old when she died, or the equivalent of a 6-year-old human.

A book and a History Channel documentary (both suggestively titled *The Link*) soon followed the announcement, accompanied by the launch of a Website, and it seemed that the discovery of the Ida Fossil was indeed as sensational as Dr. Hurum had claimed it to be. However, many scientists, including Dr. Chris Beard, curator of the Carnegie

Museum of Natural History, Pittsburgh, began to express concern about the highly publicized way in which the fossil had been revealed to the world, before enough information had been made available for scrutiny by the academic community. A number of scientists—Dr. Henry Gee, a senior editor at *Nature*, for example—also raised questions about the relative importance of the Ida Fossil and whether claims of it being a potential ancestor to humans were justified. Indeed, many scientists thought Dr. Hurum's assessment of the fossil as possibly representing a missing link between the two main branches of living primates highly questionable. They pointed out that *Darwinius masillae* bears very little resemblance to the earliest-known anthropoids.

A recent article in the science journal *Nature* (*Vol. 461, No. 7267*; October 22, 2009) by Dr. Seiffert, Assistant Professor in the Department of Anatomical Sciences at Stony Brook University, New York, and colleagues has cast serious doubts on the conclusions of Dr. Hurum and his team. The research represents the first independent evaluation of the claims made by Dr. Hurum in his paper in *PLoS ONE* and the History Channel television program. Dr. Seiffert and his team of researchers, which included Jonathan Perry, a Midwestern University paleoanthropologist, analyzed primate fossils to establish where their own discovery, a new genus and species dubbed *Afradapis*, and one of Ida's close relatives, belongs on the evolutionary tree. The 37-million-year-old *Afradapis* was discovered in 2001 by National Science Foundation (NSF)–supported paleontologists from three American universities near the Fayum Depression in northern Egypt, about 40 miles outside Cairo. Like *Darwinius, Afradapis* is an adapid, a diverse group of extinct lemur-like primates. Although *Afradapis longicristatus*, to give the fossil its full scientific name, was less-well-preserved than *Darwinius*, fragments of the teeth and jaw enabled the scientists to make some detailed comparisons between *Afradapis* and other primates.

To test these relationships, Dr. Seiffert and his colleagues compared the characteristics of 117 relevant fossils using cladistic analysis (a method of biological analysis that classifies organisms on the basis of shared ancestry). This is the type of analysis that should have been carried out by Hurum's team on *Darwinius* before holding a press conference, but it never was. The results of Seiffert and Perry's analysis showed that *Darwinius* and *Afradapis* were close together within the adapids, but that both were at the opposite side of the evolutionary tree to the anthropoids, situated nearer to the ancestors of living lemurs, lorises, and galagos, which are prosimian primates. In fact, the researchers discovered that *Darwinius* and *Afradapis* were even relatively distant on the tree from prosimians, which would suggest that they belonged to a group of specialized adapids that probably became extinct near the Eocene-Oligocene boundary, around 34 million years ago, leaving no living descendents. The implications of Dr. Seiffert and his team's work on the Ida Fossil are that *Darwinius*'s importance lies not in any supposed connection with human ancestry, but in our understanding of the origin of lemurs and lorises, which are our most distant primate relatives.

So does the Ida Fossil represent an evolutionary dead end rather than the sensational missing link claimed by Dr. Hurum and his colleagues? Although Dr. Hurum has described Dr. Seiffert's paper in *Nature* as "interesting" and was pleased that the scientific discussion around the specimen had begun, he naturally did not agree with the study's conclusions. In an e-mail to *The Scientist* (*www.the-scientist. com/blog/display/56110*), Hurum explained that he and his team had never claimed that *Darwinius* was an anthropoid. He went on to say:

> Although most [lemur-like primates] have obviously no phyloge-netic descendants and some are contemporaneous with the earli-est anthropoids, this does not exclude at least some of them from being members of the stem group from which all higher primates evolved.

Philip Gingerich, a University of Michigan paleontologist and member of the original team that analyzed the *Darwinius* fossil, is much more vociferous in his rejection of Dr. Seiffert's findings. Gingerich has stated that the conclusions of the article in *Nature* were implausible because of the *Afradapis* fossil's resemblance to a monkey. He points out that *Darwinius* exhibits other anthropoid-like characteristics, such as flat front teeth and interlocking canines, and still maintains that the Ida Fossil probably belongs to a primate group that led directly to anthropoids. The dispute over the Ida Fossil is not likely to be settled quickly, but in a sense that is how it should be; science works through such continued debate, assessment, and examination. Only after Dr.

Hurum's original data has been thoroughly scrutinized and criticized, and emerges in tact (or not), will it finally be accepted or rejected as a bona fide theory. High-profile press conferences, best-selling books, and TV documentaries cannot replace this process.

It is perhaps this PR angle of the whole Ida Fossil-as-missing-link story that has alienated the science community so much. Indeed the authors of the paper in *PLoS ONE* seem to have organized publicity on an unprecedented scale for a scientific discovery. Such was the PR surrounding the Ida Fossil that one got the impression that selling books and making popular TV programs were the prime concerns rather than communicating good science to the public. The fact that Dr. Hurum had apparently decided to sell film and book rights to *Darwinius* before details had been published in a peer-reviewed scientific journal is certainly worrying. If in the future science requires such absurd hype to promote its discoveries, then both the image of science and the understanding of evolution could become hopelessly distorted. In the end it is the data that matter, and the Ida Fossil, though it probably does not represent a "missing link" that challenges everything we knew about human evolution, is still a fascinating and important scientific discovery that adds considerably to our knowledge of the human evolutionary line.

Chapter 30

Hypatia of Alexandria
(Egypt)

Hypatia, *1885, by Charles William Mitchell.*

Hypatia (AD c. 380–415) was a mathematician, teacher, and philosopher who lived in the great intellectual capital of Alexandria, northern Egypt. The city was in Hypatia's time under Roman rule but had originally been founded by Alexander the Great c. 331 BC, around the small Egyptian port of Rhacotis. Hypatia is considered the first noteworthy female in mathematics, and has also come to prominence for being both a woman and a pagan at a time when Christianity was sweeping through the Roman Empire. However, the name Hypatia has entered history books mainly because of her brutal murder at the hands of a Christian mob around AD 415. Since her death, the figure of a tragic and heroic Hypatia has become established in the popular mind by legions of writers, artists, poets, and feminists, so much so that the real woman has become obscured by the legend.

Despite the facts known about her infamous death, Hypatia remains today somewhat of a mysterious figure. Though 19th-century romantics envisaged Hypatia as a Classical beauty, no images of her are known to exist. Details of her life are also vague, and only fragments of her writings have survived. The main primary sources for her life and work are extremely limited. There are letters written to her and fellow students by her pupil Synesius of Cyrene (Cyrene was an ancient Greek colony in present-day Libya), an entry in the *Suda Lexicon* (a 10th-century Byzantine Greek historical encyclopedia of the ancient Mediterranean world), a passage in the *Ecclesiastical History* of Greek Christian church historian Socrates Scholasticus (completed AD c. 439), and an excerpt from *The Chronicle* of John of Nikiû, a seventh-century Egyptian Coptic bishop of Nikiou (in the Egyptian Delta).

From these sources we can form at least the bare bones of the life and death of this remarkable woman. Hypatia was born somewhere between AD 355 and AD 380, the daughter of Greek mathematician and astronomer Theon (AD c. 335–c. 405), who, according to some sources, was the last fellow of the Museum of Alexandria, part of the great Library of Alexandria. Theon is best known today as the source of the text of Euclid's *Elements*. Hypatia's father seems to have guided her in the study of mathematics, and she was an exceptional pupil. She became a teacher at the Museum, though sources state that she instructed her pupils privately in her home. Hypatia was a gifted and charismatic teacher who donned the philosopher's cloak rather than typical women's attire. The *Suda Lexicon* describes her as a virtuous and beautiful woman that remained a virgin throughout her entire life. To illustrate this virtue and perhaps also Hypatia's view of romantic love, the *Suda* records a story that involved a pupil who was overcome with infatuation for her. To cool his passion, Hypatia is said to have shown him her bloody menstrual rags, telling him, "This is what you love, young man, and it isn't beautiful" (*The Life of Hypatia*, from Damascius's *Life of Isidore*, reproduced in the *Suda*; translated by Jeremiah Reedy). Understandably shocked at this action, the pupil's feelings changed instantaneously, and he went away a better human being for the experience.

Hypatia traveled to both Athens and Italy to study before, around AD 400, she was appointed head of the Platonist school of Alexandria, teaching philosophy, mathematics, astronomy, and astrology. According to the *Suda*, Hypatia's teaching included the works of Plato and Aristotle, and other sources state that she also based much of her teachings on those of Plotinus (AD c. 204–270), the founder of Neoplatonism, and Iamblichus (AD c. 250–325) author of the influential treatise *Theurgia*, or *On the Mysteries of Egypt*, which deals with a higher magic operating through the influence of the gods. Hypatia was honored more for her mathematics than her philosophy and astronomy. It is recorded that she worked on the on the ideas of conic sections (a curve created by intersecting a cone with a plane) introduced by Greek mathematician Apollonius of Perga (c. 262–c. 190 BC), and edited the work *On the Conics of Apollonius.*

Many of Hypatia's students seem to have been Christians, and some went on to successful careers in politics and religion. One of these was Synesius of Cyrene, who later became the Bishop of Ptolemais (in Libya). The fact that Hypatia's pupils included Christians would indicate that for a time there was very little if any tension between her pagan teachings and the church leaders in Alexandria. Nevertheless, during Hypatia's lifetime there was frequent conflict between pagans and Christians, as well as in-fighting between competing Christian sects, and contemporary political and ecclesiastical events in Alexandria were bound to affect her sooner or later. In 391, Roman Emperor Theodosius I (AD 347–395) ordered the closure of all pagan temples, and pagan worship was forbidden under threat of harsh punishment. In the same year, Theophilus, the patriarch (Christian bishop) of Alexandria, destroyed a number of pagan temples in the city, including the Serapeum (a temple of the Hellenistic-Egyptian god Serapis, whose precinct housed a daughter library of the great Library of Alexandria).

Theophilus's successor in Alexandria was his nephew Cyril (later St. Cyril), who was made the patriarch in AD 412, and soon became involved in a power struggle with the prefect of the city Orestes, a close friend of Hypatia. It is reasonable to suppose that Orestes had the support of Hypatia in this conflict, and probably a number of her politically influential pupils too. It is believed that Hypatia was the source of the problems between the two leaders; perhaps a mix of her paganism, her popularity, and the fact that she was a woman made her a dangerous figure in the eyes of Cyril. It has also been suggested Hypatia, with her public profile and support of Orestes, may have become the focal point of riots between Christians and pagans. For whatever reason Cyril began spreading rumors that Hypatia was a witch involved in sorcery and black magic. In the *Suda*, a single incident is recorded as being responsible for provoking Cyril to have Hypatia murdered. Though such a simple explanation is unlikely, something of this sort may have been one contributing factor:

> Thus it happened one day that Cyril, bishop of the opposition sect [i.e. Christianity] was passing by Hypatia's house, and he saw a great crowd of people and horses in front of her door. Some were arriving, some departing, and others standing around. When he asked why there was a crowd there and what all the fuss was about, he was told by her followers that it was the house of Hypatia the philosopher and she was about to greet them. When Cyril learned this he was so struck with envy that he immediately began plotting

Accounts vary regarding what happened next, but the basic facts are that in March AD 415, Hypatia was seized in the street (in some versions she was driving her chariot at the time) by a mob led by a band of fanatical Christian monks, with a Christian magistrate named Peter (believed to be *Peter the Reader*, a cohort of Cyril) at its head. The mob stripped her and dragged her through the streets to the Alexandrian church of the Caesareum (formerly a pagan temple), where they brutally murdered her by repeatedly hacking at her flesh with jagged pieces of broken pottery and/or bits of oyster shell. Her dismembered body was then taken to a place named Cinaron and burned.

Sometime after these horrific events a distraught Orestes sanctioned the execution of a Christian monk named Hierax for his supposed part in the murder of Hypatia. It was probably because of this, and also because Orestes was strongly opposed to Cyril's expulsion of the Jews from Alexandria, that within days of the execution of Hierax, Orestes was himself murdered by Christian monks. After the murders of Hypatia and Orestes, Bishop Cyril is reported to have informed the people of Alexandria that Hypatia had gone to Athens and that the prefect Orestes had resigned and fled the city.

The explanations put forward for Hypatia's murder are numerous, but outside the most likely reason—her friendship and public support of the prefect Orestes—a very plausible and interesting theory has been put forward by author Maria Dzielska in her book, *Hypatia of Alexandria (Revealing Antiquity)* (Harvard University Press, 1996). Dzielska proposes that Hypatia was not murdered for her pagan philosophy but because she was falsely accused of sorcery. She notes that the gruesome manner of Hypatia's murder (the use of oyster shells to hack at her body) matches the prescribed punishment for witchcraft at the time. Perhaps the monks also used the biblical verse "Thou shalt not suffer a witch to live" (Exodus 22:18) as justification for their brutal actions. Controversially, Dzielska also believes that, rather than being a relatively young or middle-aged woman, Hypatia was in fact in her 60s when she was murdered. However, this seems unlikely: if Hypatia had been born in AD 350, then her father Theon would only have been 15 years old at the time. It is much more probable that Hypatia was born between AD 370 and AD 380, and was thus either in her mid-30s or 40s when she died.

There has been much speculation over the centuries as to Hypatia's actual contribution to science, mathematics, and philosophy, and to the exact works she authored. For example, some sources credit Hypatia as the inventor of the astrolabe. The astrolabe was in some senses an ancient astronomical computer, which could have multiple purposes, but was basically used to show how the sky looked at a specific place at a given time. In a letter to a certain Paeonius, Hypatia's pupil Synesius claims that he designed the astrolabe himself with help from Hypatia, and had it manufactured by the very best silversmiths. Although Hypatia's father, Theon, did write a treatise on the astrolabe that became the basis for much that was written on the subject in the Middle Ages, the oldest-known astrolabes date back a century before his time, perhaps more. Claudius Ptolemy, an astronomer, geographer, and mathematician who died in Alexandria around AD 168, wrote extensively about the astrolabe in his work the *Planisphaerium*, from which it can be deduced that he may have owned such an instrument.

Another letter by Synesius, written to Hypatia herself, asks her to construct a hydrometer for him, giving detailed specifications for the work. A hydrometer is a sealed tube about the size of a flute, weighted at one end, and was the first laboratory device to measure the specific gravity (or relative density) of liquids. Synesius's letter is the first-known reference to the hydrometer in history, and it remains possible that Hypatia may have been its original inventor, though there are conflicting opinions as to the instrument's true origins.

Unfortunately, the written works of Hypatia are known to us today only through the writings of others who quoted them. Perhaps some of her works disappeared with the destruction of the Great Library of Alexandria (though this disaster may have been a gradual process lasting centuries, rather than a single catastrophic event). Hypatia's main works, attributed to her by later writers, are a commentary on the 13-volume *Arithmetica* of Diophantus, a commentary on the *Conics* of Apollonious, and possibly a commentary on Ptolemy's astronomical works, though this is far from certain. She also edited the third book of her father Theon's commentary on the *Almagest* of Ptolemy, and may also have assisted him in producing a new version of Euclid's *Elements*. On the evidence available, historians doubt that Hypatia carried out any original mathematical research herself, though they are in agreement that she was a highly skilled compiler and editor of earlier mathematical works.

Despite the limited amount of Hypatia's work surviving, her influence remained strong throughout the centuries, with Descartes, Newton, and Leibniz all expanding on her work. For a woman of her time, in the volatile atmosphere of late-fourth/early-fifth-century

Alexandria, Hypatia's achievements remain extraordinary. The legend of Hyptia has grown from the nature of her death, rather than her life. The graphic image of the beautiful young pagan torn to shreds by the fanatical Christians for preaching the old gods, though only partially true, has remained etched on the brains of artists and thinkers for 1,600 years. Like all legends surrounding great women in history, from Joan of Arc to Amelia Earhart, it has taken on a life of its own, tailored to suit the fashions and needs of the times or of whomever chooses to look back on the "martyrdom" of Hypatia of Alexandria.

⧗

Chapter 31

Cleopatra: The Last Pharaoh of Egypt (Egypt)

Statue of Cleopatra as Egyptian goddess, first century BC, Hermitage, Saint Petersburg.

Regarded by the Romans as "fatale monstrum"—a fatal omen—Cleopatra is one of the ancient world's most popular, though elusive, figures. The Egyptian queen has been immortalized by numerous writers and film-makers, most popularly by Shakespeare in *Antony and Cleopatra*, and by Hollywood in *Cleopatra* (1963), starring Elizabeth Taylor and Richard Burton. The latter work features the memorable image of the enticing young Cleopatra emerging gracefully from an unfurled carpet in front of Roman general Julius Caesar. Who was the real Cleopatra? Is she to be regarded merely as the lover of Julius Caesar and Mark Antony? Or did she play an important role not only in the history of Egypt, but also in that of the mighty Roman Republic?

Cleopatra VII Philopator ("father-loving") was born in January 69 BC in the city of Alexandria, and died on August 12, 30 BC. She was the daughter of Ptolemy XII Auletes (117–51 BC) and possibly Cleopatra V Tryphaena (c. 95–c. 57 BC), and was to become the last monarch of the Ptolemaic Empire, ruling Egypt from 51 BC to 30 BC.

The Ptolemaic Kingdom was established following the death of Alexander the Great in Babylon in 323 BC, when his generals divided up his Empire, each setting up their own kingdoms. One of these generals, Ptolemy I Soter, declared himself Pharaoh of Egypt in 305 BC, establishing the last dynasty that would rule Egypt under the title of Pharaoh. One extraordinary feature of the Ptolemaic monarchy was the important role played by women (there were no less than seven Ptolemaic queens named Cleopatra), who attained the throne because their sons or brothers were too young.

After the death of her father, Ptolemy XII, in 51 BC, 17-year-old Cleopatra and her 12-year-old brother, Ptolemy XIII, whom she probably also married in accordance with her father's will, became joint rulers of Egypt. In 49 BC, after a power struggle over the throne with her brother, who was backed by various members of the Egyptian court at Alexandria, mainly the eunuch Pothinus (who acted as regent for him), Cleopatra was forced from the palace and fled to Syria, where her father had many friends. Here she assembled a small army of Arab tribesmen and attempted to invade Egypt, via Pelusium, a city on the country's northeast frontier. Cleopatra and her army were defeated by Ptolemy XIII's forces.

A few months later, a Roman army of 10 warships and around 4,000 men led by Julius Caesar were heading for Alexandria in pursuit of Gnaeus Pompeius Magnus (also known as Pompey the Great), who was attempting to find refuge with Ptolemy XIII. However, factions in the Ptolemaic court led by Pothinus viewed the arriving Pompey as a danger to their relationship with Caesar, and so, on September 28, 48 BC, they had the Roman general stabbed to death as he stepped ashore. He was decapitated and his body was left lying on the shoreline, the embalmed head later being presented to Caesar, who reportedly turned away in disgust at the sight.

In Caesar and his army, Cleopatra saw an opportunity to return to power, and Caesar shrewdly observed in Cleopatra someone who could help him obtain a repayment of the debts incurred by her father, Ptolemy XII Auletes—funds that he desperately needed in his struggle to retain his throne. It seems probable that Cleopatra arranged to have herself smuggled into the presence of the 54-year-old Caesar wrapped up inside a sleeping bag (or a bundle of bedclothes, in other sources). After this daring exploit, Caesar and Cleopatra became lovers, and Caesar had her officially returned to the throne as co-ruler with her brother, probably because her saw her as a monarch who could be manipulated from Rome. However, realizing the relatively small size of the army Caesar had brought over with him, Ptolemy XIII allied himself with his (and probably also Cleopatra's) sister, Arsinoë IV, in an attempt to depose Cleopatra. The resulting Alexandrian War took place in mid-December 48 BC within the city of Alexandria itself, and was decided in Caesar's favour by the arrival of Roman reinforcements from Pergamum (a city in modern western Turkey).

Ptolemy XIII and Arsinoë IV were forced to flee the city, and Ptolemy was reportedly drowned on January 13, 47 BC, while attempting to cross the Nile. Arsinoë escaped and joined the Egyptian army under Achillas, who gave her the title of Pharaoh in opposition to her possible sister, Cleopatra. She was later captured by Caesar's army and transported to Rome. Cleopatra VII was now the unchallenged sole ruler of Egypt, though tradition dictated that she name her younger brother, Ptolemy XIV, her new co-ruler. In 46 BC, Caesar returned to Rome in triumph, bringing with him Cleopatra and their newborn son, Caesarion ("little Caesar"). Soon after his arrival in Rome, Caesar organized a four-day Triumph to celebrate his victories over foreign enemies, which included Cleopatra's hostile possible sister, Arsinoë, being paraded through the streets in chains. The Roman public's unexpected sympathy for the pathetic figure of Arsinoë tramping through the streets in irons persuaded Caesar to spare her life, and she was exiled to the temple of Artemis at Ephesus (in modern western Turkey).

Cleopatra returned to Rome just more than a year later, in 44 BC, and was in the city when, on March 15th of that year, Caesar was assassinated. With her ally and lover gone, Cleopatra left Rome and returned to Alexandria. The death of Caesar threw Rome into turmoil, with various factions competing for control, the most important of these being the armies of Mark Antony (83–30 BC) and Octavian (63 BC –AD 14), the former a supporter and loyal friend Caesar, the latter his adopted son. Cleopatra had to tread carefully in this potentially lethal political climate.

Soon after Cleopatra's return to Egypt, her brother and co-ruler, Ptolemy XIV, died mysteriously—possibly poisoned on her instruction. Cleopatra's hold on power in Egypt was now secure, ruling with her infant son, Ptolemy XV Caesar. But there were difficulties ahead: In the years 43 and 42 BC she was faced with severe famine and plague in Egypt, caused by the extremely low levels of the Nile flood. Through astute political dealings, Cleopatra managed to guide Egypt through these difficult years, and in 41 BC she was summoned to Tarsus (in modern southern Turkey) by Mark Antony. Cleopatra is said to have entered the city by sailing up the Cydnus River in a decorated barge with purple sails, while dressed in the robes of the Greek goddess Aphrodite. Antony, who equated himself with the god Dionysus, was instantly won over. Much like the meeting between Cleopatra and Caesar, both sides saw something in the other that they needed. For Cleopatra, it was another opportunity to achieve power both in Egypt and in Rome; for Antony, the support of Rome's largest and wealthiest client states in his campaign against the might of the Parthians (Parthia was a region in modern northeastern Iran) was highly desirable. At the meeting, Cleopatra allegedly requested Arsinoë, still living in protection at the Temple of Artemis at Ephesus, be executed to prevent any future attempts on her throne.

Antony and Cleopatra soon became allies and lovers, and he returned with her to Alexandria in 40 BC. In Alexandria, Cleopatra and Antony formed a society of "inimitable livers," which some historians have interpreted as an excuse to lead a life of debauchery, though it was more likely to have been a group dedicated to the cult of the mystical god Dionysus. In that year Cleopatra bore Antony twins Alexander Helios (the Sun) and Cleopatra Selene (the Moon).

The political situation in Rome compelled Antony to return to Italy, where he was forced to conclude a temporary settlement with Octavian, part of which was that he married Octavian's sister, Octavia. It was three years before he and Cleopatra met again, at the city of Antioch (near the modern Turkey/Syria border) under the shadow of Octavian's growing military power in the West. One result of this meeting was that Cleopatra became pregnant with her third child by Antony (the future Ptolemy Philadelphus); another was that parts of Rome's eastern possessions came under Cleopatra's control.

In 34 BC, despite the fact that Antony's Parthian campaign had been an extravagant failure, Antony and Cleopatra celebrated a mock Roman Triumph in the streets of Alexandria. Crowds flocked to the Gymnasium to see the couple seated on golden thrones surrounded by their children, and Antony made a proclamation known today as the "Donations of Alexandria." In this declaration, Antony distributed lands held by Rome and Parthia among Cleopatra and their children, and proclaimed Caesarion as Caesar's legitimate son. Not surprisingly, the Donations of Alexandria caused outrage in Rome, where the rumor began to spread that Antony intended to transfer the empire's capital from Rome to Alexandria. In 32 BC, Octavian had the Senate deprive Antony of his powers and declare war against Cleopatra, calling her a whore and a drunken Oriental. To avoid another civil war, Antony was not mentioned in the declaration, but this was to no avail, as Antony decided to join the war on Cleopatra's side. The culmination of the war came at the naval Battle of Actium, which took place near the town of Preveza, northwestern Greece, on September 2, 31 BC. Here Mark Antony and Cleopatra's combined force of 230 vessels and 50,000 sailors were defeated by Octavian's navy commanded by Marcus Vipsanius Agrippa, effectively handing control of the Roman world over to Octavian.

In 30 BC, Octavian invaded Egypt and laid siege to Alexandria. Hopelessly outnumbered, Anthony's forces surrendered and, in the honorable Roman tradition, Antony committed suicide by falling on his sword. After Antony's death, Cleopatra was taken to Octavian, who informed her that she would be brought to Rome and paraded in the streets as part of his triumph. Perhaps unable to bear the thought of suffering the same humiliation as Arsinoë many years earlier, on August 12, 30 BC, Cleopatra dressed in her royal robes and lay upon a golden couch with a diadem on her brow. According to tradition (found in ancient historian Plutarch, for example) she had an asp (an Egyptian cobra) brought to her concealed in a basket of figs, and died from the bite. Two of her female servants died with her. The asp was a symbol of divine royalty to the Egyptians, so by allowing the asp to bite her, Cleopatra became immortal. Other historians (including Joyce Tyldesley) believe that Cleopatra used either a poisonous ointment or a took a vial of poison to commit suicide. Cleopatra lived 39 years; for 22 years she reigned as queen; and for 14 years was Antony's partner in his empire. After her death, her son Caesarion was declared pharaoh, but he was soon executed on Octavian's orders. Her other children were sent to Rome to be raised by Antony's wife, Octavia.

Cleopatra represented the last significant threat to Roman authority, and her death also marks the end of the Ptolemaic Kingdom. The vast treasures of Egypt were plundered by Octavian, and Egypt itself became a new Roman province. Within a few years, the Senate named Octavian *Augustus*, and he became the first Roman Emperor, consolidating the western and eastern halves of the Republic into a Roman Empire.

Octavian later published his biography, in which he stripped Cleopatra of her political ability and portrayed her as an immoral foreigner and a temptress of upright Roman men. A number of Roman historians and writers (poets Horace [65–8 BC] and Lucan [AD 39–65], for example) reinforced the image of Cleopatra as an incestuous, adulterous whore who used sex to try to emasculate the Roman Empire. Unfortunately, this result of Roman propaganda has had a profound influence on the image of Cleopatra that has passed into Western culture. The real Cleopatra was highly skilled politically (though ruthless with her enemies), was popular with her subjects, spoke seven languages, and was said to be the only Ptolemy to read and speak Egyptian intelligently. It is also a sobering thought to remember how different the history of Western civilization might have been if she had managed to create an Eastern empire to rival the increasing might of Rome, which she very nearly succeeded in doing.

Recent archaeological work has cast interesting light on two aspects of Cleopatra's life: the location of her tomb, and the death of her possible sister, Arsinoë. Greco-Roman historian Plutarch wrote that Antony and Cleopatra were buried together and, in 2008, archaeologists from the Egyptian Supreme Council of Antiquities and from the Dominican Republic, working at the Temple of Taposiris Magna, 28 miles west of Alexandria, reported that one of the chambers in the building probably contained the bodies of Cleopatra and Mark Antony. The team have so far discovered 22 bronze coins inscribed with Cleopatra's name, and bearing her image, a bust of Cleopatra, and an alabaster mask believed to represent Mark Antony. Work at the site is ongoing, and only time will tell if the archaeologist are correct in their theory that the great couple were interred at such a distance from Alexandria.

In 1926 the body of a young aristocratic woman of approximately 15–18 years of age was discovered in an octagonal tomb in Ephesus, dating to the period 50 to 20 BC. Some researchers, including Hilke Thür of the Austrian Academy of Sciences, believe that this skeleton is the murdered Arsinoë. Although the skull was lost in Germany during World War II, Caroline Wilkinson, a forensic anthropologist, has reconstructed the missing skull using computer technology based on measurements taken in the 1920s. According to Wilkinson, the long head shape indicates a possible black African origin, which led to various newspapers (including the *Times Online*; *www.timesonline. co.uk/tol/news/world/middle_east/article5908494.ece*) to proclaim that Cleopatra herself was not ethnically Greek or Macedonian, but of mixed race, at least part African. The story of the discovery was also the subject of a BBC documentary, sensationally (and unnecessarily) entitled *Cleopatra: Portrait of a Killer*.

However, it is important to remember that these conclusions have been reached not by examining the actual skull of the body (which has long since disappeared) but by studying the measurements of the skull left by the first excavators of the Octagonal Tomb in the 1920s.

Furthermore, as the identity of Cleopatra's mother is uncertain, we don't actually know that Cleopatra and Arsinoë were full sisters—or even related by blood at all. Two nagging doubts also remain about the body in the Octagonal Tomb being that of Arsinoë. First, if Arsinoë had been banished to Ephesus, why would she have been buried in a rich ornate tomb at all? Second, if the age of the body is 15–17, possibly 18, with a death date of 41 BC, that would mean that Arsinoë was born between 59 and 55 BC. Consequently, at the time of the Alexandrian War in 48 BC, she was between 8 and 11—surely far too young to have played such a pivotal role in events? Perhaps detailed DNA tests on the skeleton from the Octagonal Tomb will one day help clear the matter up and give us further insight into the fascinating life of Cleopatra VII of Egypt.

Chapter 32

Who Were the Phoenicians?
(Lebanon)

Stelae on the Tophet of Carthage.

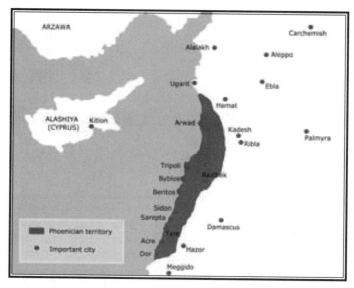

Map of Phoenicia.

The ancient land of Phoenicia was centered on coastal areas of what is now Lebanon, and extended into parts of Israel, Syria, and Palestine. The Phoenicians were an enterprising maritime trading culture that was descended from the original Canaanites, who lived in the region during the Bronze Age (c. 3000–1200 BC). By 700 BC, the Phoenicians had expanded to dominate the Mediterranean area, establishing emporiums and colonies from Cyprus in the east to the Aegean Sea, Italy, the coast of North of Africa, and the Atlantic coast of Spain in the west. According to ancient Greek historian Herodotus, the Phoenicians even managed to circumnavigate Africa, a feat that would not be repeated until the 15th century AD. Perhaps the most important gift from the Phoenicians to the Western world was the alphabet, whose signs and names still exist today through the medium of Greek. Recently, DNA testing has been revealing some intriguing facts on the location of the living descendents of the Phoenicians.

Although the Phoenicians established a number of large cities throughout the Mediterranean and are mentioned in a number of ancient sources, we know surprisingly little about them. The earliest references to the antecedents of the Phoenicians, the Canaanites, come in the form of clay cuneiform tablets from Ebla, in northwestern Syria. This archive dates from the mid-third millennium BC, and, when examined in conjunction with Egyptian inscriptions from around the same period (which mention ships from the city of Byblos transporting cedar wood and oil), we can already see at this early date the seeds of the great maritime trading culture that was to become the Phoenicians.

Texts from the the great port city of Ugarit (modern Ras Shamra), on the Mediterranean coast of Syria, dating to the 14th and 13th centuries BC, are a vital source for information about Phoenician religion and myth. Phoenician inscriptions of usually no more than a few lines, many on funerary stele (an upright stone with an inscribed or sculptured surface), both from their own coastal cities and from their colonies further afield, add a little more detail to our knowledge of the culture. In the 14th century BC, in the Amarna tablets from the Upper Egyptian site of Amarna, mostly written in Akkadian cuneiform (the writing system of ancient Mesopotamia), the Phoenicians refer to themselves as *Kenaani* or *Kinaani* ("Canaanites"), not Phoenicians, which is a word of Greek origin.

There are also numerous, usually hostile, references to Canaan and the Canaanites in the Bible, as well as to Phoenicia. In the Gospel of Mark, for example, we have "The woman was a Greek, born in Syrian Phoenicia. She begged Jesus to drive the demon out of her daughter" (Mark 7:26). Hiram, king of the Phoenician city of Tyre (in modern-day Lebanon), is also mentioned in the Bible as sending a master craftsman to King Solomon to help in the construction of the First Temple of Jerusalem:

> I am sending you Huram-Abi, a man of great skill, the son of a Danite woman and a Tyrian father, who knows how to work in gold, silver, bronze, iron, stone and wood, and in purple, violet, linen and crimson fabrics, and who knows how to make all kinds of engravings and to execute any design which may be assigned to him, to work with your skilled men and with those of my lord David your father.
>
> 2 Chronicals 2:13-14

The high point of Phoenician civilization was between the ninth and the sixth centuries BC, when they established the first trading system ever to dominate the entire Mediterranean. Apart from the great trading cities in their homeland, such as Tyre, Sidon, Byblos, Acco, and Berytus (modern Beirut), the Phoenicians established colonies in Cyprus; Sardinia; Sicily; Malta; North Africa, such as the great city of Carthage (in Tunisia), Tripolis (in Libya), and Ikosim (Algiers); and Spain, such as Gadir (Cádiz), Malaca (Malaga), and Ibossim (modern Ibiza). What drove the Phoenicians so far west in search of trade seems to have been the rich deposits of silver, copper, and tin in the Iberian Peninsula (modern-day Spain, Portugal, Andorra, and Gibraltar). First-century BC Greek historian Diodorus Siculus states that the Phoenicians made considerable profit from exploiting the silver mines of southern Spain and transporting the produce to Greece and the Near East. The Phoenicians would have been able to trade products such as wine, olive oil, the timber from the famous cedars of Lebanon, and "Tyrian Purple" for these metals. In fact, Phoenician trade was in part founded on Tyrian Purple, a purple-red dye derived from various species of marine molluscs, notably murex, once widely available in coastal waters of the eastern Mediterranean. In many ancient cultures this color was reserved for the use of royalty or nobility.

One result of the extensive and far-reaching trading activities of the Phoenicians in the Mediterranean was the spread of the Canaanite-Phoenician alphabet. The Phoenician alphabet developed from the North Semitic alphabet, used in Syria as early as the 11th century BC, and is the ancestor to Arabic, Hebrew, Latin, and Greek scripts. In Phoenicia proper, the Phoenician script remained in use until around the first century BC; variants of the parent alphabet developed in its colonies, such as the Punic and neo-Punic alphabets of Carthage, which continued to be written until about the third century AD. St. Augustine (Augustine of Hippo; AD 354–430), Berber (North African) philosopher and theologian, is believed to be the last important ancient writer with knowledge of the Punic script.

The Phoenicians have also been credited with the rebirth of Mediterranean economy and culture after the Late Bronze Age collapse (in the 12th century BC) of important cultures, such as the Mycenaeans and the Hittites. It is believed that beginning in the 10th century BC, the Phoenicians re-established long-distance trade and reopened sea routes, and also played a significant role in the beginning of the Orientalizing Period in Greece in the late eighth century BC. This cultural revolution in Greece, based on renewed contact with the Near East and Egypt, brought Greece out of the isolation of the Dark Ages (c. 1200–800 BC) and laid the foundations for the Classical Greece of the sixth to fourth centuries BC.

One achievement attributed to the Phoenicians by Herodotus (c. 484–c. 425 BC) that has caused a good deal of controversy among scholars is their supposed circumnavigation of Africa. Herodotus describes it thus:

> Libya is washed on all sides by the sea except where it joins Asia, as was first demonstrated, so far as our knowledge goes, by the Egyptian king Necho, who, after calling off the construction of the canal between the Nile and the Arabian gulf, sent out a fleet manned by a Phoenician crew with orders to sail west about and return to Egypt and the Mediterranean by way of the Straits of Gibraltar. The Phoenicians sailed from the Arabian gulf into the southern ocean, and every autumn put in at some convenient spot on the Libyan coast, sowed a patch of ground, and waited for next year's harvest. Then, having got in their grain, they put to sea again, and after two full years rounded the Pillars of Heracles in the course of the third, and returned to Egypt. These men made a statement which I do not myself believe, though others may, to the effect that as they sailed on a westerly course round the southern end of Libya, they had the sun on their right—to northward of them. This is how Libya was first discovered by sea.
>
> (Herodotus, *The Histories* 4.42, tr. Aubrey de Selincourt)

According to this statement, Phoenician sailors in the employ of Pharaoh Necho II of Egypt (c. 600 BC) circumnavigated the continent of Africa some 2,000 years before Portuguese mariner Bartolomeus Diaz reached the Cape of Good Hope in 1488. Ironically, the part of the story that Herodotus did not believe—that the sailors had their sun on their right—is what would appear to confirm the truth of the voyage. Sailing around the Cape of Good Hope, the Phoenicians would have sailed into the southern hemisphere, where the sun does appear on the right when traveling westward. If the Phoenicians did not round Africa, it seems unlikely that they would have known this fact. Although there is no other evidence for the circumnavigation of the continent apart from the account in Herodotus, the voyage is not completely unfeasible; sailing around Africa the Phoenicians would have been in site of land almost the whole time. If this incredible expedition did indeed take place, then it must rank as one of the greatest exploration voyages in history.

The decline of Phoenician dominance in the Mediterranean began when the Persian leader Cyrus the Great conquered their homeland in 539 BC. A large amount of the population probably migrated to Carthage and other colonies following the Persian conquest, and Phoenician culture and trade were maintained from these cities. After Alexander the Great conquered Tyre in 332 BC, and Hellenic Greece rose to prominence in the Eastern Mediterranean, the Phoenicians lost control of trade in the area and gradually their culture vanished almost entirely from their motherland.

The greatest and most prosperous of Phoenician colonies was Carthage (Latin—*Carthago*, from the Phoenician *Qart-hadašt*, meaning "new town"), located near modern Tunis and founded by the Phoenicians in the ninth century BC. The colony developed into a large, rich city and became a major power in the Mediterranean with the decline of Tyre in the sixth century, after Cyrus the Great's conquest. Such was the importance of Carthage that it soon became a rival to the Greek city of Syracuse (in Sicily) and eventually to Rome also. This rivalry resulted in several wars known as the Punic Wars, which were fought between Rome and Carthage from 264 to 146 BC. Hannibal's famous invasion of Italy took place during the Second Punic War, and culminated in a Carthaginian victory near the town of Cannae in Apulia, southeast Italy, in 216 BC. This victory posed a serious threat to the spread of the Roman Empire, but, despite years of fighting in Italy, Hannibal was never able to follow it up and was recalled to Carthage in 205 BC. After the end of the Third Punic War (149–146 BC), Carthage was destroyed by the Romans: most of its citizens were killed, and the city was left burning for 10 days.

According to Diodorus Siculus, during a political crisis in the city in 310 BC, the Carthaginians publicly sacrificed 200 children to make amends to Cronus (in other words, to Ba'al Hammon, the supreme god of the Carthaginians). Greek historian Plutarch (AD c. 46–120) also mentions the practice. Were these writers merely passing on Roman propaganda against the "foreigners" from the East who had the tenacity to challenge the might of Rome?

It is worth remembering that the Hebrew Bible attributed child sacrifice and other wickedness to the ancestors of the Phoenicians, the Canaanites, for many of the same reasons as the Romans did with the Carthaginians: primarily to indicate the "otherness" and the depravity of the foreign culture that was being conquered. Nevertheless, there is some intriguing archaeological evidence from Carthage, in the form a large number of children and infant burials that have been interpreted in the light of child sacrifice. In a huge cremation cemetery that archaeologists have termed "The Tophet," an estimated 20,000 urns were deposited between 400 BC and 200 BC, all containing the charred bones of children and in some cases the bones of fetuses. Although some historians, Lawrence Stager and Samuel. R. Wolff, for example, believe these remains are evidence of child sacrifice, perhaps during difficult periods in the city's history, others, including scholar Sergio Ribichini, have argued that the cemeteries contained the cremated remains of children who had died naturally and stillborn infants. The evidence is ambiguous, and the debate over whether of not the Carthaginians practiced child sacrifice continues.

Some fascinating new light is being cast on the possible living descendents of the Phoenicians by DNA studies. In 2005, the National Geographic Society and IBM launched the Genographic Project, a five-year study that aims to analyze historical patterns in DNA from hundreds of thousands people around the world to better understand our human genetic roots. After analyzing the Y chromosome of 1,330 men from Phoenician trading centers in the Mediterranean regions of Syria, Palestine, Tunisia, Morocco, Cyprus, and Malta, Project Director Spencer Wells found that one in 17 of these men still have Phoenician DNA. The presence of this distinctive Phoenician genetic signature means that around 6 percent must be descended from those ancient seafarers. The spectacular findings of Spencer Wells and his colleagues show that, although the vast majority of Phoenician material culture has vanished, these enterprising and unique maritime traders of the

Mediterranean left behind a significant genetic footprint in the region, which is only now being explored. As more DNA samples continue to be analysed, who knows what further insights into the mysterious Phoenicians the research of the Genographic Project will bring.

⧗

Chapter 33

The Mound Builders
(United States)

Grave Creek Mound, Moundsville, West Virginia.

The great earthen mounds of North America are scattered across the country, from the Great Lakes to the Gulf of Mexico, and from the Mississippi River to the Appalachian Mountains. The earliest of these impressive and important monuments dates back to around 3000 BC, and they were still being built when the Spanish arrived in the country in the 16th century AD. "Mound Builder" is a general term used to describe several prehistoric cultures who built these structures, mainly along river valleys in North America. However, in the 19th century, "Mound Builder" was also applied to a hypothetical mysterious race that was thought to have been responsible for the construction of these enigmatic monuments. The ancient mounds of North America differ widely in size and design from area to area, and the building of the larger mounds, such as those at Cahokia, Illinois, must have been vast engineering projects, which would require highly organized societies. Why were these monuments built, and did they serve the same function in each part of the country?

Earth-built mounds in North America were first noticed by European settlers after the end of the Anglo-French War of 1756, as they traveled further westward across the North American continent. When the land-hungry colonists came upon the fertile plains of the Ohio River Valley, for example, they found a wide variety of earthworks and effigy mounds, some geometric in shape, others in the form of birds, deer, alligators, lizards, bears, and felines. However, no matter how astonished they were at these monuments, the settlers' main concern was the use of the land for agriculture; consequently they proceeded to plough a large number of the mounds into the ground.

These early settlers were at a loss to explain the origin of these great monuments, and came to the conclusion that they must be the work of some long-vanished civilization that probably migrated to North America from the Old World at some unspecified past date. This "superior" race later became known as the Mound Builders, and from the colonial period right up until the end of the 19th century they were variously described as the Ten Lost Tribes of Ancient Israel, Egyptians, Phoenicians, Greeks, Chinese, Mongols, Vikings, Hindu colonists from India, or even refugees from Atlantis. In fact, just about any ancient Old World culture that white settlers in North America could think of was suggested as the original builders of the mounds. Because Native American culture appeared to white immigrants too "primitive" to have organized and constructed such vast and complex monuments, the myth of the "vanished race" of Mound Builders gained currency.

In 1787, American botanist and physician Benjamin Smith Barton published a monograph entitled *Observations on some Parts of Natural History*, which discussed the Indian mounds of North America and ascribed their construction to the Danes, whom he believed then migrated to Mexico and became the Toltec. In the 19th century, the most popular of the lost race theorists was Josiah Priest, a harness-maker whose 1834 book, *American Antiquities and Discoveries in the West*, sold 22,000 copies in its first 30 months, according to Priest's publishers. Priest's views on the origins of North American mounds are apparent from the first page of this work, where he states that, many centuries before Columbus, America was peopled by "an ancient population of partially civilized nations, differing entirely from those of the present Indians." Priest does not stop there. By the time we get to the Preface, his theories have encompassed almost the whole of the "civilized" world:

> As it respects some of the ancient nations who may have found their way hither, we perceive a strong possibility that not only Asiatic nations, very soon after the flood, but that all along the different eras of time, different races of men, as Polynesians, Malays, Australasians, Phoenicians, Egyptians, Greeks, Romans, Israelites, Tartars, Scandinavians, Danes, Norwegians, Welsh, and Scotch, have colonized different parts of the continent. We have also attempted to show that America was peopled before the flood that it was the country of Noah, and the place where the ark was erected.
>
> *(American Antiquities and Discoveries in the West,* Preface IV)

A rational discussion of such a jumble of biblical and pseudo-historical nonsense would be pointless, but the fact remains that Priest's book offered a romanticized version of North America in antiquity that had a huge appeal for those eager to exclude Native Americans from the country's history. The influence of Priest's work is apparent even today among writers entirely unconcerned with the facts of North American prehistory.

Even when the mounds were opened up and "investigated," the often-rich array of goods discovered inside them only served to reinforce the prevailing idea that the "savage" American Indians could not have constructed such monuments. Large-scale looting of the mounds in the 18th and 19th centuries revealed human burials accompanied by grave goods such as obsidian, mica, soapstone, shell, meteoric iron, and copper. The technology involved in the crafting of metal artifacts in particular was thought to be well beyond the capabilities of Native

Americans. Such views were the result of a general ignorance of the numerous separate cultures of Native American peoples, and of how widely these cultures varied throughout the country.

However, not everyone shared these opinions of the origins of North America's mounds. Geologist and ethnologist Henry Schoolcraft (1793–1864) and Thomas Jefferson (1743–1826), third president of the United States, carried out excavations of these mysterious mounds and concluded that Native Americans were entirely capable of constructing such monuments. After examining the numerous skeletons discovered in his excavations, Jefferson even stated that the people buried inside the mounds were no different from modern Native Americans. Finally, in 1894, ethnologist Cyrus Thomas submitted a lengthy and detailed report to the Bureau of American Ethnology concluding that the prehistoric earthworks of the eastern United States were constructed by Native Americans. One of the sources Thomas referred to in this report was the largely forgotten work of Spanish chronicler Garcilaso de la Vega (c. 1539–1616).

De la Vega, also known as "El Inca" because of his Incan mother, was record-keeper of the infamous De Soto expedition that landed in present-day Florida on May 31, 1538. In his *Historia de la Florida* (published in Lisbon in 1605, as *La Florida del Inca*), Garcilaso de la Vega gives detailed descriptions of Native American Mound Cultures still practicing their traditional way of life, which included constructing earthen mounds and temples. De la Vega was not the only one to witness the Mound Builders in action. French artist Jacques Le Moyne was a member of Jean Ribault's 1562 expedition to the New World and produced a series of historically important watercolor paintings depicting scenes of native life, including Native American tribes using existing mounds and constructing others. Most of his paintings were unfortunately lost, and his work only exists in the form of engravings created by Belgian printer and publisher Theodor de Bry, based on Le Moyne's work. In the early 17th century, French Jesuit priest Maturin Le Petit observed the Natchez tribe of Mississippi constructing and using mounds for public buildings and burials, as did the French explorer Le Page du Pratz in the mid-18th century.

The oldest mound complex in North America is Watson Brake, in the floodplain of the Ouachita River near Monroe in northern

Louisiana. The site has been carbon dated to c. 3400 BC, and consists of at least 11 mounds, measuring from 3 to 25 feet tall, connected by ridges to form an oval 853 feet across. Investigations of Watson Brake led by archaeologist Joe W. Saunders of Northeast Louisiana University suggest that the mobile hunter-gatherers may have been used the site as a base from summer until autumn.

Archaeologists have, to date, identified four main distinct mound cultures: Poverty Point, Adena, Hopewell, and Mississippian. This grouping is based on the shared architectural practice of mound construction and radiocarbon dating of the sites. The Mound Builder sites of the Poverty Point culture are named after a site near Floyd, Louisiana, whose massive earthworks (one of which reaches 70 feet high) were constructed between 1800 BC and 1000 BC. The mounds of the Poverty Point culture do not seem to have been used for burials but probably had a ceremonial purpose. The Poverty Point culture developed from nomadic tribes into societies living in villages extending for almost 100 miles along the lower Mississippi Valley and surrounding Gulf coast. Artifacts associated with the Poverty Point culture include beautifully crafted flint tools, animal effigy figures, and stone beads and pendants. Many of the raw materials used, such as copper, jasper, lead, and soapstone, came from regions often more than 600 miles away, indicating widespread trade contacts.

Around 1000 BC, a new culture began in North America, radiating out from the Ohio River Valley to include what is now Kentucky, West Virginia, Indiana, Pennsylvania, and New York. The Adena culture, which lasted to about AD 1, constructed mounds, ranging in size from 20 to 300 feet in diameter, in and around their villages, indicating a high degree of social organization. The larger mounds were constructed over small log-lined tombs and were often used more than once. These huge earthworks contained multiple burials at different levels, which meant that over time the mounds gradually increased in size. The dead of the Adena culture were laid to rest with a variety of grave goods, including engraved stone tablets, bone masks, tubular stone pipes, flints, pearl beads, and mica and copper ornaments. The nature of this material indicates that, like their predecessors, the Adena were great traders.

The best known of the Adena burial mounds is Grave Creek Mound, in Moundsville, West Virginia, which, at 62 feet high and 240 feet in diameter, is the largest conical-type burial mound in the United States of America. The multiple burials at different levels within the giant structure indicate that it was built in successive stages from about 250 BC to 150 BC, toward the end of the Adena period. A controversial object, known as the Grave Creek stone, was allegedly found at the site in 1838 during excavations. This object, a sandstone disc engraved with 22 mysterious hieroglyph-like characters, is now thought to be a hoax fashioned by a local physician, Dr. James W. Clemens, who had financed the excavations at Grave Creek by borrowing large amounts of money. The current location of the Grave Creek stone is unknown.

The culture that gradually replaced the Adena is known as the Hopewell. The Hopewell culture survived from about AD 1 to AD 700. Although they possessed many of the same elements as their predecessors, the Hopewell culture appear to have been a more sophisticated culture, with richer burials, larger earthworks, a higher level of artwork, and more developed agriculture. The Hopewell culture was centered in Southern Ohio and Illinois, but there is evidence of a large and wide-ranging trading network in the form of obsidian from the Rocky Mountains and the Black Hills (South Dakota and Wyoming), copper from the Great Lakes of eastern North America, and shells from the Atlantic and Gulf coasts. The largest set of geometric earthworks built by the Hopewell culture are known as the Newark Earthworks (Newark, Ohio), which consists of three sections of preserved earthworks, of which the 1,180-foot-wide Newark Great Circle is the largest. These huge earthwork enclosures were probably used as ceremonial and social centers. Like the Adena, many Hopewell mounds covered multiple burials. The Hopewell culture also constructed effigy mounds, earthworks in the shape of animals (such as bears, birds, buffalos, deer, snakes, or turtles). A number of these effigy mounds contain burials, though not all of them.

The last of the Mound Builder cultures is known as the Mississippian. The peoples of this culture were master farmers and traders who established the most extensive trade network the northeast of North America had ever seen. Their culture spread through the east of the country, mainly along the river valleys. In the Mississippian culture there were not only the domed burial mounds of the previous Adena and Hopewell cultures, but vast pyramidal temple mounds. These temple mounds were rectangular, flat-topped earthen platforms with temples or chiefly residences constructed on top.

The prime example of the Mississippian culture is the site of Cahokia, located near Collinsville, Illinois, across the Mississippi River from St. Louis. Cahokia was a great regional ceremonial center of the Mississippian culture, at its peak from around AD 1050 to 1150, during which period it was among the largest metropolitan centers on earth, covering an area of 6 square miles, with a population of about 15,000 living in the city, and between 20,000 and 30,000 dwelling in surrounding houses and farms. The remains of Cahokia consist of 80 surviving earthen mounds of an estimated total of around 120. The most spectacular of these structures is Monks Mound, a flat-topped multi-terraced platform mound, which still stands 100 feet tall and covers an area of 14 acres. Located within the central ceremonial area of Cahokia, Monks Mound was once topped by a large 50-foot-high building, probably a palace or temple from which Cahokia's elite ruled the area. Cahokia's prominence was, however, relatively short-lived: from about AD 1200, the population of the great center began to decline and the site was abandoned by AD 1400.

An Ohio Valley–based mound-building society known as the Fort Ancient culture were at one time thought to be related to the Mississippian, but are now believed to have been an independently developed culture, probably descended from the Hopewell culture. The Fort Ancient culture was responsible for perhaps the most famous of North America's earthworks: the Serpent Mound. This effigy earthwork, which lies on a plateau overlooking the Miami River near Peebles, Adams County, Ohio, was fashioned in the shape of an undulating snake with coiled tail and open jaws. The jaws are depicted holding or eating a large hollow oval feature, variously interpreted as an egg, the sun, or an enlarged eye. Radiocarbon tests carried out in 1995 dated the construction of the Serpent Mound to AD c. 1070. The Fort Ancient culture flourished until around AD 1650, when, like the Mississippian to the south, their culture collapsed.

The disruption of these Mound Builder cultures had in reality begun a century earlier, when first European contact had brought diseases like measles and smallpox, which decimated Native American populations, and thus undermined the social and political structure of their societies. The Mound Builder cultures changed irrevocably, tribal elders died in the waves of epidemics brought over by the Europeans, and many groups migrated great distances from their original homelands. Although the oral traditions of some tribes, such as the Cherokee, kept alive links to their former way of life, such was the break in cultural continuity brought about by European colonization that the vast majority of Native Americans did not know that it was their own ancestors who had constructed the great mounds that spread across the North American landscape.

Chapter 34

The Olmec
(Mexico)

*One of the four Olmec colossal heads at
La Venta.*

The mysterious Olmec culture of Central America flourished 1,500 years before the Maya and 2,500 years earlier than the Aztec. The Olmec were Central America's first great civilization, building large settlements, establishing far-reaching trade routes, possibly developing an early hieroglyphic writing system, and originating the ceremonial ball games that were to become such a feature of Mesoamerican culture. They also crafted beautiful and distinctive objects of art, the best known of which are the colossal stone heads that have caused so much controversy over the last few decades in the debate over the possible African origins of the Olmec. Around 300 BC, the Olmec civilization vanished from the archaeological record. What happened to this once-great civilization, and how much influence did they have on their better-known Mesoamerican successors—the Maya and the Aztec?

The name Olmec is a misnomer. The word means "rubber people" in Nahuatl, the Aztec language, and was the Aztec name for the Olmeca-Xicalanca people living in the tropical Lowlands of the Gulf of Mexico in the 15th and 16th centuries AD, long after the Olmec culture had disappeared.

We do not know what the people living in the lowlands of the Gulf of Mexico around 3,000 years ago called themselves. The term *rubber people* refers to the ancient practice of harvesting latex from *Castilla elastica*, a rubber tree in the area, then processing it using liquid extracted from *Ipomoea alba* (a species of night-blooming morning-glory), and fashioning rubber balls and other rubber artifacts from the resulting material.

It was not until the 19th century that the Olmec culture became known to historians. In 1869, Mexican explorer José Melgar y Serrano published the first-known report on an Olmec artifact, a colossal head found by a farmer in Hueyapan in the State of Veracruz. Systematic research into the Olmec culture did not begin for many years, when, between 1939 and 1946, Matthew W. Stirling, head of the Smithsonian Institute's Bureau of American Ethnology, led a small group of individuals on eight archaeological expeditions into Olmec territory. The team made a series of spectacular archaeological discoveries, including several colossal stone heads at the sites of La Venta, San Lorenzo, and Tres Zapotes, which brought the Olmec culture and their achievements to the attention of the world.

The Olmec civilization originated between 1400 BC and 1000 BC in the sticky, humid jungles of Mexico's southern Gulf Coast. The rich soil and tropical climate of the area made it possible for the Olmecs to develop a highly structured society that was based primarily on the production of maize (corn). The prosperity of the Olmec culture led to class distinction, which provided the social basis for the development of a significant artistic element among the civilization, which were able to produce the sophisticated luxury artifacts that characterize the Olmec culture. Olmec influence soon spread as far as modern Guatemala, Honduras, Belize, Costa Rica, and El Salvador.

The first recognizable signs of the Olmec culture appear around 1400 BC, in San Lorenzo Tenochtitlán (or San Lorenzo)—a collective name for a large area containing three main related archaeological sites: San Lorenzo, Tenochtitlán, and Potrero Nuevo, located in the southeast part of the Mexican state of Veracruz. The other three major Olmec sites in the culture's heartland (the coastal plain of the Gulf of Mexico), an area about 125 miles long and 50 miles wide, with the Coatzalcoalcos River system running through the middle, were La Venta, Tres Zapotes, and Laguna de los Cerros.

San Lorenzo was a complex of temples, plazas, roadways, and royal residences covering an area of about half an acre, within which around 1,000 people lived. In its heyday, between 1200 BC and 900 BC, San Lorenzo was the largest city in Mesoamerica. It was set in a rich agricultural area and had an elaborate drainage system, which is thought to be the first water control system in the New World. The houses at San Lorenzo were made of wooden walls with clay and palm rooftops; it seems that elaborate housing was constructed for the elite classes and simpler accommodations for the poorer, indicating a simple, but nonetheless important, social structure within Olmec society.

Around 900 BC, San Lorenzo began to decline. At about the same time, La Venta, located on an island on a coastal swamp in the present-day Mexican state of Tabasco, rose to prominence, with a population reaching an estimated 18,000 at this time. A major religious complex and political center, La Venta has provided some of the most notable archaeological discoveries from Mesoamerica. These finds include four colossal stone heads, numerous jade figures and ornaments, mosaic pavements of serpentine blocks, and a large number of beautifully carved stone sculptures. One of the main features at La Venta is the Great Pyramid, a 110-foot-high clay mound, originally rectangular in shape with stepped sides and inset corners. Like all the great mounds built at La Venta, it was aligned to eight degrees west of north, probably for astronomical reasons.

Laguna de los Cerros, in the southern foothills of the Tuxtla Mountains in Veracruz, is the third of the major Olmec sites, though it has not been extensively excavated. However, we know that by 1200 BC it had become a large regional center, covering an area of around 370 acres, and by 1000 BC it had grown to encompass 47 smaller sites within a 3-mile radius. Laguna de los Cerros was located close to important sources of basalt in the Tuxtla Mountains, a stone used to manufacture Olmec monuments and tools, though unlike other major Olmec sites, no colossal stone heads have been discovered at Laguna de los Cerros.

The fourth major Olmec site was Tres Zapotes, located on the slopes of the Tuxtla Mountains, in the Papaloapan River plain, in the Mexican state of Veracruz. The first occupation of Tres Zapotes may date back as early as 1500 BC, but the site came to prominence between 1200 and 900 BC. In contrast to the other sites in the Olmec heartland, Tres Zapotes continued to be occupied well into the Early Postclassic period (AD 1000–1200).

By the beginning of the fourth century BC, the major Olmec center at La Venta was abandoned, and the Olmecs all but disappeared as a distinct culture. We do not know exactly why this happened, but internal political strife could have divided the population into archaeologically invisible smaller groups, or perhaps serious environmental change, such as important rivers changing their courses and thus affecting agriculture, hunting and gathering, and transportation, could have occurred. A related explanation is that the rivers silted up due to the intensive agriculture practiced by the Olmec. Other suggestions are more dramatic and include an invasion from outside the Olmec region, a volcanic eruption, or a catastrophic earthquake. The Olmec did not vanish entirely, however; elements of the population were absorbed by other peoples, and at Tres Zapotes the culture was gradually transformed into what has come to be called the Epi-Olmec.

Among the many achievements of the Olmec is their possible development of the earliest pre-Columbian writing system. The main evidence for this, if it is genuine, is the Cascajal Block, a large serpentine slab dating to around 900 BC, when Olmec culture was at its peak. The block was discovered in 1999 in a gravel quarry, not far from San Lorenzo. It weighs about 26 pounds, and is 14.2 inches long, 8.2 inches wide, and 5.1 inches thick. The stone is incised with 62 notations of 28 different glyphic signs, some of which appear to be depictions of insects, plants, fish, and animals; others are abstract shapes.

The authenticity of the Cascajal Block has been called into question for a number of reasons. Firstly, it was not found in an archaeological context but in a pile of bulldozer debris, and thus cannot be reliably dated. The uniqueness of the block has also drawn criticism from some researchers (there are no other known examples of Olmec drawing or writing on a serpentine slab) such as archaeologist Christopher Pool of the University of Kentucky in Lexington, author of one of the standard books on the archaeology of the Olmec culture, *Olmec Archaeology and Early Mesoamerica* (Cambridge University Press, 2007). Another objection is that the symbols on the slab bear no resemblance to any other Mesoamerican writing system. Furthermore, the symbols also seem to be randomly grouped, rather than written either vertically or linearly, as in other Central American writing systems.

In 2006, an international archaeological team undertook an investigation into the Cascajal Block. The team comprised a number of experts on the Olmec civilization, including Stephen D. Houston of Brown University, Providence, Rhode Island; Ma. del Carmen Rodríguez Martínez and Alfredo Delgado Calderón of the Centro del Instituto Nacional de Antropologia e Historia of Mexico; and Richard A. Diehl of the University of Alabama. The conclusion of their study, published in the journal *Science* (September 2006; *Vol. 313. no. 5793*, pp. 1610–14) was that the Cascajal Block was a genuine and vastly important artefact in terms of Mesoamerican civilization. Despite this report, a list of objections to the team's conclusions by archaeologists Karen Bruhns and Nancy Kelker were published in a letter to *Science* magazine (March 9, 2007). Consequently, for the time being at least, the authenticity of the Cascajal Block must remain unproven.

Olmec art and its distribution around ancient Mesoamerican sites give us important insights into Olmec culture. The presence of luxury artifacts of jade and obsidian at major Olmec centers located a long distance from any source for these materials indicates an extensive trade network. The existence of such a network is also shown by the presence of Olmec artifacts and iconography hundreds of miles outside the Olmec heartland. Olmec art consists primarily of fine pottery, carved jade jewelry, and exquisite sculptures. Motifs in Olmec art include jaguars (or "were-jaguars"—half-human and half-jaguar), serpents, monkeys, and fish. The distinctive and often highly stylized decoration present in Olmec art became a model for the Maya, Aztec, and other later civilizations in the area.

The most famous pieces of Olmec artwork are the colossal stone heads. Olmec stone heads, 17 of which have been discovered so far, were probably carved between 1200 BC and 900 BC, and are sculpted from blocks of volcanic basalt. The colossal heads range in height from 5 feet to 11 feet, weigh as much as 20 tons, and are believed to be representations of individual male (and occasionally female) Olmec rulers. No two statues are alike, and some include headgear, indicating that they represent ballplayers, or rather Olmec royalty dressed as ballplayers. Indeed the majority of the evidence for the Olmec ballgame comes in the form of artwork, mainly figurines depicting male and female ballplayers wearing padded protection on their stomach, arms, and legs. These ballplayer figurines have been radiocarbon-dated as far back as 1250–1150 BC, though the simple earthen ball court discovered at San Lorenzo Tenochtitlán is more recent, dating back to 600–400 BC.

The facial features of the Olmec stone heads—slanted eyes and large lips—have persuaded many people, including José Melgar, as far back as 1862, that they represent a former occupation of the area by an African race, probably Nubians. Based primarily on their interpretation of the facial features of these statues, writers like Ivan Van Sertima (*They Came before Columbus*, originally published in 1976) have postulated theories of transatlantic diffusion, with the inherent suggestion that Native Americans were incapable of such artistic achievement.

There are a number of objections to this theory. The deformed skull shown on many of the Olmec heads was likely the result of the binding of the head at birth for noble children, as was done in the later Mayan culture. The African presence in Mesoamerica is also refuted by the complete lack of African objects discovered in the thousands of controlled excavations that have taken place in Central America.

Perhaps the most convincing proof that the Olmec heads represent native Mesoamerican rulers is that their facial characteristics can still be found in modern Mesoamerican Indians. In the 1940s, Mexican artist and art historian José Miguel Covarrubias published a series of photos of Olmec artwork and of the faces of modern Mexican Indians, which showed very similar facial characteristics. Indeed the photos of modern Mexican people from the Olmec area published in the article "Robbing Native American Cultures: Van Sertima's Afrocentricity and the Olmecs" by Gabriel Haslip-Viera, Bernard Ortiz de Montellano, and Warren Barbour (*Current Anthropology, Volume 38, Number 3,* June 1997, pp. 419–41) show beyond doubt the indigenous character of the Olmec heads.

Because so little is known of the Olmec (few intact human remains have been discovered, for example) compared to the Maya and Aztec, the culture is rife for "alternative" speculation such as their posited African origin. Though such speculations are not considered credible by the majority of Mesoamerican researchers, dozens of unanswered questions remain about the Olmec culture, not least of which is their origin. The mystery surrounding the Olmec is partly due to the fact that their great centers have not been completely excavated. Unfortunately, this situation is not likely to change easily as the vast majority of Olmec territory has now been converted from jungle to cow pastures and sugar-cane fields, making archaeological work extremely difficult. However, recent excavations at the probable Olmec trading center at Chalcatzingo, located in the Valley of Morelos in the southern part of the Central Highlands of Mexico, provide some hope of future discoveries that may cast new light on the enigma of the Olmec.

⧗

Chapter 35

The Extinction of the Neanderthals (The World)

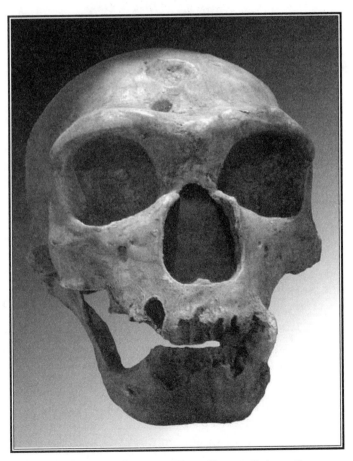

Neanderthal skill from La Chapelle aux Saints, France.

Reconstruction of a Neanderthal child from Gibraltar (Anthropological Institute, University of Zürich).

Although the Neanderthals are our closest prehistoric relatives, we know relatively little about them. Neanderthals were a type of early hominid that evolved, as all hominids did, in Africa, and migrated into Europe and Asia between 230,000 and 300,000 years ago. For almost 200,000 years this enigmatic member of the *Homo* genus dominated Europe and parts of western and central Asia. Between roughly 30,000 and 45,000 years ago, Neanderthals shared this large area with anatomically modern humans, and there has been much speculation about whether the two species interbred, and if this happened whether it left any traces of Neanderthal mitochondrial DNA in the cells of living people. Perhaps the biggest mystery surrounding the Neanderthals is that by around 20,000–28,000 years ago they were gone forever, and no one is quite sure why. Researchers have speculated that they were forced out by modern humans spreading out of Africa, that they interbred with *Homo sapiens* and disappeared through absorption, or that the species failed to adapt to the severe climate change during the last Ice Age. All three explanations for this prehistoric enigma have supporters and detractors.

The Neanderthal is named after the Neander Valley, 7 1/2 miles east of the German city of Düsseldorf. In 1856, during industrial mining operations in this small limestone valley, the bones of the original Neanderthal man—Neanderthal 1—were discovered in a cave known as the Feldhofer Grotto. Although some scientists believe

Homo neanderthalensis (Neanderthal man) to be a subspecies of *Homo sapiens*, the prevailing opinion nowadays is that it is a species unto itself. Several hundred examples of Neanderthal remains have been found all over Europe and western Asia. These include a fossilized skull (known affectionately as "the Old Man") from La Chapelle-aux-Saints, a cave in central France; more than 800 fossil remains representing almost 75 Neanderthals individuals, along with tools and weapons, from a hill called Hušnjak Krapina near modern Krapina, northern Croatia; nine skeletons of Neanderthals of varying ages from the cave site of Shanidar, in the Zagros Mountains of Kurdistan, Iraq; and the remains of a Neanderthal boy approximately 11 years old from Bontnewydd Cave, northeast Wales. The latter, dated to 230,000 years ago, are some of the oldest Neanderthal remains ever found.

At an average height of 5 feet 6 inches, Neanderthals were a little shorter than modern humans, but similar to contemporaneous *Homo sapiens*. Neanderthals were heavily built with robust bone structure, likely an adaptation to the cold climate of Europe during the Pleistocene era, and would have been extremely powerful by modern standards. At birth, Neanderthals had brains as large as modern humans and slightly larger than ours as adults, which is probably connected with their larger body size in general. A 2007 report in *Science* (October 25, 2007) stated that DNA retrieved from the bones of two Neanderthals suggested that at least some of the species had red hair and pale skin. The Neanderthals' stone tool industry is called by archaeologists "Mousterian," after the rock shelter site of Le Moustier in southwestern France, where a rich assemblage of predominantly flint tools was discovered along with the remains of a Neanderthal adolescent and a newborn child, dating to around 40,000–50,000 years ago. Mousterian tools found in Europe were fashioned by Neanderthals between 30,000 and 300,000 years ago.

Between 40,000 and 45,000 years ago, modern humans moved into Europe. The earliest evidence so far discovered of modern humans in Europe, at least 40,000 years ago, comes from a group of sites near the village of Kostenki, along the Don River, central Russia. No skeletal remains have been recovered from the site; the evidence for modern humans comes in the form of the artifacts (of bone, shell and ivory), which include types completely unknown at Neanderthal sites. Modern humans co-existed with Neanderthals for several thousand years—though the exact duration is not certain—before the Neanderthals were eventually forced out and vanished from the archaeological record. Although the Neanderthals seem to have died out about 30,000 years ago, there is a possibility that they hung on longer in isolated areas. One site that is claimed to be one of the last-known inhabited by the Neanderthals is Gorham's Cave in Gibraltar, the narrow strip of rocky land that extends off southern Spain and faces Morocco. Carbon dates obtained from hearths at the natural cave site have suggested that Neanderthals might have survived there until 28,000 years ago, or even as recently as 24,000 years ago, though the accuracy of these dates has been challenged. Stone tools rather than skeletal remains have been used to identify the occupation at Gorham's Cave as Neanderthal.

One of the most intense controversies in human evolution revolves around the question of whether Neanderthals and modern humans interbred. Finds from the Lagar Velho rock shelter site in the Lapedo valley, 87 miles north of Lisbon, Portugal, have been put forward as proof that the two species did interbreed. The main discovery was the largely complete skeleton of a child between 3 1/2 and 5 years old (known as the "Lapedo child"), buried with pierced shells and red ocher, which is dated to around 24,500 years ago. Examination of the skeletal remains suggested that the proportions of its robust lower limbs resembled those of a Neanderthal rather than an anatomically modern human. A number of researchers believe that the features exhibited by the skeleton represent a Neanderthal/modern human hybrid—in other words, evidence that successful interbreeding of the two species took place. However, not everyone agrees with the conclusions drawn from the "Lapedo child" and similar skeletons from a site Pestera Muierii, Romania, dated to 30,000 years ago. Anthropologists Ian Tattersall and Jeffrey Schwartz, for example, believe that Velho child was either an unusually well-built modern human child or one with a growth abnormality.

Svante Paabo, director of genetics at the Max Planck Institute for evolutionary Anthropology, Leipzig, Germany, has stated that he believes the Neanderthals and modern humans met and had sex, though his research has proved that Neanderthals did not contribute mitochondrial DNA to modern humans. In other words, there was at least no direct maternal line originating with Neanderthals that has survived into modern times. Nevertheless, if there was interbreeding, then it may explain what happened to the Neanderthals. Perhaps the species didn't disappear as such, but was absorbed into the modern human population by interbreeding.

Some researchers have suggested a quicker, more violent end for the Neanderthals. In the early 20th century, French palaeontologist Marcellin Boule, and more recently Jared Diamond, professor of geography and physiology at the University of California, Los Angeles (UCLA), have hypothesized a genocidal replacement of Neanderthals by modern humans. Diamond also adds that Neanderthals may have been more susceptible to pathogens introduced by anatomically modern humans, paralleling the situation with the colonialists' arrival in America.

If battles between the two species did take place, some researchers, including Karen L. Steudel of the University of Wisconsin, believe that anatomical differences between the limbs of Neanderthals and modern humans would have been crucial. One result of the fact that Neanderthals had shorter, stockier limbs than modern humans, so they would not have been able to run as fast, thus giving humans a decided advantage in battle. This argument is also given some support by analysis of the only complete Neanderthal pelvis yet recovered, from the 60,000-year-old occupation at Kebara cave, Mount Carmel, Israel. Paleoanthropologist Yoel Rak, from Tel-Aviv University, has shown that the pelvis, which came from a female skeleton recovered at the site, is fundamentally different from that in anatomically modern humans. The Neanderthal pelvis is considerably wider; consequently it would have been much more difficult for Neanderthals to absorb shock and to "spring" from one step to the next, giving modern humans superior running and walking ability.

However, perhaps there wasn't the need for large-scale fighting between the two competing species. It may well be that the modern humans were more intelligent, possessed better technology, or were better adapted to the environment. One hypothesis is that, when Neanderthals and anatomically modern humans encountered each other, the Neanderthals soon disappeared because they simply could not compete with modern humans' superior adaptations in terms of behavior and technology. However, for many researchers this explanation is far too simplistic. They believe it is more likely that a number of factors contributed to the disappearance of the Neanderthals, one of which was the climate.

An event that must have affected both the Neanderthal and the anatomically modern human population was the deterioration in temperatures beginning around 35,000–40,000 years ago. As temperatures fell, ice caps moved farther south, snow cover increased, and the once-forested landscape that sustained the large herbivores disappeared. As the landscape was transformed into a sparsely vegetated steppe, big-game species like mammoth bison, red deer, and other animals moved south, and Neanderthals and indeed early humans had no choice but to follow them. However, there may have been an additional reason for the Neanderthal's move south. Researchers like Professor John Shea, from Stony Brook University, New York, believe that anatomically modern humans, with their lighter throwing spears and more mobile hunting strategy, were better adapted to hunting in the open plains than Neanderthals, with their thrusting spear and ambush tactics. According to this theory, if climate deterioration resulted in competition for increasingly limited food resources, then the Neanderthals would have lost out to anatomically modern humans.

The Neanderthal population seem to have moved mainly into Iberia (present-day Spain and Portugal), especially the southern coastal areas, where resources were more plentiful than in the semi-desert farther north. Indeed the most recent Neanderthal remains are from sites in this region, such as the previously mentioned sites of Lagar Velho in Portugal, and Gorham's Cave in Gibraltar. Another example is a cave (*Cueva del Boquete*) in Zafarraya, in the province of Granada, southern Spain, where a Neanderthal mandible dating to 30,000 years ago was unearthed in 1983. As the ice crept further south, even these isolated pockets of Neanderthal habitation became affected, as southern Iberia was slowly transformed into a semi-arid steppe. It may well be that Gorham's Cave, located at the southernmost tip of the Iberian Peninsula, was the final outpost of a particularly hardy group of Neanderthals, who perhaps survived there as recently as 18,500 years ago, according to some estimates, before the climate finally overcame them. There is certainly no evidence of modern humans in southern Iberia until some time after the Neanderthals were gone.

The question of why a large-brained intelligent hominid, in many respects so similar to us, who had dominated Europe for so long, vanished completely may never be resolved satisfactorily. It is more than likely that there is not a single cause for the Neanderthal's extinction; they did not disappear overnight in one huge group. Neanderthals covered a vast area of Europe and western Asia, and there were probably localized factors affecting their disappearance in different regions at various times between 25,000 and 45,000 years ago. Perhaps the question should not be why Neanderthals became extinct, but why did *they* disappear and *we* survive? Professor Clive Finlayson of the Gibraltar Museum, expresses this point succinctly: "It is quite sobering that at one point in the history of the planet, there were different types of us of which one—possibly by chance—survived. In other words, we might be the Neanderthals discussing this today." (*news.bbc.co.uk/2/hi/science/nature/7873373.stm*)

⧗

Photo Credits

*Unless noted here, photos are in the public domain.

Chapter 1: Lyonesse
Creative Commons Attribution ShareAlike 2.0 License

Chapter 4: Cape Sounion
Photo by Frank van Mierlo (GNU Free Documentation License, version 1.2)

Chapter 5: Akrotiri and the Destruction of Thera
Photo by Klearchos Kapoutsis (GNU Free Documentation License, version 1.2)

Chapter 6: Solomon's Temple and the Jehoash inscription
Inner Court and House of the Temple: Photo by Gabriel Fink (GNU Free Documentation License, version 1.2)
Temple Mount: GNU Free Documentation License, version 1.2)

Chapter 9: The Taj Mahal
Photo by Buyoof (Creative Commons Attribution ShareAlike 3.0)

Chapter 11: The World's Oldest Pyramid
Photo by Dhirad (Creative Commons Attribution ShareAlike 2.5)

Chapter 12: Great Zimbabwe
Conical Tower: Photo by Marius Loots (GNU Free Documentation License, version 1.2)

Chapter 13: Newport's Mystery Tower
Newport Tower: Photo copyright 2004 by Matthew Trump (GNU Free Documentation License, version 1.2)

Chapter 14: The Abandonment of Mesa Verde

Photo by Massimo Catarinella (Creative Commons Attribution ShareAlike 3.0)

Chapter 16: The Stone of Destiny

Photo by sarniebill1 (Creative Commons Attribution 2)

Chapter 17: The Mystery of the Ogham Stones

GNU Free Documentation License, version 1.2)

Chapter 22: The Uluburun Shipwreck

Photo by Georges Jansoone (GNU Free Documentation License, version 1.2)

Chapter 24: The Dendera Lamps

Dendera Light: Photo by Twthmoses (Creative Commons Attribution 2.5 License)

Dendera Light 2: Photo by Twthmoses (Creative Commons Attribution 2.5 License)

Chapter 25: The Oak Island Treasure

Photo by NormanEinstein (GNU Free Documentation License, Version 1.2)

Chapter 27: Boudica

Photo by A. Brady (GNU Free Documentation License, Version 1.2)

Chapter 29: The Ida Fossil

Photo source: Jens L. Franzen, Philip D. Gingerich, Jörg Habersetzer1, Jørn H. Hurum, Wighart von Koenigswald, B. Holly Smith (Creative Commons Attribution ShareAlike 2.5)

Chapter 31: Cleopatra

Photo by George Shuklin (GNU Free Documentation License, Version 1.2)

Chapter 32: Who Were the Phoenicians?

Phoenicia: Photo by Kordas (Creative Commons Attribution 3.0 Unported)

Chapter 33: The Mound Builders

Photo by Tim Kiser. (Creative Commons Attribution ShareAlike 2.5)

Chapter 34: The Olmec

Photo by Hajor. (Creative Commons Attribution ShareAlike 2.0)

Chapter 35: The Neanderthals

Neanderthal: Photo by Luna04 (GNU Free Documentation License, Version 1.2)

Neanderthal Child: Photo by Christoph P.E. Zollikofer (public domain)

Bibliography

Chapter 1

The Lyonesse Project Website. *www.cornwall.gov.uk/default. aspx?page=20.*

Pennick, Nigel. *Lost Lands and Sunken Cities.* London: Fortean Tomes, 1987.

Westwood, Jennifer, and Jacqueline Simpson. *The Lore of the Land: A Guide to England's Legends, from Spring-heeled Jack to the Witches of Warboys.* London: Penguin Books Ltd., 2005.

Chapter 2

Beamon, Sylvia P. *The Royston Cave: Used by Saints or Sinners? Local Historical Influences of the Templar and Hospitaller Movements.* Baldock, Hertfordshire, UK: Cortney Publications, 1992.

Fitzpatrick-Matthews, Keith. "Royston Cave: A Secret Templar and Masonic Shrine?" Bad Archaeology.net Website. *www.badarchaeology.net/conspiracy/royston_cave.php.*

Houldcroft, Peter T. *A Pictorial Guide to the Royston Cave.* Royston, UK: Royston and District History Society, 1998.

Pennick, Nigel. "The Royston Cave—A 'Templar' Circular Sacred Building." *At the Edge* magazine Website. *www.indigogroup.co.uk/edge/Royston.htm.*

Chapter 3

Polidoro, Massimo. "The Secrets of Rennes-le-Château." *Skeptical Enquirer Volume 28.6,* November/December 2004. Committee for Skeptical Enquiry (CSI) website. *www.csicop.org/si/show/secrets_of_ rennes-le-chacircteau.*

Putnam, Bill, and John Edwin Wood. *The Treasure of Rennes-le-Château.* Stroud, Gloucestershire, UK: The History Press, 2005.

Rennes-le-Chateau.com Website. *www.renneslechateau.com/default-uk.htm.*

Rennes-le-chateau-rhedae.com Website. *www.rennes-le-chateau-rhedae.com/.*

Chapter 4

Camp, John M. *The Archaeology of Athens.* New Haven, Conn.: Yale University Press, 2001.

Mee, Christopher, and Antony Spawforth. *Greece (Oxford Archaeological Guides).* Oxford, UK: Oxford University Press, 2001.
Sheldon, Natasha. "The Archaeology of Sounion—Exploring the Buildings and History of an Ancient Greek Sanctuary." Suite 101 Website. *archaeology.suite101.com/article.cfm/the_archaeology_of_sounion.*

Chapter 5

"Akrotiri of Thera." Hellenic Ministry of Culture Website. *odysseus.culture.gr/h/3/eh351.jsp?obj_id=2410.*

Dickinson, Oliver. *The Aegean Bronze Age.* Cambridge, UK: Cambridge University Press, 1996.

LaMoreaux, P.E. "Worldwide Environmental Impacts from the Eruption of Thera." *Environmental Geology* 26:172–81 (1995).

Thera Foundation Website. *www.therafoundation.org/.*

Chapter 6

Brodie, Neil. "James Ossuary." The Stanford Archaeology Center Cultural Heritage Resource Website. *www.stanford.edu/group/chr/drupal/ref/james-ossuary.*

Burleigh, Nina. *Unholy Business: A True Tale of Faith, Greed, and Forgery in the Holy Land.* New York: HarperCollins, 2008.

Hamblin, William, and David Seely. *Solomon's Temple: Myth and History.* London: Thames and Hudson, 2007.

Milstein, Mati. "Solomon's Temple Artifacts Found by Muslin Workers." *National Geographic* News Website. *news.nationalgeographic.com/news/2007/10/071023-jerusalem-artifacts.html.*

Shanks, Hershel. *Jerusalem's Temple Mount: From Solomon to the Golden Dome.* New York: Continuum, 2007.

Chapter 7

Curry, Andrew. "Gobekli Tepe: The World's First Temple?" *Smithsonian magazine* Website. *www.smithsonianmag.com/history-archaeology/gobekli-tepe.html*.

"Göbekli Tepe." Website of the German Archaeological Institute Website. *www.dainst.de/index_642_en.html*.

Scham, Sandra. "The World's First Temple." *Archaeology Volume 61, Number 6,* November/December 2008. *Archaeology* magazine Website. *www.archaeology.org/0811/abstracts/turkey.html*.

Thomas, Sean. "Gobekli Tepe—Paradise Regained?" *Fortean Times* Website. *www.forteantimes.com/features/articles/449/gobekli_tepe_paradise_regained.html*.

Chapter 8

Herodotus. *The Histories*. Trans. Aubrey de Sélincourt. Harmondsworth, England: Penguin, 1972.

Lendering, Jona. "Etemenanki (The Tower of Babel)." Livius Articles on Ancient History Website. *www.livius.org/es-ez/etemenanki/etemenanki.html*.

The Virtual Babel Encyclopedia Website. *www.towerofbabel.info*.

Walton, John H. "It There Archaeological Evidence of the Tower of Babel?" Associates for Biblical Research Website. *www.biblearchaeology.org/post/2008/05/10/Is-there-Archaeological-Evidence-for-the-Tower-of-Babel.aspx*.

Chapter 9

"The Controversy Surrounding the Origins of the Taj Mahal." BBC h2g2 Website. *www.bbc.co.uk/dna/h2g2/A5220*.

Koch, Ebba. *The Complete Taj Mahal: and the Riverfront Gardens of Agra*. London: Thames & Hudson, 2006.

Okada, Amina, and Mohan C. Joshi. *Taj Mahal*. New York: Abbeville Press, 1993.

"World Heritage Sites—Agra—Taj Mahal." Archaeological Survey Of India Website. *www.asi.nic.in/asi_monu_whs_agratajmahal.asp*.

Chapter 10

Alberge, Dalya. "UN Vandals Spray Graffiti on Sahara's Prehistoric Art." The Times Online Website. *entertainment.timesonline.co.uk/tol/arts_and_entertainment/visual_arts/article3280058.ece.*

"PlanetQuest: The History of Astronomy—Nabta Playa." PlanetQuest Website. *www.planetquest.org/learn/nabta.html.*

Stankek, Steven. "Egypt's Earliest Farming Village Found." *National Geographic* Website. *news.nationalgeographic.com/news/2008/02/080211-egypt-farming.html.*

Wendorf, Fred, and Romuald Schild. "Late Neolithic structures at Nabta Playa, southwestern Egypt." Comparative Archaeology Website. *www.comp-archaeology.org/WendorfSAA98.html.*

Wendorf, Fred, Romuald Schild, and Kit Nelson (eds). *Holocene Settlement of the Egyptian Sahara: The Archaeology of Nabta Playa.* New York: Kluwer Academic/Plenum Publishers, 2001.

Chapter 11

Edwards, I.E.S. *The Pyramids of Egypt.* Harmondsworth, England: Penguin, 1993.

Lehner, Mark. *The Complete Book of the Pyramids.* New York: Thames and Hudson, 1997.

"Step Pyramid of Djoser—Egypt's First Pyramid." *National Geographic* Website. *www.nationalgeographic.com/pyramids/djoser.html.*

Winston, Alan. "Egypt Feature Story—The Step Pyramid of Djoser at Saqqara in Egypt Part I: An Introduction." Alan Winston. *Tour Egypt.net* Website. *www.touregypt.net/featurestories/dsteppyramid1.htm.*

Chapter 12

Clark, Stuart, and Damian Carrington. "Eclipse Brings Claim of Medieval African Observatory." *New Scientist* Website. *www.newscientist.com/article/dn3137-eclipse-brings-claim-of-medieval-african-observatory.html.*

Garlake, Peter S. *Great Zimbabwe (New Aspects of Archaeology).* Harare, Zimbabwe: Zimbabwe Publishing House, 1985.

"Heilbrunn Timeline of Art History—Great Zimbabwe (11th–15th century)." Metropolitan Museum of Art (New York) Website. *www.metmuseum.org/toah/hd/zimb/hd_zimb.htm.*

McIntosh, Roderick J. "Riddle of Great Zimbabwe." *Archaeology Volume 51, Number 4*, July/August 1998. *Archaeology* magazine online. *www.archaeology.org/9807/abstracts/africa.html.*

Tyson, Peter. "Lost Tribes of Isreal—Mystery of Great Zimbabwe." Nova Online. *www.pbs.org/wgbh/nova/israel/zimbabwe.html.*

Chapter 13

Barstad, Jan. "The Newport Tower Project – An Archaeological Investigation into the Tower's Past." Chronognostic Research Society Website. *chronognostic.org/pdf/tower_project_report_2007.pdf.*

"History of the Chesterton Windmill." Warwickshire County Council Website. *www.warwickshire.gov.uk/Web/corporate/pages.nsf/Links/B4 E46C93E89E769F802571020053A992.*

Maier, Chris. "Newport's Mystery Tower." Unexplained Earth Website. *www.unexplainedearth.com/newport.php.*

"Special Salvage Excavation May 30–June 4, 2008." Chronognostic Research Society Website. *www.chronognostic.org/daily_logs. php?id=6.*

"A Visitor's Guide to Nathan Tufts Park." City of Somerville Website. *www.somervillema.gov/CoS_Content/documents/NathanParks%20 Brochure_10_23.pdf.*

Weller, Doug. "The Newport Tower and the Plowden Petition." Hall of Maat Website. *www.hallofmaat.com/modules.php?name=Articles&fil e=article&sid=99.*

Chapter 14

FitzGerald, Michael C. "The Majesty of Mesa Verde. *Wall Street Journal* Website. *online.wsj.com/article/SB123697765848223641.html.*

Kantner, John. *Ancient Puebloan Southwest.* Cambridge, UK: Cambridge University Press, 2004.

The Mesa Verde National Park Website. *www.mesa.verde.national-park.com.*

Chapter 15

Broda, J., J.D. Carrasco, and E. Matos Moctezuma. *The Great Temple of Tenochtitlan.* Berkeley, Calif.: University of California Press, 1987.

Del Castillo, Bernal Diaz. *The Conquest of New Spain.* Trans. J.M. Cohen. Baltimore, Md.: Penguin, 1963 (1632).

Hassig, Ross. *Mexico and the Spanish Conquest. 2nd edition.* Norman, Okla.: University of Oklahoma Press, 2006.

Chapter 16

Aitchison, Nick. *Scotland's Stone of Destiny.* Stroud, UK: Tempus, 2000.

Kannard, Brian. "The Stone of Destiny." Unexplained Mysteries Website. *www.unexplained-mysteries.com/column.php?id=100577.*

Lister, David. "Stone of Destiny a 'Fake to Dupe Invading English'." *The Times Online* Website. *www.timesonline.co.uk/tol/news/uk/scotland/ article4144587.ece.*

Ritchie, John. "Shadow of a Dream—The History of the Stone of Destiny." John.bravepen.com Website. *www.john.bravepen.com.*

Chapter 17

McManus, D. *A Guide to Ogam.* Maynooth, Co. Kildare, Ireland: An Sagart, 1991.

The Ogham Stone Website. *ogham.lyberty.com/index.html.*

"The Victorian Excavations of 1893—The Ogham Stone." The Silchester Project at the University of Reading Website. *www.silchester.rdg. ac.uk/victorians/vic_ogham.php.*

Chapter 18

Bonsing, John. "The Celtic Calendar." Caer Australis Website. *caeraustralis.com.au/celtcalmain.htm.*

Brennan, Martin. *The Stones of Time: Calendars, Sundials, and Stone Chambers of Ancient Ireland.* Rochester, Vt.: Inner Traditions, 1994.

"Celtic Found to Have Ancient Roots." *New York Times* online. *www. nytimes.com/2003/07/01/science/celtic-found-to-have-ancient-roots. html.*

Koch, John T. *Celtic Culture: A Historical Encyclopedia* (Five-Volume Set). Santa Barbara, Calif.: ABC-CLIO, 2005.

Matthews, Caitlin. *The Celtic Tradition.* Dorset, UK: Element Books, 1994.

Chapter 19

Fitzpatrick-Matthews, Keith, and James Doeser. "Glozel." Bad Archaeology.net Website. *www.badarchaeology.net/controversial/ glozel.php.*

Gerard, Alice. *Glozel: Bones of Contention*. Bloomington, Ind.: iUniverse.com, 2005.

Glozel.net Website. *www.glozel.net/index.html.*

Chapter 20

Harding, A.F. *European Societies in the Bronze Age* (Cambridge World Archaeology). Cambridge, UK: Cambridge University Press, 2000.

Nawroth, Manfred. "Golden Hats of the Bronze Age: Symbols of Power and Calendar Systems." Virtual Museum of European Roots Website. *www.europeanvirtualmuseum.it/Deepenings/deepberlin4.htm.*

Paterson, Tony. "Mysterious Gold Cones 'Hats of Ancient Wizards'." *Daily Telegraph* Website. *www.telegraph.co.uk/news/worldnews/europe/germany/1388038/Mysterious-gold-cones-hats-of-ancient-wizards.html.*

Chapter 21

Amos, Jonathan. "German 'Venus' may be oldest yet." BBC News Website. *news.bbc.co.uk/2/hi/8047319.stm.*

Bahn, Paul G. *The Cambridge Illustrated History of Prehistoric Art* (Cambridge Illustrated Histories). Cambridge, UK: Cambridge University Press, 1998.

Fagan, Brian. *The Oxford Companion to Archaeology*. Oxford, UK: Oxford University Press, 1997.

Witcombe, Christopher L.C.E. "Venus of Willendorf." Christopher L.C.E. Witcombe's Website. *witcombe.sbc.edu/willendorf/.*

Chapter 22

Bass, G.F. "Oldest Known Shipwreck Reveals Splendors of the Bronze Age." *National Geographic Magazine* 172, no. 6 (December 1987), 692–733.

Pulak, Cemal. "The Uluburun Shipwreck: An Overview." *The International Journal of Nautical Archaeology* 27.3 (1998), 188–224.

"Report—Uluburun, Turkey." Institute of Nautical Archaeology Website. *inadiscover.com/projects/all/southern_europe_mediterranean_aegean/uluburun_turkey/report/.*

Chapter 23

Anantharaman, T.R. "The *Iron Pillar* at *Kodachadri* in Karnataka." *Current Science 76* (1999): 1428–30.

Balasubramaniam, R. "Delhi Iron Pillar" (in two parts). *IIM Metal News Volume 7, No. 2*, April 2004: 11–17; and *IIM Metal News Volume 7, No. 3*, June 2004: 5–13.

——. "New Insights on the 1600-Year-Old Corrosion Resistant Delhi Iron Pillar." *Indian Journal of History of Science, 36* (2001): 1–49.

——. *Story of the Delhi Iron Pillar*. New Delhi, India: Foundation Books, 2005.

Story, Ronald. *The Space Gods Revealed*. London: Book Club Associates, 1977.

Von Daniken, Erich. *Chariots of the Gods*. London: Corgi, 1975.

Chapter 24

Andrews, Mark. "Dendera and the Temple of Hathor." Tour Egypt Website. *www.touregypt.net/featurestories/dendera.htm.*

"The Dendera Lightbulb." Ancient Egypt online. *www.ancientegyptonline.co.uk/Denderahlightbulb.html.*

Dörnenburg, Frank. "Electric Lights in Egypt?" World Mysteries Website. *www.world-mysteries.com/sar_lights_fd1.htm.*

Orcutt, Larry. "The Dendera Reliefs." Larry Orcutt's Catchpenny Mysteries of Ancient Egypt Website. *www.catchpenny.org/dendera.html.*

Chapter 25

Joltes, Richard. "History, Hoax, and Hype: The Oak Island Legend." Critical Enquiry Website. *www.criticalenquiry.org/oakisland/index.shtml.*

Nickell, Joe. "The Secrets of Oak Island." *Skeptical Inquirer,* March/April 2000. The Committee for Skeptical Inuiry Website. *www.csicop.org/si/show/secrets_of_oak_island.*

Oak Island Treasure Website. *www.oakislandtreasure.co.uk/.*

O'Connor, D'Arcy. *The Secret Treasure of Oak Island: The Amazing True Story of a Centuries-Old Treasure Hunt*. New York: The Lyons Press, 2004.

Chapter 26

Barber, Richard. *King Arthur Hero and Legend*. Woodbirdge, Suffolk, UK: The Boydell Press, 1986.

"Celtic Gods: The Cymric Bard and Seer, Myrddin Wyllt (Madman, the Wild)." Celtnet's Nemeton Website. *www.celtnet.org.uk/gods_m/ myrddin_wyllt.html.*

Geoffrey of Monmouth. Lewis Thorpe, ed. *The History of the Kings of Britain.* Harmondsworth, UK: Penguin Books, 1977.

"Merlin." The Camelot Project at the University of Rochester Website. *www.lib.rochester.edu/camelot/merlmenu.htm.*

Chapter 27

De la Bédoyère, Guy. "The Roman Army in Britain." Guy de la Bédoyère's Roman Britain Website. *www.romanbritain.freeserve. co.uk/Legions.htm.*

Hingley Richard, and Christina Unwin. *Boudica: Iron Age Warrior Queen.* London: Hambledon & London, 2006.

"Is Boudicca Buried in Birmingham?" BBC News Website. *news.bbc. co.uk/2/hi/uk_news/england/west_midlands/5016126.stm.*

Trow, M.J. *Boudicca: The Warrior Queen.* Stroud, UK: Sutton Publishing, 2004.

Webster, Graham. *Boudica: The British Revolt Against Rome AD 60 (The Roman Conquest of Britain).* London: Routledge, 2000.

Chapter 28

Champlin, Edward. *Nero.* Cambridge, Mass.: Harvard University Press, 2003.

Griffin, Miriam. *Nero: The End of a Dynasty.* London: Routledge, 2000.

"Secrets of the Dead—The Great Fire of Rome." Public Broadcasting Service (PBS) Website. *www.pbs.org/wnet/secrets/previous_seasons/ case_rome/index.html.*

Chapter 29

Keim, Brandon. "Bone Crunching Debunks 'First Monkey' Ida Fossil Hype." Wired News Website. *www.wired.com/wiredscience/2009/10/ reconfiguring-ida/.*

McGourty, Christine. "Scientists Hail Stunning Fossil." BBC News Website. *news.bbc.co.uk/2/hi/8057465.stm.*

The Messel Pit Fossil Website. *messel-fossils.eu/.*

"So Ida's Not the 'Missing Link': Questions and Answers with Erik Seiffert." Eureka Zone—*The Times Online* Website. *timesonline. typepad.com/science/2009/10/so-idas-not-the-missing-link-questions-and-answers-with-erik-seiffert.html.*

Tudge, Colin, and Josh Young. *The Link: Uncovering Our Earliest Ancestor.* New York: Little, Brown and Company, 2009.

Chapter 30

Deakin, Michael A.B. *Hypatia of Alexandria: Mathematician and Martyr.* Amherst, N.Y.: Prometheus Books, 2007.

Dzielska, Maria. *Hypatia of Alexandria (Revealing Antiquity).* Cambridge, Mass.: Harvard University Press, 1996.

"The Life of Hypatia." From Damascius's *Life of Isidore,* reproduced in *The Suda.* Translated by Jeremiah Reedy. Alexandria Website. *cosmopolis.com/alexandria/hypatia-bio-suda.html.*

Chapter 31

Bradford, Ernle. *Cleopatra.* New York: Penguin Group, 2001.

Crawford, Amy. "Who Was Cleopatra?" *Smithsonian* magazine Website. *http://www.smithsonianmag.com/history-archaeology/biography/cleopatra.html.*

Hashash, Sara. "Flamboyant Archeologist Believes He Has Identified Cleopatra's Tomb." *The Times Online* Website. *www.timesonline. co.uk/tol/news/world/africa/article3998944.ece.*

Tyldesley, Joyce. *Cleopatra: Last Queen of Egypt.* New York: Basic Books, 2008.

Walker, Susan, and Peter Higgs. *Cleopatra of Egypt, From History to Myth.* Ewing, N.J.: Princeton University Press, 2001.

Chapter 32

Aubet, Maria Eugenia. Translated by Mary Turton. *The Phoenicians and the West: Politics, Colonies and Trade.* New York: Cambridge University Press, 2001.

Gore, Rick. "Who Were the Phoenicians?" *National Geographic* magazine Website. *ngm.nationalgeographic.com/ngm/0410/feature2/index.html.*

James, Peter, and Nick Thorpe. *Ancient Mysteries*. New York: Ballantine Books, 2001.

Moscati, Sabatino. *The Phoenicians*. New York: Rizzoli International Publications, 2000.

Chapter 33

Abrams, Elliot M., and AnnCorinne Freter (eds). *The Emergence of the Moundbuilders: The Archaeology of Tribal Societies in Southeastern Ohio*. Athens, Ohio: Ohio University Press, 2005.

Feder, Kenneth L. *Frauds, Myths, and Mysteries: Science and Pseudoscience in Archaeology. 5th ed.* New York: McGraw Hill, 2006.

Milner, George R. *The Moundbuilders: Ancient Peoples of Eastern North America (Ancient Peoples and Places)*. New York: Thames & Hudson, 2004.

Priest, Josiah. *American Antiquities and Discoveries in the West*. Albany, N.Y.: Hoffman & White, 1834.

Squier, Ephraim, and Edwin Davis. *Ancient Monuments of the Mississippi Valley. Smithsonian Contributions to Knowledge, vol. 1*. Washington, D.C., 1848.

Waldman, Carl. *Atlas of the North American Indian*. New York: Checkmark Books, 2000.

Chapter 34

Diehl, Richard. *The Olmecs: America's First Civilization (Ancient Peoples and Places Series)*. London: Thames & Hudson, 2004.

Haslip-Viera, Gabriel, Bernard Ortiz de Montellano, and Warren Barbour. "Robbing Native American Cultures: Van Sertima's Afrocentricity and the Olmecs." Hall of Maat Website. *thehallofmaat.com/modules.php?name=Articles&file=article&sid=73.*

Pool, Christopher A. *Olmec Archaeology and Early Mesoamerica (Cambridge World Archaeology)*. New York: Cambridge University Press, 2007.

Van Sertima, Ivan. *They Came Before Columbus*. New York: Random House, 2003.

Chapter 35

Finlayson, Clive. *The Humans Who Went Extinct: Why Neanderthals Died Out and We Survived*. New York: Oxford University Press, 2009. Hall, Stephen S. "Last of the Neanderthals." *National Geographic* Website. *ngm.nationalgeographic.com/2008/10/neanderthals/hall-text*.

Rincon, Paul. "Did Climate Kill Off the Neandertahls?" BBC News Website. *news.bbc.co.uk/2/hi/science/nature/7873373.stm*.

Schrenk, Friedemann. *The Neanderthals (Peoples of the Ancient World)*. Abingdon, Oxon, UK: Routledge, 2008.

Index

D

E

F

G

H

I

About the Author

A qualified archaeologist, Brian Haughton is an author and researcher on the subjects of prehistoric megalithic sites, ancient sacred places, and supernatural folklore.

Haughton's first book, *Hidden History: Lost Civilizations, Secret Knowledge, and Ancient Mysteries*, was published in January 2007, and has been translated into 11 languages, including German, Russian, Greek, and Thai. His second book, *Haunted Spaces, Sacred Places,* which concentrates on the folklore and strange tales surrounding ancient sacred sites, was published by New Page Books in July 2008. His third book for New Page, *The Lore of the Ghost,* was published in September 2008.

Brian's work has been featured in various print publications across the world, including *Doorways Magazine, Awareness,* and *All Destiny,* and on Websites such as the BBC's Legacies, World Mysteries, and the Book of Thoth. He is a member of the Folklore Society (England) and serves as a consultant for UK-based research and investigative organization Parasearch. He long ago fell for the lure of the ancient world and tales of the supernatural, initially inspired by visiting the Neolithic chambered tombs of the Cotswold Hills in England and by reading the ghost stories of Sheridan Le Fanu and M.R. James.

In his spare time, Brian plays guitar in the band The Electric Rays.